BYRON:
Wrath and Rhyme

BYRON:
Wrath and Rhyme

edited by
Alan Bold

VISION
and
BARNES & NOBLE

Vision Press Limited
Fulham Wharf
Townmead Road
London SW6 2SB

and

Barnes & Noble Books
81 Adams Drive
Totowa, NJ 07512

ISBN (UK) 0 85478 355 5
ISBN (US) 0 389 20373 4

Printed and bound in Great Britain by
Unwin Brothers Ltd.,
Old Woking, Surrey.
Phototypeset by Galleon Photosetting,
Ipswich, Suffolk.
MCMLXXXIII

Contents

Introduction

by ALAN BOLD

In Harold Pinter's *The Homecoming* the domestic tyrant Max
throws out a casual rhetorical question: 'How many other
houses in the district have got a Doctor of Philosophy sitting
down drinking a cup of coffee?' By the same irreproachable
irrationality it is worth asking how many poets are notorious
enough to command an entry in *The Intimate Sex Lives of Famous
People* (1981). Quite a few, actually, including Ezra Pound,
Robert Burns and (of course) Byron who, according to Walter
Kempthorne,

> was sexually initiated at the age of nine by the family nurse,
> May Gray. For three years, the devout, bible-quoting Scottish
> girl seized every chance to creep into the child's bed and 'play
> tricks with his person'. Arousing the boy physically by every
> variation she could think of, May also allowed him to watch
> while she made love with her uninhibited lovers. Thus primed,
> Byron—eager for continued stimulation—moved with ease into
> sexual activities during his four years at Harrow. There he
> preferred the company of young boys. . . . In July 1813, Byron
> flouted the ultimate sexual taboo—incest—by seducing his
> married half-sister, Augusta Leigh.

So there you have it all in a few well-chosen words: the mad-
bad-dangerous Byron, the Freudian slip of a lad who indulged
in infantile sexuality, then graduated to homosexuality and
incest. No wonder a book calling itself *The Dirty Bits: The Book
That Falls Open at Every Page* (1981) begins with a quotation
from *Don Juan*:

> His classic studies made a little puzzle,
>   Because of filthy loves of gods and goddesses,
> Who in the earlier ages raised a bustle,
>   But never put on pantaloons or boddices.

7

Byron became mythical in his own lifetime and immortal after it, so it is helpful to demythologize the man in order to appreciate the extent of the poetic achievement. The literary taste of the Romantic period valued content above style, and emotionally compelling content at that, and Byron's work was received largely as a projection of his personality. If it had only amounted to that, then it would have been crippled by psychological failings. However, Byron aspired to something less ephemeral than metrical self-promotion. He believed that the act of creation enabled him to transcend his physical limitations as a person and to become an example to us all. He is quite specific about this in *Childe Harold's Pilgrimage* (III, vi):

> 'Tis to create, and in creating live
> A being more intense, that we endow
> With form our fancy, gaining as we give
> The life we image, even as I do now.
> What am I? Nothing: but not so art thou,
> Soul of my thought! with whom I traverse earth,
> Invisible but gazing, as I glow
> Mix'd with thy spirit, blended with thy birth,
> And feelings still with thee in my crush'd feelings' dearth.

Whether one approves of it or not, that stanza contains the message of the Byronic philosophy. It defines art as an impulse that is larger than life and portrays the artist as a man possessed by this all-consuming urge that has the power to transfigure him. In making his poems Byron is not merely advertising himself; he is declaring himself willing to abandon the distractions of the earthly life in order to become 'A being more intense'. The same sacrificial concept of the artist is developed in Thomas Mann's *Tonio Kröger*, where the hero

> worked, not like a man who works that he may live; but as one who is bent on doing nothing but work; having no regard for himself as a human being but only as a creator.

Hugh MacDiarmid, who incorporated that passage into his *The Kind of Poetry I Want*, was likewise fascinated by the sacrificial status of the really dedicated artist. In *A Drunk Man Looks at the Thistle* his protagonist begins as a man intoxicated by alcoholic spirit and ends as a spiritually transformed creator ready for the supreme sacrifice:

Introduction

A Scottish poet maun assume
The burden o' his people's doom,
And dee to brak' their livin' tomb.

Byron, who was 'half a Scot by birth, and bred/ A whole one', does not perhaps immediately impress the reader as a sacrificial poet, though he has frequently been cast in the role of political saviour. Like Scott and Hemingway and other impetuous artists he did not like to dwell on the sedentary nature of literary composition, so drew attention to his more obvious activities. The fiction of his myth shows a devil-may-care man-of-action who knocks off cantos with effortless ease in his spare time; the facts of his life tend to give the impression of a cynic who could treat intelligent women, such as Claire Clairmont, with contempt. Yet if we prefer the evidence of Byron's poetry to the combination of gullibility and gossip that constitutes his myth, it is possible to see Byron as a self-conscious artist with a vision of the human race as he knew it and of himself as a representative individual willing to sacrifice his life on the altar of artistic integrity. Given his unusual experiences, this vision is not only interesting, it is illuminating. In pursuit of this vision it is important to respond to what Byron himself wrote rather than accepting the anecdotal evidence of his ostentatiously public private life.

As a person Byron was not what an impartial observer would call noble; he could be insufferably arrogant and off-hand in his dealings with other people. Even an ineffectual angel like Shelley felt like throttling him over his decision to put his daughter Allegra in a convent rather than into the arms of her mother Claire Clairmont. The poetic ideal he envisaged, though, does have nobility, and Byron's personal affairs do not invalidate his artistic vision. This was always understood by those who read him most attentively and Engels shrewdly observed, in 1845, that

> it is the workers who are most familiar with the poetry of Byron [who] attracts their sympathy by his sensuous fire and by the virulence of his satire against the existing social order.

Engels was wrong, however, in supposing that it was only Byronic satire that appealed to the newly literate sections of society. A Lancashire weaver, Benjamin Brierley, tells in his autobiography *Home Memories and Recollections of a Life* (1886) that he did not really take to literature until he was given a poetic insight into the potential of humanity:

> I must confess that my soul did not feel much lifted by the only class of reading then within my reach. It was not until I joined the companionship of Burns and Byron that I felt the 'god within me'.

That is the value of great poetry. In Byron's lifetime poetry was seen, by the poets anyway, as a sublime expression of the human spirit, and though this romantic approach has limitations, it is more profound than twentieth-century critical attempts to cut poetry down to the size of manageable text. It is not surprising, of course, that modernism encouraged the cult of the fragment which, by its broken image, simulated breakdown. Poetry was involved in the general cultural collapse associated with World War One, and when the war was over it was not easy to put poetry together again. Poets became adept at incongruity, used the method of montage, relied on contrast and counterpoint, retreated from the grand statement to the ambiguous aside. In criticism F. R. Leavis and I. A. Richards encouraged a microscopic examination of selected texts, and though this led to an awareness of linguistic texture and irony, it also meant a lack of concern for poetry that ambitiously extended itself over the whole range of human thought. The megapoets like Milton and Byron were out of favour and poetry generally shrank in size and scope. The defeatist tone that was critically established after World War One prevented the postwar public from accepting long poems from modern poets. Pound's *Cantos*, Williams's *Paterson*, MacDiarmid's *Mature Art*, Zukovsky's *A*—all these are addressed to the many and known only by the few.

Byron is a big poet. 'My poem's epic', he declares in *Don Juan* and he means what he says. He is at his best in long stretches as he sets up an irresistible rhythm and carries the reader along with him. It is absurd that Byron should have been out of favour with the modernists until Auden wrote his 'Letter to Lord Byron' and included it in *Letters from Iceland* (1937). After all, the modernists advocated an allusive, irreverent and

10

rhythmically unfussy poetry and Byron is erudite, witty and a master of the conversational mode. Auden understood this and addressed Byron as a misunderstood colleague:

> You've had your packet from the critics, though:
>   They grant you warmth of heart, but at your head
> Their moral and aesthetic brickbats throw.
>   A 'vulgar genius' so George Eliot said,
>   Which doesn't matter as George Eliot's dead,
> But T. S. Eliot, I am sad to find,
> Damns you with: 'an uninteresting mind'.

A thematic (not to say sartorial) survey of the English poetry scene would reveal a cult of drabness entirely appropriate to a country whose critics value the poetic understatement more than the visionary affirmation. The notion of what is seemly in a poet and becoming to his calling was established in England, this century, by T. S. Eliot. The 'Reverend' Eliot, as Ezra Pound called this 'most bank-clerkly of Englishmen' in the *Cantos*, had good reason to regard emotional stability as a prerequisite of poetic security. He had had one clash with social convention and it was one too many. His marriage to Vivien Haigh-Wood in 1915 was a traumatic involvement for Eliot; his disapproving father cut off his allowance and thereby cast him out of the Edenic safety of his family and into the arms of an unlikely Eve. Eliot's masterpiece, *The Waste Land*, was composed (or at least concluded) when the poet was in Lausanne undergoing psychotherapy as a result of his divorce from the family and marriage to Vivien. When he returned to England it was to re-establish himself as a pillar of the critical, ecclesiastical and publishing community. He established *The Criterion* (which carried the noteless text of *The Waste Land* in the first issue of October 1922); he was accepted into the established Church of England in 1926; and he helped establish Faber & Faber (formerly Faber & Gwyer) as the Englishman's poetic castle.

To Eliot, the image of Byron was anathema. In an essay he contributed to Bonamy Dobrée's *From Ann to Victoria* (1937) he compared busts of Scott and Byron. Scott was, like Eliot, a man who seemed to value his social standing more than his literary readiness for action. Scott's bust, therefore, has 'an air of nobility':

Byron: Wrath and Rhyme

> But Byron—that pudgy face suggesting a tendency to corpulence, that weakly sensual mouth, that restless triviality of expression, and worst of all the blind look of the self-conscious beauty; the bust of Byron is that of a man who was every inch the touring tragedian.

Eliot's answer to this anomaly was to rid the realms of English poetry of Byron and reclassify him 'as a Scottish poet'. Byron himself sanctioned the assessment in the celebrated passage of *Don Juan* (X, xvii) when he describes himself as 'half a Scot by birth, and bred/ A whole one' and goes on to conclude the aside as follows (X, xix):

> And though, as you remember, in a fit
>   Of wrath and rhyme, when juvenile and curly,
> I railed at Scots to show my wrath and wit,
>   Which must be owned was sensitive and surly.
> Yet 'tis in vain such sallies to permit;
>   They cannot quench young feelings fresh and early.
> I 'scotched, not killed', the Scotchman in my blood
> And love the land of 'mountain and of flood'.

That confession implies that Byron has outgrown his 'fit/ Of wrath and rhyme', but *Don Juan* is as full of it as ever. Byron's ability to control his indignation by giving it a memorable artistic form is the essence of his art from the juvenilia to the consummate artistry of *Don Juan*. Byron always approached life with passion and so, naturally, he produced poetry that is animated by a huge emotional appetite for life. Remarkably, he gave all this artistic shape.

In 'Darkness', his Gothic evocation of the Apocalypse, Byron shows a world at war with itself:

> Morn came and went—and came, and brought no day,
> And men forgot their passions in the dread
> Of this their desolation; and all hearts
> Were chill'd into a selfish prayer for light . . .
> And War, which for a moment was no more,
> Did glut himself again:—a meal was bought
> With blood, and each sate sullenly apart
> Gorging himself in gloom: no love was left;
> All earth was but one thought—and that was death.

It will not escape the notice of the reader that for Byron the most dreadful aspect of this nightmare is the paucity of

12

passion: for 'men forgot their passions' and 'no love was left'. Despite his erratic behaviour and occasionally cynical acts, Byron regarded himself, rightly, as a man motivated by passion for his fellow men and, less philosophically, for women. He was, for all his affectations and neoclassical stylistic mannerisms, a genuine romantic who believed it was the push of passion that made the world revolve. Shelley's verse was addressed to some ideal assembly where he would be at last acknowledged as a legislator; Keats longed for a life of self-indulgent sensuality; Byron, alone of the great romantic trio, lived his life with existential urgency, but if he put his heart into the business of living, then it is in his art that we find the authorized version of the passion of the poet.

David Hume's supposition (in *A Treatise of Human Nature*) that 'Reason is, and ought only to be the slave of the passions' could have been formulated in anticipation of Byron's coming for his reason was punctuated, even disturbed, by passion. But whatever he was in person he was not, as an artist, passion's slave. In the poetry Byron masters his passion and makes it into endurable art. Despite the wildness of some of his descriptions and the audacity of some of his assertions, Byron—in form and on song—never loses technical control, and this allows him to express his vision of a human race emancipated from what he regards as antisocial rules and regulations. Byron is a positive poet who expects to be criticized by devotees of negativity and he is ready for them:

> The lawyer and the critic but behold
> The baser sides of literature and life,
> And nought remains unseen, but much untold,
> By those who scour those double vales of strife.

So he says in *Don Juan* (x, xiii), but if Byron is opinionated about others, his attitude to himself also comes across clearly in his poetry.

Intent on realizing his vision of human liberation, Byron sees himself as a suitable subject for verse and as a creative artist willing to make whatever sacrifice is necessary for the perfection of his art. Since he felt it was possible to surmount criticism by making himself superior to it, he has been judged as a human failure whose flaws are preserved in his poetry.

13

Not so. It is when we see Byron's life and literature as expressions of an ontological and artistic experiment that we understand how personal mistakes in his life allowed him to adjust his image of mankind in his poetry. The distance between *Childe Harold* and *Don Juan* is a great one and the massive gain in quality demonstrates that Byron's priority was his poetry. This, again, is something he pondered in *Don Juan* XIV, xii):

> I think that were I certain of success,
>   I hardly could compose another line.
> So long I've battled either more or less
>   That no defeat can drive me from the Nine.
> This feeling 'tis not easy to express
>   And yet 'tis not affected, I opine.
> In play there are two pleasure for your choosing:
> The one is winning and the other losing.

Byron may have lost in life but he was more careful in his art. It is recognition of his artistic triumph that has brought this book into being.

Part One:
RHYME AND CRITICISM

1

Byron as a Scottish Poet

by TOM SCOTT

My attention to the Scottish nature of Byron's genius was first drawn by T. S. Eliot in an essay, still to my mind the best on the subject, first published in 1937 and again in *On Poetry and Poets*, in 1957. Till then I had vaguely regarded him as an English romantic inferior to the luscious Keats and ecstatic Shelley. In fact Byron has more in common with Dryden and Pope, from whom he learned his early poetics, and in spirit and nature still more with Burns and Scott. He is a misfit in the English scene precisely because, like the Scott of the verse romances, he belongs mainly in the very different Scottish tradition in poetry, and it is with some account of the nature of that tradition that I must begin.

Scottish poetry is characterized by great extrovert energy, both verbal and intellectual, sensational rather than intuitive, common-sensible rather than philosophic, comic rather than tragic, social rather than solitary, humour rather than solemnity of subject and treatment. Its main strands are narrative and lyric, with little meditative poetry of length, and almost no drama. It tends also to be earthy rather than exalted, though the natural and the supernatural are on easy terms with each other. One need think only of the ballads, our staple poetry, to see there narrative, lyric, earthy, supernatural, social, comic, the humorous, hard-headed common-sense in abundance. There is little of the high-falutin (some aureation among the makars apart, and that but little of their work) and idealistic. One cannot imagine Shakespeare, Spenser, much less Blake, coming out of the Scottish tradition—leaving aside the fact that the Scots language never developed such poetic potential as Elizabethan English. Neither can one imagine Barbour (the main poetic influence on Scott) or Henrysoun, Dunbar or Burns coming out of the English tradition: but John Gay, even Crabbe whom Byron called 'Nature's sternest painter [note the words] yet her best', we might almost be persuaded to gie the kilt. Our poetry is rarely courtly, often folksy and hamely, rarely pious but often irreverent, outrageous even, rumbustious and orgiastic. There is nothing in English quite so outrageous as our flyting tradition. Satire is common, but usually of the humorous sort rather than the excoriating hatred of a Swift, and we are more given to cursing than blessing, to abusing than praising. We have an easy familiarity with both God and the Deil, though the heroic Satanism of Milton is beyond us. Scottish poetry also has a flair for nature-painting, to echo Byron, a keen sense of weather, of the passing seasons and their phenomena, of the everyday, and expresses these in physical, often onomatopoeic language, objective rather than subjective. Almost all of the above qualities can be found in two key poems: 'The Tretis of the tua mariit Wemen and the Wedo' and 'Tam o' Shanter', but also in most works by Dunbar and Burns. It is interesting, incidentally, that in the one poem *Childe Harold* where Byron makes the mistake of trying the Spenserian stanza, it is the Scotsmen Beattie and Thomson he mentions as his models, not Spenser himself.

I could go on, but I think enough has been said for my purpose. Born in 1788, Byron was 8 when Burns died, and Walter Scott 25. His boyhood in Aberdeen, where he lived till he was 10, plus the fact that his mother was an heiress of that fiery, proud clan the Gordons, was a harsh and painful schooling of the man. His scoundrelly English father no sooner got his hands on Catherine Gordon's money than he squandered it, as he had done the fortune of his first wife, and left her and her son in Aberdeen to dree out a wretched existence in back-street lodgings, in poverty and neglect. She must have been, if not heart-broken, deeply embittered, and with her fiery Gordon temper she seems to have been driven half-mad. The boy was born with a club foot, and his unsentimental mother had him subjected to excruciating tortures to try to straighten it out. These facts, plus the habitual cruelty of children to each other, especially the afflicted, must have made his childhood a season in hell. Geordie Byron was nae spoilt bairn, at least until he inherited the title and Newstead Abbey, itself encumbered with debts, in 1798. The surprising thing, and very much to our purpose, is not that he never came back to live in Scotland, but that his love of things Scottish and pride in being Scottish remained throughout his life and he was to boast that he was born half a Scot 'and bred a whole one'. It is not only in such a song as 'Lachin y Gair' that this proud assertion of his Gordon blood is to be found, but, as T. S. Eliot pointed out, in this triumphant stanza which breaks the turgidness of so much of *Childe Harold* like a blast from the bagpipe:

> And wild and high the 'Cameron's gathering' rose!
> The war-note of Lochiel, which Albyn's hills
> Have heard, and heard, too, have her Saxon foes;—
> How in the noon of night that pibroch thrills,
> Savage and shrill! But with the breath which fills
> Their mountain-pipe, so fill the mountaineers
> With the fierce native daring which instils
> The stirring memory of a thousand years,
> And Ewan's, Donald's fame rings in each clansman's ears!

Nevertheless an alienation from Scotland, and from his poor Scottish childhood, set in after the move south, and this was encouraged by his education at Harrow and Cambridge. Even more than most Scots, his feelings about Scotland and its people were ambivalent, veering between violent love and equally violent hate, with little in-between. This encouraged a split between head and heart, an escape into an aloof, disdainful, intellectually superior persona, from the tormented, turbulent feelings in his heart, the pain of the hurt sensitive boy. Byron became, in a sense, an inversion of Jekyll, the Satanic Hyde his normal self, the gentle Dr. Jekyll only breaking out here and there. He was an actor who made himself a suitable role and then played it for all he was worth, in and out of season and reason. And in his childhood background too was Calvinism with its presbyterian egalitarianism, its doctrine of predestination of the elect and the damned. Byron of course saw himself as one of the damned and

19

deliberately created a suitably Satanic role for himself to play in life. It was of course pseudo, if only for one good reason: to be good enough to think oneself damned is to be nearly saved. Not even T. S. Eliot seems to have noticed that Byron is in fact a very religious poet, perhaps the most so of his generation, and that much of the inner torment between pride and damnation, good and evil which is at the core of his work stems from his religious background and temperament. The accompanying feelings of inferiority stemming from his club foot and miserable childhood merely enhance his conflict as an aristocratic presbyterian—even if a lapsed presbyterian. He was no Justified Sinner, who by contrast is genuinely Satanic in denying his own evil.

Byron's life and work were immensely influenced also by two other main factors: his failure to fit in with the English social scene of his time, and that which finally ensured his exile from that society, his love for Augusta. His maiden speech to the House of Lords on behalf of the oppressed Nottingham weavers and other industrial workers, while showing the innate goodness of the man, would not endear him to the Establishment; but that was only a sign of the essential incompatibility between him and English society. His rather passive, intersexual nature, with its strong homosexual side however latent and unexpressed, led him to seek in older women something of the good, loving mother he had never known. His relations with Lady Oxford and Lady Melbourne may be evidenced. But even with his half-sister Augusta there was an element of the son-mother relationship. If Byron ever loved anyone not himself, he loved Augusta, truly, wholly, and exclusively. The incestuous, or semi-incestuous, nature of the relationship made it a doomed one in that society, indeed probably would even today. His outraged, prim wife not only left him but tried to poison Augusta against him, with some success. The breach with Augusta—their final meeting is almost as full of pathos as the tale of Paolo and Francesca—and his exile from England as an Ishmael wanderer on the face of the earth is to my mind the most important single factor in Byron's life. He loved Augusta as Orpheus did Eurydice, and the pain of that blighted love is responsible for much of the ensuing story, including his Don-Juanism. He was marked out

20

for destruction. One is reminded again of Walter Scott's blighted love of Williamina: but of course there is as much contrast as comparison here. And Byron's treatment of his daughter by Augusta is a despicable tale, only less so than that of his treatment of Allegra.

I think we have now said enough about Scottish poetry and of Byron the man to proceed to our subject: Byron as a Scottish poet. The first, most obvious thing about his work is that it is written in English, not Scots or Gaelic (of which he would have but little anyway). He is an example of Scottish genius finding itself as best it may in the alien medium of English, which he writes like a brilliant foreigner. He is an example of Edwin Muir's contention that no Scot can write anything but second-rate English. Virginia Woolf made a similar point about Scott's prose, saying the only time it came alive was when he wrote in Scots. The first evidence of Byron's Scottishness therefore is a negative one, the fact that he did not write English as a native, is largely insensitive to its subtleties and poetic potential—compare Keats e.g. Byron was a brilliant verse-writer, but he used the language as if it were prose. This is true of his first book *Hours of Idleness*, in which we get excellent, correct versification, 'poetical works', and no inspired utterance, with the possible exception of 'Lachin y Gair'. But even there the inspiration is of its Scottish subject, not its English language. These poems mark him a child of the eighteenth century and of Pope in particular, though here and there he reads like Tom Moore not at his best. Even in 'When I roved a young Highlander', a poem about his boyhood in Aberdeenshire, the language is pedestrian, the verse correct rather than inspired. Even in 'To my Son', written in 1807 to his illegitimate son, only the subject reminds us of Burns. Throughout the lyrics we get a poet who is trying to live up to his models, to write Poetry, rather than break new ground with something new to say. But they have vigour, skill, even virtuosity and fluency, a rare energy which, indeed, calls for a more energetic tongue than English: Scots. He rarely equals the best in English lyric poetry—perhaps only in *Hebrew Melodies* (his best and most original book of songs) and in it perhaps only in 'She walks in beauty, like the night'. The fondness for couplets, with him all his life, and for triple verse

21

such as anapaestic, in these poems suggests a talent more epic in nature than lyric, a thronging, sustaining energy rather than a flair for catching fleeting moods, feelings, thoughts and such. And epic indeed, as we know, his talent proved, or at any rate narrative, in the wonderful tales which are his major work. One lyric stands apart, though: 'So we'll go no more a-roving.' This is simply a translation of a Scots song attributed to James V:

> We'll gang nae mair a-rovin,
> A-rovin in the nicht
> Tho the hert be neer sae lovin
> And the muin be still as bricht.

The original has also a beautiful tune. The poems to Augusta, which we know to spring from the most important experience of his life, still somehow never seem to break through the conventional corsetry of his verse into passionate utterance and poetic fire. He tends to be rather sentimental than passionate, to take up poses rather than attitudes, to be more concerned with what he and his imagined readers think 'poetry' than with genuine utterance. His rhythm in most of these short poems is mechanical, lacking a discriminating ear, his diction is conventional and prosaic. One notes that sentimentality too is a (bad) characteristic of Scottish literature of the eighteenth century (one thinks of *The Man of Feeling* for instance), and that the uncertainty in the English tongue is characteristic of Scottish poets even today. But the sheer vitality and energy of Byron's mind, its hard-headed extroversion, its jocularity and satiric edge, and a certain sense of the colloquial, almost at times slangy, and the occasional religiosity here and there, are also Scottish traits. If there is one poem among these minor pieces which foreshadows the later Byron, and at the same time, shows the unmistakable note of the Scottish tradition of comic rhyming which he brought over into English in his later verse, via Pulci and Frere, it is 'Granta'. Listen to the echo of Skinner's 'Tullochgorum' in this stanza:

> If David, when his toils were ended,
>   Had heard these blockheads sing before him,
> To us his psalms had ne'er descended,—
>   In furious mood he would have tore 'em.

Slightly Scoticized, we get:

> Gin Dauvit, when his tyles were endit,
>   Had hard thir dunnerheids sing afore 'im,
> Til us his psaulms had ne'er descendit,—
>   In tearan rage he wad hae tore 'em.

I invite the reader to try putting other poems, such as 'Lachin y Gair', into light Scots: Awa, ye braw landscapes, ye gairdens o roses. . . . There you hear the true voice trying to get through the thinner English.

Byron's first poem of some length is *English Bards and Scotch Reviewers*. The title is a bit of a misnomer for, unfortunately for the Edinburgh reviewers who savaged the boy's first book (he was 19), this Bard was a Scot, and he replied not with a satire, as it is miscalled, but a flyting of his enemies. Satire attacks the abuse, not the person(s): flyting abuses the person(s). He might have sub-titled it with Scotland's motto: *nemo me impune lacessit*. That Byron was unconscious of the flyting tradition he was working in and presented it as (failed) Popean satire makes no difference to the fact: indeed, it reveals his problem as a Scot working in English. The poem rather falls between two stools, the flyting being somewhat tamed by the English tradition yet too much present to make good satire in that tradition. Also, Byron was essentially a chatty, digressive poet (his greatest virtue in *Don Juan*) and that is the enemy of sustained intensity. Like a retriever puppy loose in a field of smells, he couldn't stick to one scent but followed up every one he happened on, dashing about all over the place.

It is as well to consider all his 'satires' here. The *Hints From Horace* is simply a rehash of that rather humdrum poet's *Arte Poetica*, of little real use to Byron, and the Horatian precepts were ignored in practice, luckily. *The Curse of Minerva* is really another flyting, this time of Lord Elgin for his rape of the marbles from the Parthenon, the so-called Elgin marbles. The heroic couplets are mostly in his imitation eighteenth-century Poetic vein, too high-falutin for the most part. But here and there it comes to life in passages of flyting, not only of Elgin but of Scotland for producing him; and even in this he writes from his Scottish experience:

23

And well I know within that bastard land
Hath Wisdom's goddess never held command;
A barren soil, where Nature's germs, confined
To stern sterility, can stint the mind;
Whose thistle well betrays the niggard earth,
Emblem of all to whom the land gives birth;
Each genial influence nurtured to resist;
A land of meanness, sophistry, and mist. . . .

So he goes on, lashing the negative side of Scotland and the Scots as only a native can. So Byron looks at the thistle, and flytes Elgin for his reiving. But he also goes on to praise the good side of Scotland, which he sees chiefly in her writers and soldiers.

The Waltz is not so much a satire as a mock-puritan *jeu d'esprit*, poking fun at the sexiest dance of the time and at Terpsichore, the 'least vestal' of the Muses. He has fun finding rimes for 'waltz', including 'Galt's', the Scottish novelist he met on his travels, salts, assaults, exalts, halts, and so on. *The Blues* is more truly satiric, on blue-stocking women, but again exuberant fun, with here and there crambo-clink riming of the kind common in Scots poetry and his hall-mark in his later major works: scamp ill/example, shock it/pocket, Madeira with pleasure/Windermere treasure, but it is slight. *The Vision of Judgment* is probably the best of these pieces, an uproarious flyting of Southey who had written a sycophantic poem on the death of George the Third with that title, and in the preface attacking Byron as leader of the Satanic School. Southey was to Byron a despicable turncoat, a republican turned monarchist for venial reasons. Parodying Southey, Byron paints a comic picture of heaven which is folksy and irreverent and indeed in places reminiscent not only of Scots poetry but of certain medieval plays such as the Townley ones. St. Peter's keys are rusty, the lock dull, the angels sing out of tune, wind up the sun and moon, curb a runaway star or two, or a wild colt of a comet—it all bustles with exuberant energy. But under it is withering scorn and real outraged sensibility at the social evils of the time, the carnage of Waterloo, and much else, including an indictment of George's reign. On that score there is one gem which to me is hall-marked Scottish:

24

Byron as a Scottish Poet

'God save the king!' It is a large economy
  In God to save the like. . . .

That surely is the kind of thing we might have heard from
one of the Bodies, or Gourlay himself, in *The House with the
Green Shutters*. Him—his mither used ti waash oor sterrs! He
can turn the comedy on himself too, but revealing the presbyterian Calvinist in him:

God help us all! God help me too! I am
  God knows, as helpless as the devil can wish,
And not a whit more difficult to damn
  Than is to bring to land a late-hook'd fish. . . .

Here, too, much of the fun is in the riming, such as 'his
perspiration was but ichor/ Or some such other spiritual
liquor'. . . . More than in any previous work we note a quality
I've not seen much spoken of re Byron, his sheer intelligence, a
large and vigorous mind, immensely read and alert to society
and all its vices and evils. He missed little and his range of
historical and literary reference is vast and accurate. His was a
very well-furnished mind indeed, and in many tongues. There
is much impassioned, angry social satire in the work as well as
the hilarious flyting of Southey.

Other features of the poem seem to me to have Scottish
affiliations. There is his joke about George being a better farmer
than he was a king, which reminds us of Allan Cunningham's
satirical song about George the First, 'The Wee, Wee, German
Lairdie' 'delvin in his kail-yairdie, sheughin kail and layin
leeks'. The dialogue between Michael and Satan has something of the comedy of 'Death and Dr. Hornbook', while the
slinking into heaven of George after he had been thrown out
by St. Peter and 'practicing the hundredth psalm' reminds me
of the middle Scots poem 'Kynd Kyttok': the humour is very
similar.

On the face of it few poems could be less Scottish than *Childe
Harold*, with the Spenser pastiche of the early cantos, soon to
be dropped, but a deeper look is necessary. I have already
quoted the stanza about the 'Cameron's Gathering', but there
are other features. The poem is the first to give us the Byronic
hero, and he has much of the wandering Scot in his make-up,
something goliardic (and later poems have more of the soldier),

25

more at home in Europe than in England, more international than the insular Englishman. We note too that he is inspired by mountain scenery and the Rhine and such nature scenes as touch off unconscious reminiscence of similar Scottish scenes, the 'Lachin y Gair' strain, by wild scenery and wild tribesmen of the mountains with whom he has a curious empathy: the Albanian scenes, e.g. if not the Greek. The Byronic hero is something of an aristocratic picaro, and the picaresque novels of the Scot Smollett are to some extent plebeian precursors of the aristocratic Byronic hero, who culminates in the superb scamp, Don Juan. The title is possibly an echo of 'Childe Rowland to the dark tower came' but in the form of cheil it is still common in Scots. The mask of Harold is more and more dropped as the poem progresses (and it does progress, ending with Byron having discovered his own voice and proper subject: his own experience) and by the fourth canto Byron himself has taken over and we get his best poetry up to that time in the Italian scene. Again he responds to the mountains (Appenines) and I can't help feeling that in certain respects Italy and Italians have things in common with the Scots: torn by noble gangsters, passionate and violent natures (the douce presbyterian is not the true Scot), oppressed and divided, suffering from internal strife and external government. Is not the elegiac note in the opening brooding on Venice akin to that of the lament for 'the broken image of the lost kingdom' which Edwin Muir found in the soul of every Scot? Is it not, indeed, akin to the note that sounds through the great pibrochs of the Ceol Mor, the lament for the Celtic destiny? This canto was much admired by Scott, who saw in Byron his own successor and superior in the verse narrative. Byron himself compares Scott with Tasso and Ariosto, calling Scott the 'Ariosto of the North' and Ariosto 'The southern Scott' who both sang 'ladye-love and war, romance and knightly worth'. And in the most famous stanza of the whole canto he pays Scott the compliment of echoing his line 'Unwept, unhonour'd, and unsung' (*Lay of the Last Minstrel*): 'Without a grave, unknell'd, un-coffined, and unknown' (clxxix).

The first of the verse tales mainly drawn from his eastern journeys to my mind shows Scott's specific influence, and specifically *The Lady of the Lake*, throughout. Moore and

Southey had both written of the East of course, but neither of them had Byron's range of actual experience of it. One example may suffice to make my point. Scott in *The Lady* writes:

> The stag at eve had drunk his fill
> Where danced the moon on Monan's rill . . .

and Byron in *The Giaour* writes:

> The sun's last rays are on the hill
> And sparkle in the fountain rill . . .

and it's not that there are few rimes to 'hill': it is an echo. Incidentally, re the problem of the Scot writing in English, take the Scott couplet over into light Scots:

> The stag at een had drunk his fill
> Whaur daunsed the muin on Monan's rill . . .

is that not the true voice of his poetry? The specificity and accuracy of detailed observation in this and other poems seems to me a Scots trait, a respect for hard facts almost scientific, and of course the Byronic hero with his tormented conscience and deep sense of sin and damnation mixed with Satanic pride is very much a Calvinist product:

> The Mind, that broods o'er guilty woes,
>   Is like the Scorpion girt by fire. . . .
> So writhes the mind Remorse hath riven,
> Unfit for earth, undoom'd for heaven,
> Darkness above, despair beneath. . . .

The story of Leila and the Giaour is a screen on which Byron can project and express something of his own conflict over Augusta, the doomed love, the damned hero. Similar projections and the same type of hero can be seen in *Lara*, *The Corsair*, *The Bride of Abydos*, *The Siege of Corinth* and *Parisina*. In these tales too, especially the Levantine ones, we note the sense of fact, the poetry of fact, of history, in his careful notes giving Turkish words and meanings customs and such, Moslem lore, words and meanings, and how he himself probed and questioned people in search of information, a scholarly interest in truth and knowledge for its own sake as well as for poetic material, a natural social researcher. One is reminded

27

to some extent of the later MacDiarmid and his forays in science and technical lore. This surely is a Scots trait. It is interesting that the four 'British' writers who have most influenced Europe are Shakespeare and three Scots—Scott, Ossian Macpherson and Byron—the latter indeed is the most international, least insular of all our poets, and that too is a Scottish trait. In these tales Byron takes the verse tale of the 'Ariosto of the North' a stage further both in technique and subject matter, and the contradictory nature of his hero-figure, at once damned as a great sinner and really a fine generous nature twisted out of true by evil and hypocritical influences and people around him. We know this figure well in our literature, but perhaps he is not quite so contradictory as he seems: Byron was in fact a generous nature at odds with society: but also predestinedly damned in his own Calvinist conscience. Both traits can co-exist, each in its own sphere of experience. The religious trait is very much there in some of these tales, in *The Giaour* especially with its title meaning infidel, its motifs of sin, remorse, curse, damnation, Christianity-Moslem conflict: all stemming from some undeclared titanic conflict in Byron himself, and that stemming from his Calvinist Scottish background. He is not a non-believer, but a confused, a lapsed believer: but Byron is a heretic, unorthodox, and all the more intense for that. And this conflict is not purely personal, he expresses a crisis of faith in the soul of Europe, and it is this that all Europe recognized. This is his true greatness, recognized by Goethe and Pushkin among others, something far beyond the actorry persona he cultivated, the role he invented and played for himself. In this suffering, tortured hero, many of the best minds in Europe saw themselves and their times.

This religious conflict in Byron is best evidenced in the dramas *Manfred, Marino Faliero, Sardanapalus, The Two Foscari, Werner*, and most importantly *Cain* and *Heaven and Earth*. The typical hero in these is Hamlet bred out of Faust by Byron, a tormented puritan very close to Milton's Satan. He never resolved the conflict and one gets the impression that having worked it over, given it expression, and probably recognizing that it was insoluble anyway, he tired of it and sought refuge in lighter things with a lighter style.

In making my case for Byron as a Scottish poet I do not

suggest that there are no other cases to be made. The opposite
one, Byron as an English poet, has never been made: it has been
taken as self-evident by all and sundry, hence the lack of understanding of Byron in official Eng. Lit. I want now to try
something more daring than I have yet done to bring out his
Scottishness:

> It's kent, at least it sould be, that thurchoot
>   Aa countries o the Catholic persuasion,
> Some weeks afore Shrove Tuesday comes aboot,
>   The folk aa tak their fill o recreation,
> An buy repentance, ere they grouw devoot,
>   Houevir hiech their rank, or laich their station,
> Wi fiddlin, feastin, dancin, drinkin, maskin,
> An ither things that may be had for askin.
>
> The meenit nicht wi murky mantle covers
>   The lift (an the mair murkily the better),
> That time less lo'ed by husbands nor by lovers
>   Begins, an prudery flings aside her fetter;
> An gaiety on restless tiptae hovers,
>   Gigglin wi aa the gallants that beset her;
> An there are sangs an quavers, roarin, hummin,
> Guitars, and aakin ither sort o strummin.
>
> An there are dresses brawlik, but fantastical,
>   Masks o aa times an nations, Turks an Jews,
> An harlequins and clowns, wi feats gymnastical,
>   Greeks, Romans, Yankee-doodles, an Hindoos;
> Aa kin dresses, 'cept the ecclesiastical,
>   Aa folk that, as their fancies hit, may choose,
> But naebody in thir pairts may quiz the clergy,—
> Sae tak heed, ye Freethinkers aa, I chairge ye.

I could go on, but let it suffice. Some lost poem by Robert
Burns? Or some later, forgotten poet? These are the opening
stanzas of *Beppo*, lightly Scoticized, by Byron. And *Beppo* was
his first serious essay in the stanza and style he borrowed from
Pulci and made his own in *Don Juan*. Pulci was a fifteenth-
century Florentine who wrote in his own dialect, and Byron
read him first in Frere's translation, and was struck by the
form and its possibilities to him. In other words, the Scot in
him, having lost its own traditions, found them again, to some

extent, in this roundabout way. That this is what happened is proved, in my view, by what Byron brought to the form which is neither in Pulci nor Frere, a wilder, more elritch freedom and imagination, exhilaration, comedy, wit, outrageous flyting and satire, swift twistings and turnings of mood and attitude—in a word vitality. Here Byron for the time leaves behind his brooding, damned presbyterian-cum-proud-aristocrat self and finds his comic common-sense self, the self closest to Burns and Fergusson. The very theme of the tales is significant: Beppo returning to find his wife has acquired a lover in his absence and instead of high tragedy resulting, the three of them sensibly set up a *menage à trois*. Byron uses this common-sense to lambast the hypocritical English high society which came between him and Augusta and drove him into exile. The Scot takes revenge on the English. The comic Muse moreover liberates in him his greatest gift of all, the gift of the gab, of blethering on about everything and anything that comes into his mind, relevant or not, without for a moment being dull or uninteresting—indeed, he is more likely to lose the reader when being strictly relevant than when being outrageously digressive. This Byron would have been at home in the howfs and clubs of Edinburgh in his and earlier time, holding the floor, endlessly entertaining. He and Burns would have got on famously if they'd met. What Byron brought to the stanza was the genius of the Scottish tradition derived from his mother and her people, the irrepressible Gordons: it is a mainly comic tradition from which one cannot imagine the tragedies of Shakespeare, or any other major tragedian, emerging. Even Henrysoun, who gave us our best narrative tragedies, had essentially a comic vision of life.

Beppo was written in 1817 and in the following year Byron began his magnum opus, *Don Juan*, which occupied much of his time for the next five years. Of the seventeen stanzas of the 'Dedication' to Southey, Eliot points out (see above) that they are unlike any English satire, that they are in fact a flyting in the Scottish tradition, and he compares the opening stanza with one from Dunbar's flyting of Kennedy, and in his view 'one of the most exhilarating pieces of abuse in the language'. This is so, and Eliot further links both Burns and Dunbar with Villon, the greatest poet of the three, and by implication

ranges Byron with them all, but of lower rank, and praises him
for qualities too uncommon in English poetry and for the lack
of some vices all too common in English. I mention this
because Eliot is not only the poet he is but also our best poetry
critic since Coleridge, and further, being an American, he sees
the English and Scottish scenes unblinkered by racial prejudice, which no Englishman ever does and probably no Scots-
man either.

> BOB SOUTHEY! Ye're a poet—Poet-Laureate,
> An representative o aa the race;
> Whit tho it's true ye've turned oot a Tory at
> Last,—yours has lately been a common case;
> An, nou, my Epic Renegade! whit're ye at?
> Wi aa the Lakers, in an oot o place?
> A nest o tunefu bodies, ti my eye
> Lik 'fowr and twinty Blackbirds in a pie' . . .

Once again I have lightly Scoticized, to bring out Eliot's point.
Further on, he says:

> For me that, wanderin wi pedestrian Muses,
> Dinna contend wi you on the wingit steed,
> I wish yir fate may yield ye, when she chooses,
> The fame ye envy, and the skill ye need;
> An recollect a poet naethin loses
> In giean ti his brithers their fu meed
> o merit, and complaint o present days
> Is no the certain path ti future praise.

But no more Scoticizing for the present; the point's made.
Eliot quotes, for comparison, Dunbar's

> Lene larbar, loungeour, baith lowsy in lisk and lunye;
> Fy, skolderit skyn, thow art both skyre and skrumple;
> For he that rostit Lawrance had thy grunye,
> And he that hid Sanct Johnis ene with ane womple
> And he that dang Sanct Augustine with ane rumple
> Thy foul front had, and he that Bartilmo flaid;
> The gallowis gaipis eftir thy graceles gruntill
> As thow wald for ane haggeis, hungry gled.

One stands rather in awe at the linguistic loss between
Dunbar and Byron; a time for two minutes silence. Just think
if Byron had inherited the fowth of Scots available to Dunbar!

Byron: Wrath and Rhyme

Southey would have been shrivelled in his skin. Not the least Scottish trait in him is that he is a 'guid hater', and not only Southey but Wordsworth, Coleridge and others come in for a deal of flyting here and there throughout *Don Juan*. In Canto III, e.g. stanzas xciv to c, he attacks all three, Wordsworth particularly being flyted for *The Excursion* and other poems, his mind denounced as vulgar and unfit to comprehend classical references' and allusions, ending in the cry:

> 'Pedlars,' and 'Boats,' and 'Waggons!' Oh! ye shades
> Of Pope and Dryden, are we come to this?
> That trash of such sort not alone evades
> Contempt. . . .

The essentially flyting nature of this poem and its kind of comedy is not only to be found in particulars—and we shall see more of that as we go on—but in general. It is the very climate of the poem, the very temperament of the poet. Much has been made of Byron's aristocratism, and rightly so: but he is even more of an aristocrat on his mother's side (related to royalty) than on his father's, and a Scottish aristocrat is only that much more aristocratic. But I reject the received opinion that Don Juan is, for all his Spanishness, essentially English: on the contrary, he is well contrasted with the English Johnson in the Ismail cantos, and the Spanishness allows him to see England and its life as a foreigner—as a Scot. The poem is reductive, scornful, with that savage reductive humour of the presbyterian Scot puncturing all pretensions, hawk-eyed for the false and high-falutin, an almost philistine attack on idealism and aesthetic preciousness. In life it is a vice which militates against artistic achievement in Scotland, progress and eleva- tion, but its comic potential is obvious throughout the range of Scottish literature, even from pre-Reformation times. Byronic satire has more in common with the satire of Burns, among others, than with the great English satirists he so much admired, and this makes Byron unique in the whole range of English. His nearest affinities in later years are the Ulster Scot, Louis Macneice and, in such poems as *The Georgiad*, the South African Scot Roy Campbell. His savaging of Southey and Castlereagh among others was too much for English taste, and his publisher Murray had many an anxious moment. It is very dangerous to tell the truth, and most unsociable.

Byron could be almost as generous in friendliness as vituperative in enmity, and no less Scottish in that too, as in his saluting of his old enemy Jeffrey in Canto X (xvl–xvll):

> Dear Jeffrey, once my most redoubted foe . . .
> . . . Here's a health to 'Auld Lang Syne!'
> I do not know you . . .
> . . . but you have acted on the whole
> Most nobly, and I own it from my soul.
>
> And when I use the phrase of 'Auld Lang Syne!'
> 'Tis not addressed to you . . .
> . . . for I would rather take my wine
> With you, than aught (save Scott) in your proud city. . . .
> But I am half a Scot by birth, and bred
> A whole one, and my heart flies to my head,—
>
> As 'Auld Lang Syne' brings Scotland, one and all,
> Scotch plaids, Scotch snoods, the blue hills, and clear
> streams,
> The Dee, the Don, Balgounie's brig's *black wall*
> All my boy feelings, all my gentler dreams
> Of what I *then dreamt* . . .
> My childhood in this childishness of mine:
> I care not—'tis a glimpse of *'Auld Lang Syne'*.

The theme of being half a Scot is echoed negatively in Canto XI (xii) when he says 'half English as I am/ (To my misfortune). . .', when he identifies himself with Juan's astonished reaction to being ambushed on Shooter's Hill. In this episode too comes the remarkable stanza in cant, commented on by Eliot as 'something new in English verse' and 'first-rate' at that:

> Who in a row like Tom could lead the van,
> Booze in the ken, or at the spellken hustle?
> Who queer a flat? Who (spite of Bow-street's ban)
> On the high toby-spice so flash the muzzle?
> Who on a lark, with black-eyed Sal (his blowing). . . .

Eliot further comments: 'It is not a bit like Crabbe, but it is rather suggestive of Burns.' Even more like Villon, but that merely underlines the point. Byron himself notes that he has drawn heavily on a popular song for this stanza, in itself a

Burns characteristic. Returning to the 'Auld Lang Syne' stanza, the Burns' song begins 'Should auld aquentance be forgot'. . .: there may be some significance in the fact that Byron more than once rimes 'aquaintance' with '-entence'. His dropping of the 'g' in many 'ing' rimes might be a Scots trait, but could also be an aristocratic affectation. But when he rimes 'hour' with 'four' (as in Canto V, xxx) we can hardly doubt that he is hearing the Scots 'fowr'.

Scotland and things Scottish seem rarely to have been far from his consciousness, as in the footnote to Canto V, liii, in which he tells the story of the Scot who complained that the eating of six kittiwakes did nothing to whet his appetite. And in the same canto (lxxvii) he gives us:

> Which girt a slight chemise as white as milk . . .
> Which—as we say—or as the Scotch say, *whilk* . . .

while in xcviii he refers to the beauty of Mary, Queen of Scots. There are several references to Walter Scott, each one more complimentary than the last, and betraying a genuine fellow-feeling and admiration, in one case seeing himself as Scott's successor as a poet. He is not, therefore, unconscious of his essential Scottishness, but he does not grasp its implications for him as a Scottish genius writing in the foreign medium of English for a mainly English audience. Or if he had grasped it, he saw no alternative to trying to do what he could in English. It was not yet time for a MacDiarmid, and the folk route taken by Burns was too remote from him. But Byron was by no means purely lowland Scots, and his highland ancestry gave him no living root in the Gaelic: but that his poetry has much in common with the Gaelic tradition as well as the lowland Scots is also evident in his work, not least in his love of clear description and of rich trappings and apparel (e.g. Canto III, lxi–lxxvii), delight in the sumptuous and ornamentation, of splendour, colour, display, the hard classical light—indeed, his very Hellenism. But I leave that aspect of his Scottishness to be followed up, I hope, by those more fortunate in their Gaelic heritage than I am. It is at least as obviously present in his work as the lowland Scots affinities, if not more so: and I don't mean the kind of thing we get in Canto VI, xiii:

His Highness gazed upon Gulbeyaz' charms,
Expecting all the welcome of a lover
(A 'Highland welcome' all the world over).

And in any case the Celtic love of finery and lush description is common enough in the poetry of the Makars and elsewhere in the literature—some of the romances, e.g.

The flyting note can sometimes be so savage—and not only about Southey or Castlereagh—as to be almost Swiftian in its sweeping misanthropy:

Dogs or men!—for I flatter ye in saying
  That ye are dogs—your betters far—ye may
Read, or read not, what I am now essaying
  To show ye what ye are in every way. . . .

                    (Canto VII, vii)

But this is rare, and Byron is no misanthrope in truth, and there is much comedy in his flyting, humour in his satire, and, typical of the Scots tradition, humanity in his humour. Medicine comes in for quite a lot of mickey-taking in Scots, from Henrysoun's 'Sum practices of Medycin' to Burns's 'Death and Dr. Hornbook'. Byron too has his tilt at it in Canto X (xli, xlii).

But here is one prescription out of many:
  '*Sodae sulphat. 3vj. 3fs. Mannae optim.*
Aq. fervent. f.3 ifs. 3ij. tinct. Sennae
  Haustus' (and here the surgeon came and cupp'd him)
. . . . . .
This is the way physicians mend or end us,
  Secundum artem: but although we sneer
In health—when ill, we call them to attend us,
  Without the least propensity to jeer. . . .

The joke has its bitter irony for us, for it was almost certainly the leeching attentions of a quack doctor that cost him his life at Missolonghi in 1824, a few years after he penned these lines. Poets indeed often prophesy their own fates. The flyting note can take a more general target too at times, as in the marvellous catalogue of guests at the house party in Canto XIII. The catalogue convention is a favourite one among Scots poets (think of the one in Dunbar's 'Remonstrance to the King' e.g.), and can give rise to an elritch, abandoned comedy outrageously uncontrolled. (I may be allowed, I hope, to remark here that I wrote my catalogue of passengers on 'The Ship' some twelve years before I came across this canto of *Don Juan*: up to then I had only known some earlier, more famous cantos.) Byron gets almost the whole of the English Establishment into that fantastic house party, mocks them all, and richly enjoys doing so, running on from lxviii to xcix: all seen from outside, as a foreigner (Scottish Byron, Spanish Juan) might see them, seeing their ridiculousness from a different national tradition and set of values, as well as part of the eternal human comedy seen from a position, and values, of no time or place. I cannot agree with Eliot that the last four cantos are the best of the whole poem (my taste perhaps is too picaresque), but I do agree that they are quite unlike any other verse in English before or since. The reason is that they were written by a Scot, though in the medium of English, and the very different temperament transcends the language:

> The noble guests, assembled at the Abbey,
>   Consisted of—we give the sex the *pas*—
> The Duchess of Fitz-Fulke; the Countess Crabby;
>   The Ladies Scilly, Busey;—Miss Eclat,
> Miss Bombazeen, Miss Mackstay, Miss O'Tabby,
>   And Mrs. Rabbi, the rich banker's squaw;
> Also the honourable Mrs. Sleep,
> Who look'd a white lamb, yet was a black sheep. . . .

Note the riming of *squaw* with *pas* and *eclat*, thus giving the Scots *aw* sound a backthrow up the stanza. Such rimings are common in Byron, but how conscious he was of the Scots ear they betray I do not know: certainly he does it quite deliberately for comic effect, as when he rimes *soul* with *foul*. But whether he knows it or not, he is enjoying his Scots lug and the rich comic tradition in Scots.

Space considerations force me to end here, but indeed no more is needed. If the reader refers back to my opening description of the main characteristics of the Scottish tradition in poetry, I think he will agree that the case for considering Byron a Scottish poet of genius finding himself as best he may in the medium of English is made and sustained.

2

Byron and the English Tradition

by PHILIP HOBSBAUM

The old-fashioned kind of literary history would have it that
there were two generations of Romantic poets. Wordsworth,
Coleridge and, notionally, Southey were held to represent an
older generation; Byron, Shelley and Keats some sort of
second wave. 'Had they lived, Venetia or Umbria might
perchance have been to them, at least for a time, a selected
and common sojourn, a Lake district. . . .'[1] Readers of *Don
Juan* may well imagine what Byron would have done with a
fantasy such as that. He had views about his contemporaries
that were decidedly anti-Romantic. So far as the Lake Poets
were concerned he thought Coleridge the best of a bad bunch,
though he voiced a liking for 'Christabel'—'I won't have you
sneer at Christabel', he writes to John Murray, 'it is a fine wild
poem.'[2] Of Wordsworth he writes 'There is undoubtedly
much natural talent spilt over "the Excursion" but it is rain
upon rocks where it stands & stagnates—or rain upon sands
where it falls without fertilizing—who can understand him?'[3]
His references to Shelley as a poet are suspiciously few, and it
is clear that he preferred his friend's company to his writing.
He does, however, in a letter actually addressed to Shelley
commend *The Cenci*.[4] Of Keats he spoke severely:

> Such writing is a sort of mental masturbation—he is always
> flogging his Imagination . . . soliciting his own ideas into a state
> which is neither poetry nor any thing else. . . .[5]

37

All this should be quite enough to indicate that, unless he mistook his purpose, Byron cannot be regarded as part of any Romantic 'school'.

However, one must remember that, as Wilson Knight says, he 'had only Wordsworth's shorter poems and *The Excursion* on which to base his judgments'.[6] Nevertheless, he disliked the tendency of what he knew so much that it is hard to imagine him paying more than formal regard to, say, *The Prelude*. It is true, however, that he was to alter his opinion of Keats after the latter's death and in response to the volume that contained 'Hyperion'.[7] One can only acknowledge the fitness of the respect which the greatest anti-Romantic of the time had for this least Romantic of all Keats's works.

What, then, were Byron's positives? His preferences do not show him bearing much relationship to the groupings of the historians. In 1813 he made a kind of *Gradus ad Parnassum* of contemporary poets.[8] Scott heads the pyramid; Samuel Rogers, a figure unread today, is put in the second class; Thomas Campbell and Thomas Moore in a third; the 'Lake Poets', fourth. Later on Byron almost certainly would have set, alongside Rogers, Crabbe, in spite of that poet's 'coarse and impracticable subject'.[9] This tendency in taste is hardly, in any conventional sense, Romantic. Indeed, Byron greeted the word as an unwelcome innovation. He wrote in 1820:

> I perceive that in Germany, as well as in Italy, there is a great struggle about what they call '*Classical*' and '*Romantic*,'—terms which were not subjects of classification in England, at least when I left it four or five years ago. Some of the English Scribblers, it is true, abused Pope and Swift, but the reason was that they themselves did not know how to write either prose or verse; but nobody thought them worth making a sect of.[10]

Byron had his positives; however, except for a consistent regard for Scott, these were not initially invested in writers of his own time. Right through his career, though, he had the most unswerving admiration for Pope. There are more than 150 references to Pope and his works in the eleven-volume edition of Byron's letters and journals edited by Leslie Marchand. Fifty of the references occur in a single volume, that for 1821, when Byron was in the middle of a controversy

with William Lisle Bowles. Bowles had produced an edition of
Pope carrying a number of deprecatory comments about that
poet's life as well as his poems. Byron produced two 'letters' in
defence. One of them was published as a pamphlet in 1821;
one, presumably as a result of conciliatory gestures on the part
of Bowles,[11] was withheld. It was in the second of these, first
printed in 1835, that Byron gives voice to the most moving of
his encomia. Referring to Pope's detractors among the (hypo-
thetical) second wave of Romantic poets, Byron writes:

> If they had said nothing of *Pope*, they might have remained
> 'alone with their glory,' for aught I should have said or thought
> about them or their nonsense. But if they interfere with the
> 'little Nightingale' of Twickenham, they may find others who
> will bear it—*I* won't. Neither time, nor distance, nor grief, nor
> age, can ever diminish my veneration for him, who is the great
> moral poet of all times, of all climes, of all feelings, and of all
> stages of existence. The delight of my boyhood, the study of my
> manhood, perhaps (if allowed to me to attain it), he may be the
> consolation of my age. His poetry is the Book of Life. Without
> canting, and yet without neglecting religion, he has assembled
> all that a good and great man can gather together of moral
> wisdom cloathed in consummate beauty. . . . A thousand years
> will roll away before such another can be hoped for in our
> literature. But it can *want* them—he himself is a literature.[12]

With all this admiration on his part, why is Byron so
radically unlike Pope? He does not resemble him, even when
he essays deliberate imitation. Consider his attempt to adapt
Pope's lines on the Duke of Buckingham to himself when
recovering from a fever contracted at Patras while travelling in
the Morea:

> On a cold room's floor, within a bed
> Of iron, with three coverlids like lead,
> A coat and breeches dangling o'er a nook,
> Where sits a doctor, and prescribes a puke,
> Poor Byron sweats—alas! how changed from him
> So plump in feature, and so round in limb,
> Grinning and gay in Newstead's monkish fane
> The scene of profanation and Champagne,
> Or just as gay with scribblers in a ring
> Of twenty hungry authors banqueting,

No whore to fondle left of half a score,
Yet one thing left him, which he values more,
Here victor of a fever and its friends
Physicians and their art, his lordship *mends*.[13]

We must make every allowance for a *jeu d'esprit*, especially one undertaken in such dispiriting conditions. Even so, it is obvious that Byron has little ear for the form in which he is writing. This piece shows only a vestigial sense of its great original:

In the worst inn's worst room, with mat half-hung,
The floors of plaister and the walls of dung,
On once a flock-bed, but repaired with straw,
With tape-tied curtains, never meant to draw,
The George and Garter dangling from that bed
Where tawdry yellow strove with dirty red,
Great Villiers lies—alas! how changed from him,
That life of pleasure, and that soul of whim!
Gallant and gay, in Cliveden's proud alcove,
The bower of wanton Shrewsbury and love;
Or just as gay, at Council, in a ring
Of mimicked Statesmen and their merry King.
No Wit to flatter, left of all his store!
No Fool to laugh at, which he valued more.
There, Victor of his health, of fortune, friends,
And fame; this lord of useless thousands ends.[14]

In Byron's line 1 the scansion is clumsy and the enjambement to line 2 is a functionless lurch. The rhythm of line 2 is forced: 'iron' is unacceptably disyllabic and this occasions a stress on 'with', emphasizing a weak word and so going against the sense. Line 5 is cacophonous, and the change of rhythm after the word 'sweats', attempted in direct imitation of Pope, does not come off. A contrast between this and the original clearly would operate to the younger poet's disadvantage. 'Gallant and gay, in Cliveden's proud alcove' dances; 'Grinning and gay in Newstead's monkish fane' drags!

Of course, Byron's piece comes early, in 1810. But Pope had written imitations that were technically flawless at a far earlier period of his life. The 'Imitation of Waller' dates from 1701, when Pope was thirteen, and the 'Imitation of Spenser', which may have been Byron's favourite,[15] is no later than 1709. This suggests that Byron had less affinity with Pope than Pope had

Byron and the English Tradition

with the poets from whom he learned. But to make the point adequately we must look at works of greater distinction.

There is, in all of Byron's output, no more effective essay in couplets than 'A Sketch'. It is a satire upon Mrs. Clermont, a confidante of the estranged Lady Byron. John Murray reported that Samuel Rogers and John Hookham Frere—names important in the Byron circle—'agree that you have produced nothing better . . .'.[16]

> Mark how the channels of her yellow blood
> Ooze to her skin, and stagnate there to mud,
> Cased like the centipede in saffron mail,
> Or darker greenness of the scorpion's scale—
> (For drawn from reptiles only may we trace
> Congenial colours in that soul or face)—
> Look on her features! and behold her mind
> As in a mirror of itself defined:
> Look on the picture! deem it not o'ercharged—
> There is no trait which might not be enlarged. . . .[17]

Yet, for all its force, the venom rises too near the surface. The fault is over-explicitness. There is too much end-stopping here; there are too many rhetorical gestures. If Byron of all poets was unable to retrieve the characteristically antithetical couplet of Pope, it had gone irretrievably. This was a time when metres were growing more fluid, when forms such as the dramatic monologue were evolving, when the novel was in rapid development. These couplets of Byron look backward to a civilization that had ceased to exist. We certainly find in 'A Sketch' hints of Pope's portrait of Atticus. But the superficial similarities only point up the profound underlying difference:

> A lip of lies; a face formed to conceal,
> And, without feeling, mock at all who feel . . . (Byron).[18]

> . . . Damn with faint praise, assent with civil leer,
> And without sneering, teach the rest to sneer . . . (Pope).[19]

> . . . This female dog-star of her little sky,
> Where all beneath her influence droop or die . . . (Byron).

> . . . Like *Cato* give his little Senate laws,
> And sit attentive to his own applause . . . (Pope).

41

Byron bludgeons incontinently; Pope pierces the vital organ. 'What Byron evidently valued in Pope was his ability to achieve a high degree of rhetorical shapeliness and to make that shapeliness enforce a coherent development of meaning' writes A. B. England[20]; but there is more to it than that. Byron's own words attest, over and over again, that he regarded his own time as 'the age of the decline of English poetry',[21] and for Byron this decline was more than a matter of writing verse. In what deserves to be regarded as a central critical document he wrote to Murray:

> With regard to poetry in general I am convinced the more I think of it—that [Moore] and *all* of us—Scott—Southey—Wordsworth—Moore—Campbell—I—are all in the wrong—one as much as another—that we are upon a wrong revolutionary poetical system—or systems—not worth a damn in itself—& from which none but Rogers and Crabbe are free—and that the present & next generations will finally be of this opinion.—I am the more confirmed in this—by having lately gone over some of our Classics—particularly *Pope*—whom I tried in this way—I took Moore's poems & my own & some others—and went over them side by side with Pope's—and I was really astonished (I ought not to have been so) and mortified—at the ineffable distance in point of sense—harmony—effect—and even *Imagination* Passion—& *Invention*—between the little Queen Anne's Man—& us of the lower Empire—depend upon it [it] is all Horace then, and Claudian now among us. . . .[22]

That Byron was not alone in this opinion is shown by a comment written on the manuscript of his letter by William Gifford, whose sub-Popian couplets had influenced the younger poet greatly: 'There is more good sense, and feeling and judgment, in this passage, than in any other I ever read, or Lord Byron wrote.'[23] Byron reveals more even than Gifford seems to see: it is an almost religious yearning for a lost civilization. Repeatedly Byron avers that he wishes he had adopted a different plan in his own composition; that if he had to begin again he would model himself after the example of Pope.[24] But poetry, as Byron came to realize, cannot be remodelled in this way. If Byron was to fulfil his capabilities, it would have to be in a mode other than that of Pope.

In any case, the tradition of Pope could never have been

consonant with Byron's highly individual personality. Pope, for all his oddities of health and (given the time) religion, wrote from the centre of his society. Even at his most apparently negative, Pope implies an agreed code of behaviour:

> Oh! could I mount on the Maeonian wing,
> Your Arms, your Actions, your Repose to sing!
> What seas you traversed! and what fields you fought!
> Your Country's Peace, how oft, how dearly bought!
> How barb'rous rage subsided at your word,
> And Nations wondered while they dropped the sword!
> How, when you nodded, o'er the land and deep,
> Peace stole her wing, and wrapt the world in sleep. . . .[25]

This is from Pope's 'Epistle to Augustus'. The poem is, among other things, an ironic treatment of George II; in particular, it refers to his philistinism regarding the arts, together with his pacific foreign policy—'Your Country's Peace, how oft, how dearly bought. . . !' The irony is lightly touched: such was Pope's sense of hierarchy that he could not avoid, in imitating Horace's praise of the genuine Augustus, treating with courtesy his own, spurious, one.

In contrast to this, Byron's genius was subversive. He wrote from a position outside a society that he believed to be rotten. The portait of *his* George is a directed jet of contempt at a vulnerable target, and is couched in a deliberately indecorous metre:

> In the first year of freedom's second dawn
>   Died George the Third; although no tyrant, one
> Who shielded tyrants, till each sense withdrawn
>   Left him nor mental nor external sun:
> A better farmer ne'er brush'd dew from lawn,
>   A worse king never left a realm undone!
> He died—but left his subjects still behind,
> One half as mad—and t'other no less blind. . . .
>
> He's dead—and upper earth with him has done;
>   He's buried; save the undertaker's bill,
> Or lapidary scrawl, the world is gone
>   For him, unless he left a German will:
> But where's the proctor who will ask his son?
>   In whom his qualities are reigning still,
> Except that household virtue, most uncommon,
> Of constancy to a bad, ugly woman. . . .[26]

There is no seeking after rhetorical shapeliness here. The effect is one of instability, localized in the variegation and versatility of the rhymes. No one has written better about Byron's metric than W. H. Auden:

> The stanza divides by rhyme into a group of six lines followed by a coda of two; the poet can either observe this division and use the couplet as an epigrammatic comment on the first part, or he can take seven lines for his theme and use the final one as a punch line.[27]

What are functionless enjambements and forced rhymes in Byron's earlier sets of couplets become special effects in the *ottava rima*. As Auden further remarks, the form in Byron's hands provided opportunities 'for the interpolated comment and conversational aside'.[28] The reader has to be continually on the lookout for tricks and turns and unexpected let-downs:

> 'God save the king!' It is a large economy
> In God to save the like. . . .[29]

'Economy' is audacious enough in itself—a pun on the word 'save'—and it is driven home by a series of unforeseeable rhyme-words. 'Economy' is made to rhyme, outrageously, with 'one am I' and 'alone am I'. It is all part of a debunking process, but the objects of Byron's ironic attention are catechized from no secure standpoint. It is not for him to reform; he observes, and he mocks at what he observes. This is the difference between Pope and Byron. Pope can be sublime:

> Yes, I am proud; I must be proud to see
> Men not afraid of God, afraid of me. . . .[30]

Byron, on the other hand, is audacious. Of 'the crowning carnage, Waterloo' he says:

> This by the way; 'tis not mine to record
> What angels shrink from. . . .[31]

Byron's world has no centre: 'The path is through perplexing ways', 'as the veering wind shifts, shift our sails'.[32] If there is a norm, it is specific and individual: the impulse of comradeship between man and man, the unexpected shaft of pity that causes the strong to form an alliance with the weak. There is nothing quantifiable; nothing that adds up to a philosophy.

The mode of verse seen in *Don Juan* and *The Vision of Judgment* had fluctuated in and out of English literature for some time, though Byron had the privilege of manipulating it to stage centre. It is a mode naturalized in English; but its origins, usefully anatomized by R. D. Waller, are Italian.[33] There flourished in the fifteenth and sixteenth centuries a kind of burlesque poetry related to such epics as *La Chanson de Roland*. In the *Morgante Maggiore* (*ante* 1487), for example, Charlemagne becomes a foil and Roland (or Orlando) a pawn. The author, Luigi Pulci, plays for comedy: most of the activity is ascribed to the unconventional figure of Rinaldo, and there is a good deal of digression.

The chief imitators of Pulci in the sixteenth century were Boiardo, Ariosto and Berni. Ariosto's poem, *Orlando Furioso* (1532)—Roland run mad—proved intermittently influential in English. The Elizabethan version by Sir John Harington is a masterpiece in its own right. It is full of witty, irreverent and irrelevant buffoonery. To the unhistorical eye, indeed, it would seem unmistakably Byronic:

> For at the chink was plainly to be seen
> A chamber hanged with fair and rich array
> Where none might come but such as trusty been.
> The Princess here in part doth spend the day,
> And here he saw a Dwarf embrace the Queen
> And strive awhile, and, after homely play,
> His skill was such that ere they went asunder
> The Dwarf was got aloft, and she lay under. . . .[34]

It is hard to believe that, with his early interest in Ariosto,[35] Byron had never come across Harington, Ariosto's greatest English exponent. In her helpful account of Byron's reading, Elizabeth French Boyd points out that as a boy he was given the run of well-stocked libraries at Dulwich, Harrow and Burgage Manor.[36] The vein of mocking irreverence here— 'Much did the King this foul prospect mislike'[37]—would have been congenial to Byron, even if he could not, at that stage, effectively learn from it.

One finds the mode surfacing at periods of political turmoil, especially those bearing a degree of disaffection from France. Marius Bewley[38] has drawn our attention to sundry recrudescences in the seventeenth century:

Favours are oft, unhappily, by chance
Bestowed: for, 'mongst those courtiers that did wear
The Prince's points, a Marquess was of France,
Who for some heinous fact he had done there,
Hanged in effigy, fled from France for fear,
And so for refuge to Carleon came,
Monsieur Marquis Jean Foutre was his name. . . .[39]

. . . Thus was he gulled, as once a King of France
Paid a French monsieur for a prancing steed—
Gave him a purse whose richness did enhance
The enclosed gem, supposed a noble meed,
    But when for golden mountains he did gape,
    He oped the purse, and only found a rape. . . .[40]

The work of Sir Francis Kynaston and Nathaniel Whiting, from whom these quotations are taken, forms a kind of assault upon the expectations of the reader. There are characters with far-fetched names; there are ridiculous rhymes; there are absurd situations. In *Albino and Bellama*, from which the second quotation comes, a monk disguises himself as a nun and insinuates himself into a convent where he impregnates all the inmates! This would have been a plot to engage the future author of the *oda* episode in *Don Juan*, and here again it is quite possible that Byron had come across the work of some, at least, of his seventeenth-century predecessors. There was Edward Fairfax, whose translation (1604) of Tasso's *Gerusalemme Liberata* was in Byron's own library,[41] and Sir William D'Avenant, whose *Gondibert* (1651) Byron would have come across in connection with his reading of Dryden and who, in any case, was widely excerpted. There was also William Chamberlayne whose *Pharonnida* (1659) was praised and excerpted in Southey's 'Vision of the Maid of Orleans' (1799) and which is further represented in Campbell's *Specimens of the British Poets* (1819)— also in Byron's library.[42] There is, moreover, a close resemblance between Book III Canto III of this last and the Gulbeyaz episode of *Don Juan*, though both may have had a common source in Firenzuole, whose works Byron acquired in Italy.[43] An eighteenth-century forerunner may well be a singular poem by John Gay, 'Mr Pope's Welcome from Greece', in which John Underhill, following W. J. Courthope, found echoes of Ariosto.[44]

The work of poets such as these shows a remarkable resemblance in technique and tone to that of a group of littérateurs writing in the early nineteenth century. It is with this group, more than with Pope and much more than with the second wave of Romantics, that Byron should be associated. The littérateurs in question shared a desire to bring before the public the Italian romances which had surfaced in the English tradition so far only intermittently. John Herman Merivale, William Stewart Rose and John Hookham Frere, among others, used regularly to visit Murray in his parlour and advise him on his publications. Not altogether flatteringly, when the publication of various addenda to his letters on Pope was being discussed, Byron referred to this group as Murray's Utican Senate![45]

John Herman Merivale seems to have been a key figure. Byron may have made his acquaintance as early as 1805, when he was a boy at Harrow and Merivale was a young man courting the headmaster's daughter. The acquaintance was consolidated by the fact that the headmaster's son, Henry Drury, in subsequent years became not only Merivale's brother-in-law but Byron's close friend. We do not know how much of his research into Italian poetry Merivale imparted in conversation but, between May 1806 and June 1807, he wrote about Pulci in the influential *Monthly Magazine* and illustrated his articles with copious extracts:

> Morgante had a rustic palace made
>   Of sticks, earth, leaves, in his own barbarous way,
> And here at ease his mighty members laid,
>   Securely guarded, at the close of day.
> Orlando knocked; the giant, sore dismayed,
>   Waked from the heavy sleep in which he lay;
> And, when he opened, like a thing astound,
> Scared by a frightful dream, he gazed around.
>
> He thought a furious serpent had assailed him;
>   And, when to Mahound for relief he prayed,
> That nought his Pagan deity availed him;
>   But, when Christ's holy name he called for aid,
> Straightway the serpent's wonted fury failed him.
>   Waked from this dream, towards the door he made—
> 'Who knocks?' with rough and grumbling voice he cried.
> 'Soon shalt thou know—' the Paladin replied. . . .[46]

Byron never wavered in his regard for Merivale. He praised the poem Merivale wrote in imitation of Pulci, *Orlando in Roncesvalles*,[47] and, according to Jerome McGann,[48] this poem may have encouraged Byron's first attempt at *ottava rima*. Certainly Byron repeatedly invoked Merivale as an authority on Italian poetry[49]; along with, that is, William Stewart Rose.

William Stewart Rose was, in his own way, as remarkable a figure as Merivale. He published his translation of Giambattista Casti, an eighteenth-century straggler after the great Florentines, in 1819. Byron claimed to have read Casti in the original. Nevertheless, one can be reasonably certain that Rose helped him not only with Pulci, whom he did not read till later,[51] but with his development of what was, for him, a new style. Indeed, so close was the intellectual community of the two men that Frere, well acquainted with them both, at first took Rose to be the author of Byron's first publication in his new mode.[52] One can see why Frere was of this opinion if one looks at Rose's dedication of his version of Casti to Ugo Foscolo, yet another of this circle who had attracted Byron's regard.[53] Foscolo appears to have been bilingual in Italian and English and therefore especially capable of understanding Rose's endeavour:

> Dear Foscolo, to thee my dedication's
> Addressed with reason. Who like thee is able
> To judge betwixt the theme and variations?
> To whom so well can I inscribe my fable,
> As thee? since I, upon good proof may sing thee
> *Doctum sermones utriusque linguae.*[54]

The quotation from Horace[55] may imply an ethos more ideal than the one actually inhabited by these young poets and scholars. However, they certainly operated as an intellectual community, and, under their influence, Byron came to see his need for a change of style. 'I certainly am a devil of a mannerist—& must leave off.'[56] He had completed Canto IV of *Childe Harold's Pilgrimage* and, as Leslie Marchand remarks, 'he was growing tired of that vein.'[57] During this period, however, he was much in the company of Rose,[58] and it was, according to Jerome McGann,[59] Rose who gave Byron Frere's *Whistlecraft*. The effect was galvanic. 'I have since written a

poem (of 84 octave stanzas) humourous, in or after the excellent
manner of Mr Whistlecraft (whom I take to be Frere . . .).'[60]
The poem was *Beppo*, and it was Frere of all these poets
favouring the Italians who most influenced Byron's work:

> Princes protecting Sciences and Art
>   I've often seen, in copper-plate and print;
> I never saw them elsewhere, for my part,
>   And therefore I conclude there's nothing in't;
> But every body knows the Regent's heart;
>   I trust he won't reject a well-meant hint;
> Each board to have twelve members, with a seat
> To bring them in per ann. five hundred neat:—
>
> From Princes I descend to the Nobility:
>   In former times all persons of high stations,
> Lords, Baronets, and Persons of gentility,
>   Paid twenty guineas for the dedications:
> This practice was attended with utility;
>   The patrons lived to future generations,
> The poets lived by their industrious earning,—
> So men alive and dead could live by Learning. . . .
>
> . . . Lastly, the common people I beseech—
>   Dear People! if you think my verses clever,
> Preserve with care your noble Parts of speech,
>   And take it as a maxim to endeavour
> To talk as your good mothers used to teach,
>   And then these lines of mine may last for ever;
> And don't confound the image of the nation
> With long-tailed words in *osity* and *ation*. . . .[61]

This would seem startling to a twentieth-century reader who
had never come across 'Whistlecraft' before. Superficially it is
not easy to tell Frere's work from that of Byron. Both exhibit an
extent of wild rhyming, of direct address to the reader, of
far-fetched digression.[62] However, Byron is marked apart by
the superior energy of his portraiture. It is the difference between

> But every body knows the Regent's heart;
>   I hope he won't reject a well-meant hint . . .[63]

and

> Gaunt Famine never shall approach the throne.
> Though Ireland starve, great George weighs twenty stone . . .[63]

Frere is willing to wound, but Byron is not afraid to strike. Far more than Frere, Byron takes audacious risks with tone. He draws upon Romantic attitudes only to deflate them:

> But in his native stream, the Guadalquivir,
>   Juan to lave his youthful limbs was wont;
> And having learned to swim in that sweet river,
>   Had often turn'd the art to some account:
> A better swimmer you could scarce see ever,
>   He could, perhaps, have pass'd the Hellespont,
> As once (a feat on which ourselves we prided)
> Leander, Mr. Ekenhead, and I did. . . .[65]

The romance of words like 'Guadalquivir' and phrases like 'to lave his youthful limbs' is brought down into a real world of men. It is all quite distinct from the legendary subject-matter favoured by Frere. Leander seems no longer a remote hero but a contemporary of Byron and his swimming acquaintance, the Lieutenant of Marines.[66] The effect is not only to familiarize the exotic; it is to inform a measure of the exotic into the familiar.

Especially characteristic of Byron is his control of the anti-climax. Sometimes the effect is sudden; sometimes it works in successive stages of deflation. But the result is always to eradicate convention from the verse:

> 'Go, little book, from this my solitude!
>   I cast thee on the waters, go thy ways!
> And if, as I believe, thy vein be good,
>   The world will find thee after many days.'
> When Southey's read, and Wordsworth understood,
>   I can't help putting in my claim to praise—
> The four first rhymes are Southey's, every line:
> For God's sake, reader! take them not for mine![67]

We will find nothing so immediate in Frere; nor in Merivale and Rose, either. This seems to be an extension of Byron's own speaking voice, in so far as it can be inferred from reports of his conversation and from his own remarkable letters:

> Southey should have been a parish-clerk, and Wordsworth a man-midwife—both in darkness. I doubt if either of them ever got drunk. . . .[68]

Byron projects something akin to this tone of voice in his poetry and so seems to get very close to the reader. Personal interpolation becomes, paradoxically, part of the narrative; so do highly autobiographical statements:

> No more—no more—Oh! never more on me
> The freshness of the heart can fall like dew . . .[69]

and direct appeals:

> They accuse me—*Me*—the present writer of
> The present poem—of—I know not what. . . .[70]

This gives the verse a flavour which acts as a connective through all the fluctuations of tone and contrasts of linguistic register. It is not altogether true to say that Rose and Frere, and their predecessors, outraged decorum; their importance is that they showed Byron a way to turn his outrage into poetry. He could not learn directly from Pulci. His own translation of that poet, compared with that of Merivale, is painstaking and lifeless—as Ronald Bottrall said.[71] The fact that Byron never lost faith in his effort[72] does not affect one's feeling that Byron required an English intermediary between himself and the Italians in order to evolve his greatest poetic comedy. His best work relates to Rose and Frere rather than to Casti and Pulci.

However, times were changing. Byron was not only the greatest exponent of the subversive mode in verse; he was the last. A greater degree of flexibility even than he could encompass was on the way; but it was to transpire in the form not of verse but of prose. *Don Juan*'s true successor is *Martin Chuzzlewit*; especially the American chapters, with their preposterously named characters and scalding ironies. Indeed, America was a country to which Byron might well, had *Don Juan* continued, have sent his hero; he always maintained a high regard for the new republic. 'America is a Model of force and freedom & moderation. . . .' 'I would rather have a nod from an American, than a snuff-box from an emperor. . . .' 'To be the first man—not the Dictator—not the Sylla, but the Washington or the Aristides—the leader in talent and truth—is next to the Divinity. . . !'[73] In real life Byron himself seriously contemplated going to Venezuela.[74] There is no reason why *Don Juan* could not have explored territory further flung even than that.

Its scheme was comprehensive: 'since you want *length* you shall have enough of Juan for I'll make 50 cantos . . .'; 'I meant to have made him a Cavalier Servente in Italy and a cause for a divorce in England—and a Sentimental "Wertherfaced" man in Germany—so as to show the different ridicules of the society in each of those countries . . .'; 'there shall be such a poem—as has not been since Ariosto—in length—in satire—in imagery—and in what I please. . . .'[75]

The very incompleteness of *Don Juan* as it stands seems to be an essential trait in its structure. 'Byron's logic asserts that all systems and forms being, by their nature, inadequate to life, the poet can hope to describe things as they are only by being unsystematic', writes Darrell Sheraw.[76] He is right: the poem breaks off in mid-episode; but can we picture *Don Juan* with a foreseeable conclusion? Any such outcome would have been incongruous with the general air of happy improvisation:

> the fact is that I have nothing plann'd,
> Unless it were to be a moment merry. . . .[77]

There is a pattern, but it cannot be typified in ordinary narrative terms; not even those of the picaresque novel. For example, the theme of people not finding what they are looking for is voiced early in the poem:

> Under the bed they search'd, and there they found—
> No matter what—it was not that they sought. . . .[78]

It surfaces intermittently through the discursive structure—which ends, fortuitously and yet characteristically, with that same gesture:

> he had made at first a silly blunder,
> And that in his confusion he had caught
> Only the wall, instead of what he sought.[79]

Don Juan would have found nothing more satisfactory if his author had lived to be 50 and created him Governor of Massachusetts. *Don Juan* is not a development but an accumulation. Its author is neither Romantic prophet nor Classical spokesman: either stance would have committed him to being a Master of Ceremonies. As it was, Byron found his role within the English tradition as its Lord of Misrule.

NOTES

1. Emile Legouis, Louis Cazamian and Raymond Las Vergnas, *A History of English Literature* (1926–27, rev. ed. London, 1964), Book V, Chapters 1 and 4; esp. p. 1041.
2. Byron, Letter to John Murray, 30 September 1816, but see also letter to James Hogg, 24 March 1814. References to Byron's letters, unless otherwise stated, are based on Leslie A. Marchand's edition of the Letters and Journals (London, 1973–82).
3. Byron, Letter to Leigh Hunt, 30 October 1815.
4. Byron, Letter to P. B. Shelley, 26 April 1821.
5. Byron, Letter to Murray, 9 November 1820.
6. G. Wilson Knight, *Laureate of Peace: On the Genius of Alexander Pope* (London, 1954), p. 122.
7. Byron, Note to 'Some Observations upon an Article in *Blackwood's Magazine*' (1820) dated 12 November 1821, reprinted in R. E. Prothero, *Byron's Letters and Journals* (London, 1898–1904), Vol. IV, pp. 491–92.
8. Byron, Journal, 24 November 1813.
9. Letter to Murray, 15 September 1817.
10. Byron, Dedication (to Goethe) of *Marino Faliero* (14 October 1820). Reprinted in Prothero, op. cit., Vol. V. See p. 104.
11. Byron, Letter to Lord Kinnaird, 20 November 1821.
12. Byron, 'Observations upon "Observations". A Second Letter to John Murray, Esq., on the Rev. W. L. Bowles's Strictures on the Life and Writings of Pope' (25 March 1821; not published until 1835). Reprinted in Prothero, op. cit., Vol. V. See p. 590. Quotations within this quotation are, respectively, from 'The Burial of Sir John Moore at Corunna' by Charles Wolfe and from the *Life of Pope* (1769) by Owen Ruffhead.
13. Byron, Letter to John Cam Hobhouse, 25 September 1810.
14. Pope, *Moral Essays*, Epistle III, to Allen, Lord Bathurst, ll. 299–314. Text of this and other quotations from Pope based on that given in the Twickenham Edition, ed. John Butt (London, 1963).
15. Byron, Letter to the Earl of Clare, 20 August 1807.
16. *Samuel Smiles, A Publisher and his Friends: Memoirs and Correspondence of the Late John Murray* (London, 1981), quoted by Elizabeth French Boyd, *Byron's 'Don Juan': A Critical Study* (London, 1945), p. 10.
17. Byron, 'A Sketch'; see Letter to Murray, 30 March 1816. The text of this and of future quotations from Byron's poems with the exception of *Don Juan* is based on that which appears in the relevant volume of the Oxford Edition of Standard Authors.
18. This, together with the subsequent quotation from Byron, is from 'A Sketch'.
19. This, together with the subsequent quotation from Pope, is from 'An Epistle to Dr Arbuthnot'.
20. A. B. England, *Byron's 'Don Juan' and Eighteenth Century Literature* (Lewisburg and London, 1975), p. 50.

21. Byron, 'Some Observations upon an Article in *Blackwood's Magazine*', reprinted in Prothero, op. cit., Vol. IV, p. 485.
22. Byron, Letter to Murray, 15 September 1817.
23. See Prothero, op. cit., Vol. IV, p. 169n.
24. Byron, 'Some Observations upon an Article in *Blackwood's Magazine*', reprinted in Prothero, op. cit., Vol. IV, p. 488; letter to Murray, 15 September 1817.
25. Pope, The First Epistle of the Second Book of Horace, Imitated: 'To Augustus', ll. 394–401.
26. Byron, *The Vision of Judgment* (1821), stanzas viii, xii.
27. W. H. Auden, 'Don Juan', *The Dyer's Hand* (London, 1963), p. 399.
28. Ibid., p. 398.
29. Byron, *The Vision of Judgment*, stanza xiii.
30. Pope, Epilogue to the Satires, Dialogue II: ll. 208–9.
31. Byron, *The Vision of Judgment*, stanza vi.
32. Byron, *Don Juan*, Canto I, cxxxiii; Canto II, iv. The text of this and of other quotations from *Don Juan* is based upon the edition by T. G. Steffan, E. Steffan and W. W. Pratt (Harmondsworth, Middlesex, 1973).
33. R. D. Waller, Introduction to J. H. Frere's *The Monks and the Giants* (London, 1926).
34. Ariosto, *Orlando Furioso*, translated by Sir John Harington, Book XXVIII. Text based on that in my anthology, *Ten Elizabethan Poets* (London and Harlow, 1969) and adapted from Graham Hough's edition (London, 1963).
35. Byron, Letter to John M. B. Pigot, 9 August 1806; and see Elizabeth French Boyd, op. cit., p. 171n.
36. Elizabeth French Boyd, op. cit., pp. 84ff.
37. As note 34.
38. Marius Bewley, 'The Colloquial Mode of Byron', *Scrutiny*, Vol. XVI (1949).
39. Sir Francis Kynaston, *Leoline and Sydanis* (1642), stanza xxiv; text based on *Minor Poets of the Caroline Period*, Vol. II, ed. George Saintsbury (Oxford, 1906).
40. Nathaniel Whiting, *Albino and Bellama* (1638), ll. 2296–301; text based on *Minor Poets of the Caroline Period*, ed. G. Saintsbury as above, Vol. III.
41. Elizabeth French Boyd, op. cit., p. 101.
42. Ibid., p. 100.
43. Ibid., p. 127.
44. *Poems of John Gay*, ed. John Underhill (London and New York, 1893), Vol. 1, p. 290.
45. Byron, Letters to Murray, 26 February and 12 March 1821; and see Elizabeth French Boyd, op. cit., p. 6.
46. John Herman Merivale, translated extracts from *Morgante Maggiore* by Luigi Pulci. Text as in *The Monthly Magazine*, May 1806–June 1807.
47. Byron, Letter to John Herman Merivale, January 1814; and see letters to Francis Hodgson, 29 June 1811 and 3 January 1813.
48. Jerome J. McGann, *'Don Juan' in Context* (London, 1976), p. 53.
49. See, for example, Byron's letters to Merivale, January 1814; to Murray,

10 April and 2 September 1814, and 5 March 1820; and Byron's Journal, 6 March 1814.

50. Byron, Letter to Pryse Gordon, June 1816.
51. Byron, Letters to Murray, 25 March and 12 April 1818; note on one of Rose's poems, May 1818; letters to John Cam Hobhouse, 3 March, 25 March and 11 November 1818; and see T. G. Steffan, *Byron's 'Don Juan': The Making of a Masterpiece* (Austin, Texas, 1957), p. 8n.
52. Jerome J. McGann, op. cit., p. 54.
53. Byron, Preface to Canto IV of *Childe Harold's Pilgrimage* (1818); letter to Murray, 8 October 1820.
54. William Stewart Rose, *The Court and Parliament of Beasts, freely translated from the 'Animali Parlante' of Casti* (1819).
55. Horace, Odes, III, viii—'versed in the lore of either tongue', as the Loeb edition has it; and see Jerome J. McGann, op. cit., Chapter Five.
56. Byron, Letter to Murray, 9 March 1817.
57. Leslie A. Marchand, *Byron's Poetry: A Critical Introduction* (London, 1965), pp. 145–46.
58. Byron, Letter to Murray, 4 September 1817; to Samuel Rogers, 3 March 1818; to Murray, 25 March 1818; to Hobhouse, 25 March 1818.
59. Jerome J. McGann, op. cit., p. 54; and see Byron's letter to Murray, 25 March 1818.
60. Byron, Letter to Murray, 17 September 1817; and see R. D. Waller, op. cit.,—'They angled in the same waters. . .'.
61. William and Robert Whistlecraft (*i.e.*, John Hookham Frere), *The Prospectus and Specimen of an Intended National Work* (1817): Proem. Text based upon the edition by R. D. Waller, entitled *The Monks and the Giants* (London, 1926).
62. M. K. Joseph makes an interesting attempt to quantify the various proportions of digressiveness in each episode, in his *Byron the Poet* (London, 1964), pp. 198–99.
63. As note 61.
64. Byron, *Don Juan*, Canto VIII, cxxvi; and see Canto IX, xxxix; Canto XI, lxxviii; etc. For text see note 32.
65. Byron, *Don Juan*, Canto II, cv.
66. Byron, Letter to Murray, 21 February 1821.
67. Byron, *Don Juan*, Canto I, ccxxii.
68. Byron, Letter to James Hogg, 24 March 1814.
69. Byron, *Don Juan*, Canto I, ccxiv.
70. Ibid., Canto VII, iii.
71. Ronald Bottrall, 'Byron and the Colloquial Tradition in English Poetry', *Criterion*, Vol. XVIII (1939).
72. Letter to Thomas Moore, 24 May 1820; to Hobhouse, 8 June 1820; letters to Murray, 7 August and 28 September 1820, and 19 January, 1 March and 12 September 1821; letter to Thomas Moore, 4 March 1822; to Douglas Kinnaird, 8 March 1823.
73. Byron, Letter to Hobhouse, 12 October 1821; to Moore, 8 June 1822; Journal, 23 November 1813. My attention was originally drawn to this

possibility by my wife, Rosemary; to whom I owe other, less readily assignable, perceptions in this paper.

74. Byron, Letter to Hobhouse, 3 October 1819.
75. Letters to Murray, 6 April 1819, and 16 February 1821; to Douglas Kinnaird, 31 March 1823.
76. C. Darrell Sheraw, '*Don Juan*: Byron as Un-Augustan Satirist', *Satire News Letter*, Vol. X (1973).
77. Byron, *Don Juan*, Canto IV, v.
78. Ibid., Canto I, cxliv.
79. Ibid., Canto XVI, cxxii.

3

Voice, Tone, and Transition in *Don Juan*

by EDWIN MORGAN

'Byron is a perfect chameleon', concluded his friend Lady Blessington, who recorded the gist of his frank conversations with her. She thought he had 'no fixed principles' of conduct or of belief, even if he had ruling sentiments (love of liberty, hatred of cant). If the chameleon is an animal that changes colour for self-protective purposes, is this how we are to see Byron? Certainly he gave no single constant impression. In company, he could be constrained and withdrawn, or warm and loquacious, depending on the size and congeniality of the group. Both reactions seem too spontaneous to be consciously self-protective, and their main consequence was to increase the interest and curiosity felt by observers of his unpredictable, tantalizing personality. If his silence concealed nothing more than diffidence and being ill at ease, it may be that his loquacity concealed more. He loved wit and repartee, and in the right mood he could throw out a chain of ideas of extraordinary richness, linked by lightning connections scarcely sensed by the hearer; but he disliked sustained argument, and when Leigh Hunt once tried to persuade him that good argument needed logic and reason, his answer was: 'For my part, it is the last speaker that convinces me.' This eternal impressionability, the lack of patience with reason, the search for unknown links-forward rather than known links-back, is certainly zestful and creative, and one of the keys to his poetic method, but it may at the same

time be self-protective in a man who is loath to expose a central
jostle of unresolved beliefs and counter-beliefs to the hard clear
light that step-by-step argument would place them in. He is
quite capable of making a virtue of contingency:

> The great object of life is Sensation—to feel that we exist—even
> though in pain—it is this 'craving void' which drives us to
> Gaming—to Battle—to Travel—to intemperate but keenly felt
> pursuits of every description whose principal attraction is the
> agitation inseparable from their accomplishment.
>
> (Letter to Annabella Milbanke, 6 September 1813)

This is the philosophy of a man of moods, who if often bored or
abstracted enjoys the contrast that a sudden excitement
brings. Those who expect to find the languid humours of a
world-weary Romantic may be disconcerted by bursts of brisk
no-nonsense wit; others, led to expect the wit, may find a dark
immovable object they cannot even probe. John Galt, travelling
on the same boat as Byron from Gibraltar to Malta in 1809,
noted his general waywardness, which he thought partly a
pose, but was struck more persuasively by a deeper contrast
between the sociable 'day' Byron and the abstracted solitary
'night' Byron, the latter being like 'a man forbid', sitting on a
rail in silence and staring into the darkness. When we say that
Byron was temperamental and moody, then, we have many
witnesses, not least himself. But the contrasts are not only
between sensation and sensation, as the letter to Annabella
might suggest, or between sensation and the lack of it, as Hunt
observed. Sensation, feeling, craving, pursuit, agitation—to
use the words of the letter—are not all in all. A different
contrast emerges if one compares passages from two other
letters. Writing to Thomas Moore on 2 March 1815, Byron is
the very image of a man in a down mood:

> I am in such a state of sameness and stagnation, and so totally
> occupied in consuming the fruits—and sauntering—and play-
> ing dull games at cards—and yawning—and trying to read old
> Annual Registers and the daily papers—and gathering shells
> on the shore—and watching the growth of stunted gooseberry
> bushes in the garden—that I have neither time nor sense to say
> more than
>
> Yours ever,
> B.

Yet the sharpest contrast to that passage comes in another letter to the same correspondent, five years later, from Ravenna (9 December 1820), and is not a report of the delights of some elated sensation or excitement but is concerned with right action, with duty. The local garrison commander is shot near Byron's house, and lies dying in the street. A crowd gathers, makes a great noise, but does nothing to help; there is even a doctor, who conceals the fact that he is one. Byron reacts instantly: disgusted, pragmatic, British, taking charge.

> As nobody could, or would, do any thing but howl and pray, and as no one would stir a finger to move him, for fear of consequences, I lost my patience—made my servant and a couple of the mob take up the body—sent off two soldiers to the guard—despatched Diego to the Cardinal with the news, and had the commandant carried upstairs into my own quarter. But it was too late, he was gone—not at all disfigured—bled inwardly—not above an ounce or two came out. . . . You are to know that, if I had not had the body moved, they would have left him there till morning in the street for fear of consequences. I would not choose to let even a dog die in such a manner, without succour:—and, as for consequences, I care for none in a duty.

This admirable practicality—and the splendid last phrase is set down with absolutely no self-consciousness—has the effect of almost, though possibly not quite, negating his remarks about 'sensation'. The incident *was* exciting, and in another part of the letter he describes, almost like a novelist, how the man 'only said, "O Dio!" and "Gesu!" two or three times' before he died. But mainly what he illustrates is the inculcation of certain moral ideas and habits of action which occupy an area of constancy, of reliability, in a character otherwise fluid and variable. The imprint of this, too, is seen in his poetry.

Byron in company; in the streets; in correspondence. But what of Byron in his room, writing his private journals—has he any helpful secrets? Not secrets, perhaps, but some instructive examples of association and transition, caught on the wing in a more purely unpremeditated way than in the famous digressions of *Don Juan*. Two are worth noting, and both are called 'strange'. The shorter one (*Ravenna Journal*, 2 February

1821) is a tribute to the sudden effect of music. After ruminating on his bad habit of waking too early in the morning, in a state of either despondency, or thirst, or anger, and wondering whether all this is hypochondria or a case of premature senility, he writes, without a break:

> Oh! there is an organ playing in the street—a waltz, too! I must leave off to listen. They are playing a waltz which I have heard ten thousand times at the balls in London, between 1812 and 1815. Music is a strange thing.

The music, utterly accidental as it is, makes him stop what he is doing, and yet seems to carry forward, as if in another dimension, his thoughts of time passing and place changing. In a longer passage (*Ravenna Journal*, 12 January 1821), he is kept indoors by bad weather, reading letters from England and a collection of English poetry. Suddenly there is a change of direction, as his reading of the song 'Sabrina fair' in Milton's *Comus* sets off an unforeseen train of reminiscences about a dead friend of his youth, Edward Noel Long.

> How strange are my thoughts!—The reading of the song in Milton, 'Sabrina fair' has brought back upon me—I know not how or why—the happiest, perhaps, days of my life (always excepting, here and there, a Harrow holiday in the two latter summers of my stay there) when living at Cambridge with Edward Noel Long, afterwards of the Guards,—who, after having served honourably in the expedition to Copenhagen (of which two or three thousand scoundrels yet survive in plight and pay), was drowned early in 1809, on his passage to Lisbon with his regiment in the St. George transport, which was run foul of, in the night, by another transport.

He goes on to evoke the summer days of an intense romantic friendship when he and Long, as students at Cambridge, rode, dived, swam, read, played music together, and crowns the story with a reference to his even deeper attachment to the choir-boy John Edleston. The associative triggering comes from water (the element in which Sabrina, guardian nymph of the River Severn, lived, in which Long and Byron dived and swam in the River Cam, and in which Long drowned in the Atlantic Ocean) and from music (the song invoking Sabrina, the intimate music-making of the masque in which it is set, and the flute-and-'cello evenings in Cambridge when Byron was his friend's audience); and Byron's bisexual nature makes him see, at a flash, the features of Edward Long under the wet 'loose train' of Sabrina's hair. He calls the thought-sequence 'strange' because it has arisen so quickly, 'I know not how or why'. But what is strange in the prose of a personal diary may flourish naturally in the verse of a long poem which delights in real or apparent spontaneity. Shelley, interestingly enough, used the same word to characterize the poetry as Lady Blessington had used of the poet. 'The language in which the whole [of *Don Juan* Cantos III–V] is clothed—a sort of chameleon under the changing sky of the spirit that kindles it—is such as those lisping days could not have expected' (letter to Byron, 21 October 1821). What does *this* chameleon change from, and to?

Byron said many, and sometimes contradictory, things about *Don Juan* in his letters. It was 'meant to be a little quietly facetious upon every thing' (September 1818); it was 'the most moral of poems' (February 1819); it was a '*human*' poem after so many '*divine*' ones (April 1819); he had 'no plan' but he did have 'materials' (August 1819); it was 'the sublime of *that there* sort of writing' and could not have been written by anyone 'who has not lived in the world' (October 1819); 'to how many cantos this may extend, I know not' (February 1821); but some day it would be recognized as 'a *Satire* on *abuses* of the present states of Society' (December 1822). The range of comments fits the fluidity of the man. The poem is both lightly facetious and highly moral; it has no plan and is a planned social satire; it is erotic but sublime. Clearly a poem of such great length, composed over several years, must have grown and developed in the conceptions that motivated it, but it is harder than usual to see any ruling structure, not only because the work is unfinished but because Byron never decided how many cantos it was to have (24? 100? 150?—these were all forecasts he made at different times) or what goal the narrative and chronology were making for (the French Revolution and its aftermath? the fight for Greek independence?—these he considered). Add to that the fact that the emotional and intellectual climax of the poem as we have it comes half-way (Canto VIII, the siege of Ismail), with a distinct slackening of interest in the last cantos dealing with Juan's visit to England, and any sense of a satisfying architectonics is postponed to the vista of a much longer poem where extremely powerful revolutionary or military scenes in France or Greece might have redeemed the slack and restored the balance. To a reader in the late twentieth century, however, architectonics is not everything, either in art or for that matter in life. *Don Juan* may indeed seem áll the more appealing, with a kind of proleptic modernity, in its foretaste of so many later unfinished long poems, like Pound's *Cantos*, MacDiarmid's *Mature Art*, William Carlos Williams's *Paterson*, Olson's *Maximus Poems*, Berryman's *Dream Songs*, and Lowell's *Notebook* and *History*. In all these examples, the poem eventually becomes, whatever its organizing principles may once have been (narrative, philosophical, epic), an accompaniment or doppelgänger of the poet himself, rising and falling with the fluctuations of the poet's life, a work not so much unfinished as unfinishable. There is an uneasy moment in *Don Juan*, near the end of Canto XII, when Byron realizes that this is exactly where a conventional twelve-book epic would end, and brazens out his awareness both of epic traditions (which indeed he has acknowledged and illustrated throughout the poem) and of his original way of breaking them:

> But now I will begin my poem. 'Tis
>   Perhaps a little strange, if not quite new,
> That from the first of Cantos up to this
>   I've not begun what we have to go through.
> These first twelve books are merely flourishes,
>   *Preludios*, trying just a string or two
> Upon my lyre, or making the pegs sure;
> And when so, you shall have the overture.
>
> My Muses do not care a pinch of rosin
>   About what's called success, or not succeeding:
> Such thoughts are quite below the strain they have chosen;
>   'Tis a 'great moral lesson' they are reading.
> I thought, at setting off, about two dozen
>   Cantos would do; but at Apollo's pleading,
> If that my Pegasus should not be founder'd,
> I think to canter gently through a hundred.

(XII, liv–lv)

'Success' would be *Paradise Lost, The Divine Comedy*; the great task conceived, mapped out, and completed. He is doing something else, which he cannot even define for himself, far less for his readers. But he offers them a jaunty ticket for the forward voyage.

This is an art of improvisation, though we have to use the term carefully. We know that Byron had watched, met, and talked to Tommaso Sgricci, the Italian theatrical *improvvisatore*, who strung together impromptu verses on subjects suggested by the audience, but this would interest him as a sort of parallel activity rather than influence his own style, which was already formed. He does, nevertheless, tip his hat in Sgricci's direction in *Don Juan*, when he defends what he mock-modestly calls his 'desultory rhyme' as chiming out the matters uppermost in his mind from moment to moment of writing, 'Just as I feel the *Improvvisatore* (XV, xx). And the fact that Sgricci's was an oral, public art, an art of the voice and not the pen, does help to remind Byron of the importance of 'voice' in his own art, of the effect of good lively free conversation he never had to destroy other qualities to obtain. He characteristically gives the impression of devaluing his own facility in this respect, when he says:

> I rattle on exactly as I'd talk
> With anybody in a ride or walk.   (XV, xix)

Not exactly; nor is it really rattling on. But in so far as he conveys the sense and presence of a racy speaker, within the strict confines of his chosen metrical system, an achievement that is much more remarkable than his usually non-versewriting critics give him credit for, we cannot but feel the nearness of the man to his persona, so many accounts of his conversation, and of the tone and calibre of his voice, have been recorded, quite apart from the additional evidence of his extraordinarily frank, immediate, spirited, communicative, 'speaking' letters. Colonel Leicester Stanhope, one witness among many, described his conversation as 'a mixture of philosophy and slang, of everything,—like his *Don Juan*'.

The sense of an identifiable and 'modern' speaking voice, the voice of a worldly but well-read, playful but sharp and ardent British writer of the early nineteenth century, seems to have

63

been desired by Byron for two contrasting purposes. The social reality of the 'I' in the poem, his knowledge of and comments on undisguised contemporary and recent events, helps to persuade the reader of *Don Juan*, if he is pondering the speaker's categorizing of it as an epic, that one way to accept the category is to see it as a 'true' epic, its material firmly based in the British and Mediterranean world of the period from 1789 to 1823. On the other hand, 'documentary' is scarcely a word one would apply to it, and the vigorous, versatile, descanting, reader-conscious voice, with its sudden flights and digressions, helps to keep the poem opened up, as every poem must be, towards the imagination; an unmodulating, low-keyed, deadpan voice, or a voice restrained by decorums of rhetoric, would not meet the case, but Byron's own voice, transmuted only by being raised, as it were, to a higher power by the demands of the poetry, is ideal for the variety of pursuits and targets that appear, disappear, and reappear.

The historical reality is opposed to what he calls the 'labyrinth of fables' that swallows and numbs readers of earlier epics, and he sees himself as being in the epic succession only if readers will accept, as he buoyantly believes they will, one notable jolt to their expectations:

> There's only one slight difference between
> Me and my epic brethren gone before,
> And here the advantage is my own, I ween
> (Not that I have not several merits more,
> But this will more peculiarly be seen);
> They so embellish, that 'tis quite a bore
> Their labyrinth of fables to thread through,
> Whereas this story's actually true.
>
> (I, ccii)

One cannot push this too far. Even the most diligent historical novel needs fictional characters, including very often the hero or heroine. At the beginning of the first canto, the speaker admits that only Don Juan will suit his purposes, not (as he might have chosen) Nelson or Wolfe, Danton or Buonaparte. The mention of such names, however, and the accompanying references to 'gazettes' and 'Trafalgar', are sufficiently indicative of the 'truthful' aspect of the poem, and before long Juan is seen acting within the historical framework. It is not only the historical truth of great events that Byron is interested in: he has a conception of a true portrayal of 'human things and acts', a bird's eye view of 'that wild, Society', a glance 'thrown on men of every station':

> Besides, my Muse by no means deals in fiction:
>> She gathers a repertory of facts,
> Of course with some reserve and slight restriction,
>> But mostly sings of human things and acts—
> And that's one cause she meets with contradiction;
>> For too much truth, at first sight, ne'er attracts;
> And were her object only what's called glory,
> With more ease too she'd tell a different story.
>
> Love, war, a tempest—surely there's variety;
>> Also a seasoning slight of lucubration;
> A bird's-eye-view, too, of that wild, Society;
>> A slight glance thrown on men of every station.
> If you have nought else, here's at least satiety,
>> Both in performance and in preparation;
> And though these lines should only line portmanteaus,
> Trade will be all the better for these Cantos.
>
> (XIV, xiii–xiv)

Even the wry joke at the end somehow contributes to his sense that although he has now and again to explain himself to his uneasy readers ('For too much truth, at first sight, ne'er attracts'), he has the confidence of his own wide sweep and purview of real things. The truths may be well-observed facets of human conduct, human relationships; truths such as a novelist would use. They may be moral, within traditions of satirical stripping-down and exposure, as he warns the reader in a striking stanza:

> But now I'm going to be immoral; now
>> I mean to show things really as they are,
> Not as they ought to be: for I avow,
>> That till we see what's what in fact, we're far
> From much improvement with that virtuous plough
>> Which skims the surface, leaving scarce a scar
> Upon the black loam long manured by Vice,
> Only to keep its corn at the old price.
>
> (XII, xl)

The double meaning of 'improvement', moral and agricultural, serves to remind the reader of recent changes in society and to sharpen the 'modern' edge of the attack, while not losing the older reverberations of 'plough' and 'loam' and 'manure'. Elsewhere, on a deeper level, the speaker envisages a universal midnight unmasking, when the world as it really is would be seen as almost the exact opposite of what we customarily suppose it to be. In two forceful stanzas, he uses imagery from *Othello*, supreme play of deception, to illustrate the point:

> 'Tis strange,—but true; for truth is always strange;
>   Stranger than fiction: if it could be told,
> How much would novels gain by the exchange!
>   How differently the world would men behold!
> How oft would vice and virtue places change!
>   The new world would be nothing to the old,
> If some Columbus of the moral seas
> Would show mankind their souls' antipodes.
>
> What 'antres vast and deserts idle' then
>   Would be discover'd in the human soul!
> What icebergs in the hearts of mighty men,
>   With self-love in the centre as their pole!
> What Anthropophagi are nine or ten
>   Of those who hold the kingdoms in control!
> Were things but only call'd by their right name,
> Caesar himself would be ashamed of fame.
>
>   (XIV, ci–cii)

But the poem, to be true to Byron, had to be true to his moods, to his waywardness. Here, too, he has valuable comments to make through his poem's speaker. At the beginning of the seventh canto he is in transition from a theme of love (the vengeful jealousy of the sultan's wife, Gulbeyaz, in Constantinople) to a theme of war (the Russian seige of the Turkish fortress of Ismail on the Danube). Love and Glory are invoked, but questioned. The possessive, ruthless love of Gulbeyaz, commanding that Juan and Dudù be sewn into sacks and thrown into the Bosphorus, was real enough, but hardly glorious; and the forthcoming battle, 'glorious' in conventional terms, was not going to be glorious either. This is not to say that true love and glory do not exist—the speaker is defending himself against a charge of cynicism—but that they are flickering, evanescent, hard to grasp or pin down, appearing to us as shows when we are searching for substance. To meet these shifting and inconstant visions, which flash or twist above us like a shower of meteors or the Northern Lights, the speaker's poetry will itself shift and flicker, constant in its inconstancy:

> O Love! O Glory! what are you who fly
> Around us ever, rarely to alight?
> There's not a meteor in the Polar sky
> Of such transcendent and more fleeting flight.
> Chill, and chain'd to cold earth, we lift on high
> Our eyes in search of either lovely light;
> A thousand and a thousand colours they
> Assume, then leave us on our freezing way.
>
> And such as they are, such my present tale is,
> A nondescript and ever-varying rhyme,
> A versified Aurora Borealis,
> Which flashes o'er a waste and icy clime.
>
> (VII, i–ii)

'Ever-varying' is the key word, in keeping with Byron's own voice and temperament. But the changes, like the changing, dancing, shimmering folds of the aurora borealis, are a change of patterns, or half-patterns, rather than some anarchic amorphousness. In the same way, he pauses to describe in some detail, and with great relish, the ever-changing rainbow which appears as a good omen in the sky shortly before Juan is saved from shipwreck in the second canto. It is not the fact that it might be a good omen which interests the speaker, who shows himself to be duly sceptical about sailors' superstitions while accepting their occasional usefulness ('It is as well to think so, now and then'), but the nature of the changing shapes and colours themselves—the transience that strikes a chord in his mind and makes him dissolve the rainbow in a scatter of comparisons ranging from the beautiful to the grotesque:

> Now overhead a rainbow, bursting through
> The scattering clouds, shone, spanning the dark sea,
> Resting its bright base on the quivering blue;
> And all within its arch appear'd to be

Clearer than that without, and its wide hue
  Wax'd broad and waving, like a banner free,
Then changed like to a bow that's bent, and then
  Forsook the dim eyes of these shipwreck'd men.

It changed, of course; a heavenly chameleon,
  The airy child of vapour and the sun,
Brought forth in purple, cradled in vermilion,
  Baptized in molten gold, and swathed in dun,
Glittering like crescents o'er a Turk's pavilion,
  And blending every colour into one,
Just like a black eye in a recent scuffle
(For sometimes we must box without the muffle).

Our shipwreck'd seamen thought it a good omen—
  It is as well to think so, now and then;
'Twas an old custom of the Greek and Roman,
  And may become of great advantage when
Folks are discouraged; and most surely no men
  Had greater need to nerve themselves again
Than these, and so this rainbow look'd like hope—
Quite a celestial kaleidoscope.

                                                    (II, xci–xciii)

The metaphors and similes leap over one another in their
eagerness, not to define a static object but to accompany a
richly changing one. The rainbow is a bridge; a banner; a bent
bow; a chameleon; a baby; a Turkish crescent; a black eye; a
kaleidoscope. 'It changed, *of course*'; otherwise, what use would
it have been to the speaker! Byron, no great lover of the static art
of painting, would have seen little virtue in the fixed, tubelike
rainbow of Millais' *The Blind Girl*, double though it is. But
literature, like life itself, flickers, infinitely tantalizing and
suggestive, forming and breaking up similitudes and patterns.
The final 'kaleidoscope' is a good illustration of Byron's sense of
the language as a developing and malleable medium. The
kaleidoscope was invented in 1817, and Byron saw one in 1818,
just before he wrote these stanzas. It is the quickness with which
he sees the potential of the new word that we notice, and his
figurative use of it, applied to the rainbow, is the earliest
recorded in *N.E.D.* The kaleidoscope's combination of pattern
and change would recommend it particularly to Byron.

Voice, Tone, and Transition in 'Don Juan'

Meteor—aurora borealis—rainbow—chameleon—kaleido-scope. Do we have our man there, our poem, or are they both

> like the borealis race,
> That flit ere you can point their place?

Byron's art has been found hard to define, and critics have often expressed some dissatisfaction with it, not helped in their enquiries by the poet's jokiness ('Hail, Muse! *et cetera.*'—III, i) or by his reiterated praise of spontaneity ('Why, Man, the Soul of such writing is its licence'—letter to John Murray, 12 August 1819). Yet some 2,000 stanzas of *ottava rima* had to be engineered, rhymes had to be found, cantos had to be ended and begun, a considerable range of characters had to be made psychologically convincing, and the relation and balance between story and digression had to be thought about. Too much organization would have been death to the very spirit of *Don Juan*, but is the art sufficient for Byron's unique purposes?

His best effects, like Spenser's (how he would have disliked that 'like'!), may be appealed to, or experienced, but scarcely quoted, since they emerge over many pages, out of the flux and eddying of the poem, and are cumulative rather than pointed. This is not to say that local felicities and virtuosities are not frequent, from single lines and phrases ('A mighty mass of brick, and smoke, and shipping', 'that costive Sophy', 'But they will not find liberty a Troy', 'without risk or/ The singeing of a single inky whisker', 'A lonely pure affection unopposed', 'Half naked, loving, natural, and Greek', 'Carotid-artery-cutting Castlereagh', 'gentlemen in stays, as stiff as stones', 'The calentures of music') to whole stanzas where he accepts and dispatches with éclat some peculiar challenge (the Latin prescription Juan is given when he falls sick in Russia, at X, xli; the flash or canting language used elegiacally as a tribute to the footpad Juan shoots on his entry into London, at XI, xix). His command of rhyme is a great pleasure: bold, ingenious, outrageous; he takes a positive delight in extending all the normal expectations, rhyming with words from Latin, Greek, French, German, Italian, Spanish, Russian, Arabic, Turkish, Persian, Aramaic, Gaelic, and Scots. Sometimes it is what is *not* said, as in the wonderful pause between two connected stanzas at VIII, cix–cx, where—whether through the exigencies of *ottava rima*, or by a stroke of genius, or more likely a mixture of the two—the last-ditch defence of the Khan and his five sons during the siege of Ismail is given sudden pathos:

> Nay, he had wounded, though but slightly, both
>   Juan and Johnson; whereupon they fell,
> The first with sighs, the second with an oath,
>   Upon his angry sultanship, pell-mell,
> And all around were grown exceeding wroth
>   At such a pertinacious infidel,
> And pour'd upon him and his sons like rain,
> Which they resisted like a sandy plain

> That drinks and still is dry. At last they perish'd. . . .

And sometimes a brilliant passage is created out of the revitalizing of an ancient convention, as in the much-quoted '*ubi sunt*' of XI, lxxvi–lxxxvi, where the speaker, looking back on the decade before 1822, can hardly believe the changes that have occurred, in a time of political and social ferment. As befits the chameleon, he warms to the theme of change, but the remarkable characteristic of these eleven stanzas is the way in which they manage to be highly comic, witty, cutting, and 'modern' (in 1822, but the feeling is still there), and yet at the same time shadowed with intimations of mortality in the old *ubi sunt* manner. On the one hand all seems robust satire:

> Where's Brummell? Dish'd. Where's Long Pole Wellesley?
>   Diddled.
> Where's Whitbread? Romilly? Where's George the Third?
> Where is his will? (That's not so soon unriddled.)

> (XI, lxxviii)

But somehow, and even within the robust tone, there is place for Edward Young, author of *Night Thoughts* and other works of edifying gloom and *memento mori*:

> 'Where is the world?' cries Young, at *eighty*—'Where
>   The world in which a man was born?' Alas!
> Where is the world of *eight* years past? *'Twas there*—
>   I look for it,—'tis gone, a globe of glass!
> Crack'd, shiver'd, vanish'd, scarcely gazed on, ere
>   A silent change dissolves the glittering mass.
> Statesmen, chiefs, orators, queens, patriots, kings,
> And dandies, all are gone on the wind's wings.

> (XI, lxxvi)

'A silent change dissolves the glittering mass.' Like the Love and Glory shining and vanishing at the beginning of Canto VII, contemporary history also, sharp and specific as it is, a whole world of manners and personalities and actions, nothing seeming to be more real, steals away from decade to decade, undermined by forces we cannot see or hear. It is surely a very uncommon art that can produce a hilarious *ubi sunt* which is an *ubi sunt* all the same.

The larger-scale effects, which are the least amenable to analysis and evaluation because they involve such abrupt shifts not only of subject-matter but equally of tone and atmosphere, are nevertheless important in a long poem, whose length might well be thought to accommodate its variety.

Having decided that he would not plunge *in medias res* as earlier epic poets had done but instead would 'begin with the beginning' (I, vii) because (with tongue positively rolling in cheek) the regularity of his design 'Forbids all wandering as the worst of sinning', the speaker seems to promise a straight-forward, almost novelistic narrative. This, very obviously, was not to be, and the amount of 'wandering' becomes so great as the story progresses that it can be seen eventually as a sort of equivalent of *in medias res*, with interruptions of the action not for flashback or explanatory purposes as in Virgil or Milton but for expatiatory flights into another dimension, the mental dimension of the speaker's (i.e. virtually Byron's) thoughts and opinions on a large variety of subjects. Naturally he comes to admit and comment on these 'wanderings', as he comments on almost every aspect of the poem at some point within it (not from uneasiness but out of an exuberant conviction that the reader will be interested in his originality—a mighty maze, and all without a plan!), begging our indulgence for many and unconscionable digressions. 'If I have any fault,' he says (cries of 'No!' expected), 'it is digression' (III, xcvi), neglecting his characters while he soliloquizes and gives his 'addresses from the throne'. The didactic function is developed in a later canto:

> Oh, pardon my disgression—or at least
>   Peruse! 'Tis always with a moral end
> That I dissert, like grace before a feast:
>   For like an aged aunt, or tiresome friend,

> A rigid guardian, or a zealous priest,
>   My Muse by exhortation means to mend
> All people, at all times, and in most places,
> Which puts my Pegasus to these grave paces.
>
> (XII, xxxix)

That the digressions are very often didactic would not be disputed, but the variety of mood and tone with which they are presented gives them a much greater interest than 'grave paces' might suggest. Much of Byron's art can be revealed from two of the more extended digressionary passages, in Cantos I and III.

The artistic method may be said to be being tried out in the first canto (I, cxv–cxxxvi). The youthful Juan is sitting in a summer-house on a pleasant June evening with Julia, Don Alfonso's young wife; as the sun sets, and the moon comes up, they embrace, and she consents to be his lover. 'Here', says the speaker, 'my chaste Muse a liberty must take—', but the chaste reader, whether relieved or disappointed, is quickly reassured that the 'liberty' in question is not erotic but literary: a digression is coming, to fill in the five months that we are to imagine elapsing between that embrace and the next one to be described. The digression, after the Sterne-like teasing of the previous stanzas, leads with a straight lyrical listing of things that are sweet and desirable—the distant song of a gondolier, the sound of a waterfall, a rich grape-harvest—which modulates to a more mocking tone as the sweets and desirables widen to include a woman's revenge, a belated legacy, a quarrel with a tiresome friend, and then returns briefly to the lyrical mode with praises of the sweetest thing of all, 'first and passionate love'. Immediately a tangent offers itself: Adam's first love led to the Fall, the fruit plucked from the Tree of Knowledge has led to an 'age of oddities let loose', a welter of discoveries and inventions good and bad—the guillotine, galvanism, vaccination, rockets, polar voyages, miners' safety-lamps. Man is indeed a strange phenomenon, and—with a partial return to his setting-off point, though the digression is not finished yet—'Pleasure's a sin, and sometimes Sin's a pleasure.' Man goes to his grave without knowing much about his meaning or his fate:

> What then?—I do not know, no more do you—
>   And so good night.—Return we to our story:
>   'Twas in November, when fine days are few. . . .

But this is a false start: wait for it! A little meditation on
November follows, with evocative description of the season,
indoors and outside: a dusting of snow on the far-off peaks,
rough seas breaking on the promontory, 'sober suns' setting at
five o'clock, the wind gusting while a family piles wood on the
fire, the speaker's personal (and rather delightful) summing-
up:

> There's something cheerful in that sort of light,
>   Even as a summer sky's without a cloud:
> I'm fond of fire, and crickets, and all that,
>   A lobster salad, and champagne, and chat.

And then at last: ' 'Twas midnight—Donna Julia was in
bed. . . .' And the story proceeds with Juan and Julia surprised
and unmasked by the jealous Don Alfonso. There is a con-
necting thread, if one wants it, through the whole digression,
but that thread is perhaps little more than the tight-rope on
which Byron dances his various and unforeseen steps.

The third canto offers more developed, more rich transitions,
in the long digression in its latter part (III, lxxviii–cxi). The
action stops while Juan and his ideal love Haidée are enjoying
a celebration on their island, just as her father, the pirate
Lambro, unexpectedly returns and is about to put an end to
their idyllic relationship, Juan banished and Haidée dead of
despair and grief. The digression is therefore an interlude
between love and death, and might be expected to show high
seriousness; which indeed it does, yet a seriousness mingled
with broad comedy, keen satire, and literary criticism, in a
fairly audacious amalgam that tests the reader's sympathy and
receptivity to the limit. There are, however, links and connections of a most interesting kind, some clear enough, others
more oblique or subterranean.

Juan and Haidée, exotically dressed and surrounded by
every Levantine luxury from iced sherbet to tame gazelles,
have finished their feast and now sit back to enjoy a suite of
entertainers—'Dwarfs, dancing girls, black eunuchs, and a
poet'. The presence of the poet, though natural enough in the

circumstances, gives an initial signal to the reader that the story is going to be interrupted, and so it proves. The poet is described as well-known, and 'a very pleasant fellow' in company, but a time-server, a 'sad trimmer'. He will sing encomiums on the sultan and the pasha, or 'God save the King', or 'Ça ira', as the occasion demands. He is not devoid of grace, however, and the situation of the remote island, the friendly non-authoritarian audience, encourages him to be bold for once, so that

> without any danger of a riot, he
> Might for long lying make himself amends;
> And singing as he sung in his warm youth,
> Agree to a short armistice with truth.   (III, lxxxii)

From this unworthy vessel there is then delivered the famous lyric, 'The isles of Greece, the isles of Greece!'. It well deserves its fame, and in writing it Byron had the brilliant second thought of changing the *ottava rima* to a scaled-down version of it—six lines instead of eight, four feet instead of five, but a rhyming couplet still closing the stanza—and by this means keeping both separateness and continuity. (It is one of the many features which show the hand of the artist, whatever Byron may say about his carelessness.) The poem is both a plangent elegy for Greece, once culturally and politically great and now sunk in apathy under foreign domination, and a muted call to arms. Like a Wagnerian motif, Byron's belief in the duty of a poet to act as precursor or harbinger of change sounds out here as it so often does when the authorial temperature is right. The singer of the poem is at once bitterly self-critical (the lyre of Sappho and Anacreon has grown 'degenerate' in his hands) and what we would call an 'extremist' in his nationalism (praising the ancient Greek tyrants because at least they were Greek, not Persian or Turkish). He wants the Greeks to remember their military history, and act on the recollection.

> The mountains look on Marathon—
>   And Marathon looks on the sea;
> And musing there an hour alone,
>   I dream'd that Greece might still be free;
> For standing on the Persians' grave,
> I could not deem myself a slave.

The fervent but guilt-ridden bard, having his moment of truth as he recites before Juan and Haidée, fades out and is replaced by a more general meditation on whether the pen after all is mightier than the sword. It begins straight and serious:

> But words are things, and a small drop of ink,
>   Falling like dew, upon a thought, produces
> That which makes thousands, perhaps millions, think;
>   'Tis strange, the shortest letter which man uses
> Instead of speech, may form a lasting link
>   Of ages; to what straits old Time reduces
> Frail man, when paper—even a rag like this,
> Survives himself, his tomb, and all that's his!
>
> (III, lxxxviii)

But then, with a characteristic modulation, as the speaker warms to his theme he begins to toss and turn it, look at it from unexpected angles, find modern examples which naturally resist a too solemn tone, and move it step by step towards specific literary criticism, though never quite losing the thread of a poet's obligations to society. 'Troy owes to Homer what whist owes to Hoyle.' But what state, what realm, what power owes anything to the Lake Poets and their friends? What are Wordsworth, Coleridge, and Southey but renegades whose names 'cut a convict figure,/ The very Botany Bay in moral geography'? Wordsworth (who as we know heartily returned Byron's dislike) is the main target, mocked at for puerility, for tediousness, for provinciality, as against what the speaker would no doubt claim as his own adultness, readability, and internationalism. The attack, entertaining enough in the main, in a boisterous sort of way, ends on a sour and savage note:

> 'Pedlars,' and 'Boats,' and 'Waggons!' Oh! ye shades
>   Of Pope and Dryden, are we come to this?
> That trash of such sort not alone evades
>   Contempt, but from the bathos' vast abyss
> Floats scumlike uppermost, and these Jack Cades
>   Of sense and song above your graves may hiss—
> The 'little boatman' and his *Peter Bell*
> Can sneer at him who drew 'Achitophel'!
>
> (III, c)

After this explosion, there could only be an abrupt change of tack. At first, it is an apparent return to the story, though the narrative does not in fact take up again till eighteen stanzas later (IV, viii), and all that is happening is that the reader is temporarily (helpfully!) reminded of the two lovers, now left alone at the end of the revelry. 'T' our tale', says the speaker, but really this is no more than a chord struck between two greatly different sections of his huge digression. As the lovers watch the twilight, an evocative lyrical mode suddenly emerges, the battle of the books is forgotten, and an evening hymn in praise of nature, with 'Ave Maria!' repeatedly punctuating it like a vesper-bell, shows yet another side of the speaker, and of Byron. Woven into it, with some cunning, are passages translated from Sappho and Dante (whose names preserve continuities from the earlier part of the digression), emphasizing the mysteriously softening and healing influences of the twilight hour. These influences are allowed to bring the passage to an end with an unexpected reference to Nero, a tyrant justly destroyed, but whose tomb, as Suetonius records, was strewn with flowers by 'some hands unseen'. The references to Nero links back to the mention of the Greek tyrants in the poet's song at the banquet, but makes of course an entirely different point. Bravura carries off the 'Ave Maria!' passage, but only just; examined closely, it has some elements of the factitious, almost of kitsch. Its defence is made more readily when one takes it in its place as one strand in a very long poem, and in fact, reading the poem at a natural speed, and coming to it in its context, one finds it strangely moving.

'But I'm digressing . . .' the speaker has the grace to add, and closes the canto with a sardonic joke. Read Aristotle's *Poetics*, he says, for a perfect defence of the length and variousness of epics.

The shorter digressions tend to be more manageable, involving fewer shifts of tone, but still make capital out of contrast, as for example the sprightly and perceptive discourse on money at the beginning of Canto XII, or the passage on literary fame and bluestockings at the end of Canto IV. At parts where the story is itself at its most intense and serious, as during the siege of Ismail in Cantos VII–VIII, digression is instinctively held in check, but never quite disappears. Canto VIII closes with a couple of highly effective transitions, from exalted

prophecy addressing future generations to a light familiar
address to the reader, and from that to straight narrative pathos
in a very plain style in the concluding stanza. At the end of the
carnage, when the Russians have at last taken Ismail, and
Suwarrow has sent back his boastful and blasphemous rhyming
message to the Empress, the speaker bursts out with
his promise that he 'will teach, if possible, the stones/ To rise
against Earth's tyrants', adding:

> And when you hear historians talk of thrones,
>   And those that sate upon them, let it be
> As we now gaze upon the mammoth's bones,
>   And wonder what old world such things could see,
> Or hieroglyphics on Egyptian stones,
>   The pleasant riddles of futurity—
> Guessing at what shall happily be hid,
> As the real purpose of a pyramid.

> (VIII, cxxxvii)

But immediately he turns to the reader and reminds him how he
has kept his word to write an epic with its promised 'sketches of
Love—Tempest—Travel—War'—and all of it 'very accurate,
you must allow'. However, this is a tone which will not do to end
that canto with, so he swiftly closes the digression and returns
momentarily to the story, on its most personal level, describing
an ounce of good squeezed from the horror of war, as Juan goes
off with the little Turkish girl he has saved:

> The Moslem orphan went with her protector,
>   For she was homeless, houseless, helpless; all
> Her friends, like the sad family of Hector,
>   Had perish'd in the field or by the wall:
> Her very place of birth was but a spectre
>   Of what it had been; there the Muezzin's call
> To prayer was heard no more! and Juan wept,
> And made a vow to shield her, which he kept.

> (VIII, cxli)

The quiet proleptic assurance of the last three words is a fine
touch, and one of those necessary positives which appear like
beacons in the flux throughout the poem, reminiscent perhaps,
in their emphasis on immediate, self-committing action, of
Byron's encounter with the dying soldier in Ravenna.

4

Byron as Lyricist: The Poet Among the Musicians

by RONALD STEVENSON

Academic criticism is almost unanimous in declaring 'So we'll go no more a-roving' to be Byron's outstanding lyric. Andrew Rutherford finds it one of the rare exceptions to 'the metrical banality and sentimentalism which Moore's works encouraged' and enlaurels it as 'the best of Byron's handful of great lyrics'.[1] Professor John Jump places it together with *Childe Harold's Pilgrimage*, *The Prisoner of Chillon*, 'She walks in beauty', *Stanzas for Music* and the *Epistle to Augusta* and a few other lyrics in a body of work essentially different from his major achievement of poems in *ottava rima*. He characterizes its 'poignant "lyrical cry"' and claims that it suggests something of the range of his best work, uniting 'great power and simplicity of feeling with utter clarity of style'.[2]

Such is the innocence of Academe. It arises because the majority of literary commentators appear to be musically illiterate. Were they able to read music and were their interest to engender research into folksong, they would acknowledge that Byron's 'best lyric' was lifted from the refrain of an old Aberdeenshire ballad 'The Jolly Beggar'. Byron wrote:

> So, we'll go no more a-roving,
> So late into the night,
> Though the heart be still as loving,
> And the moon be still as bright.

The refrain of 'The Jolly Beggar' is:

> And I'll gang nae mair a-rovin,
> A-rovin i the nicht.
> I'll gang nae mair a-rovin,
> Though the müne shine ne'er sae bricht.

The ballad exists in many versions, all given in Bronson's monumental study of the child ballad-tunes.[3] To quote two variants of the folksong verse:

> There was a Jolly beggar, and a-begging he was bound,
> And he took up his quarters into a land'art town.

> There was a auld beggar man
> An' he was dressed in green
> An' he was askin' lodgins
> At a place near Aiberdeen.

And there we have it. Aberdeen—the city of Byron's boyhood, where he lived with his Gordon mother on Broad Street (the Gordons of Gight—pronounced 'Gecht'—Gight on the Ythan below Fyvie in Aberdeenshire—where the laddie George Gordon attended the Grammar School and spent a summer holiday on Ballaterach farm on the Dee's south bank, opposite Cambus o' May).[4]

Bronson refers to the disputed attribution of 'The Jolly Beggar' to James V of Scotland and avers that it 'has been current for at least three hundred years'[5] and has entered oral tradition in Scotland, England, Ireland and as far west as Missouri. Two of the tunes he gives are quoted in music examples 1 and 2.*

In appropriating a folksong for one of his poems, Byron was merely continuing the tradition and practice of Ramsay, Burns and Scott. The opening stanzas of many of Burns's best-loved lyrics are actually folksong texts, such as 'Ye Banks & Braes', 'John Anderson' and 'Sweet Afton'. The same applies to Scott's 'Jock o' Hazeldean', 'Bonnie Dundee' and 'Blue Bonnets over the Border'. Moore occasionally practised the same inspired plagiarism: an example is 'The Song of Fionnula' ('Silent, O Moyle') which, in one of his scholarly footnotes, he attributes to a manuscript translation by the Countess of Moira, from the Irish Gaelic.

* All music examples are given on pp. 94–99.

Byron: Wrath and Rhyme

By the beginning of the twentieth century, the music of fashionable London salons of, say, 1820 had seeped down through the British bourgeosie to the working class. So it was that as a child of a Lancastrian family of Scots descent, in the 1930s I played piano accompaniments to my proletarian father's singing of Moore's *Irish Melodies* and Scots folksong. The kind of music—no, the *actual* music!—that Byron heard sung by his bosom cronie Tom Moore (generally to harp accompaniment) was what I was hearing as a child of 10 or so. The result was that, when I began to compose music myself (at about 14) my first essays were song-settings of poems by Moore, Scott—and Byron's 'So we'll go no more a-roving' (Ex. 3).

Years later, in the 1950s, the Australian composer and folklorist Percy Grainger drew my attention to the Victorian English composer Maude Valérie White's setting of Byron's 'So we'll go no more a-roving' (Ex. 4), a truly great song worthy of revival and a rare case of a love-lied composed by a woman—shades of 'burning Sappho'!

Those *literati* who are not particularly interested in music often forget that the root of the word 'lyric' is the Greek for the musical instrument, the lyre (*lyra*), that was introduced to Ancient Greece from Asia, through Thrace (home of the Orpheus legend). The Greek distinction between the epical and the lyrical was the difference between what was spoken and what was sung. Hegel's *Ästhetik* (1832) contends that the epic is objective, the lyric subjective. But even the epicists Homer and Hesiod were represented by the lyre, though their work is polarized to that of Pindar and Bacchylides the lyricists. Greek poetry was always accompanied by the lyre.

There is something symbolic about Byron, the lad bred in Scotland—after his many later personal Odysseys, wearing the various mantles of Manfred, Childe Harold or Don Juan—embarking on his final mission to Greece, the birthland of lyric poetry.

Lyric poetry, made for music, has its own internal music: the fundamental tones which generate the harmonics which the composer perceives in its vibrations.

What was the *specific resonance* of Byron's lyric poetry? For instance, how did he speak? What was his accent? Was it

Aberdonian? Or had the Harrovian and then the Cambridge
Standard English planed the rough grain of the Doric? We can
only guess. We have a little internal evidence. We know that his
mother had the Scots leid—and a sharp tongue at that. He had
a Scots nurse in Aberdeen in the 1790s: Agnes Grey. In later life
(1821) he wrote a sketch *Aberdeen—Old and New, or the Auldtoun
and Newtoun* (that was his orthography). He tells us that he was
sent at 5 to Mr. 'Bodsy' Bowers's School. But then he
incorrectly remembers the meaning of the Scots word *Bodsie*
(Chambers Scots Dictionary: 'a nickname given to a short,
thickset person'). He translates it (perhaps with a touch of the
Beau Brummel) as 'dapper'. But again we catch the severe
Presbyterian tones of his remembered first lesson in reading by
rote: the monosyllables 'God made man, let us love him.' He
turns a page and, not yet literate, pretends to read but goes on
repeating his seven-worded maxim. He is rewarded by getting
his ears boxed ('which they did not deserve, seeing that it was
by *ear* only that I had acquired my letters', he adds with pauky
humour). Later he had the 'saturnine' Paterson for tutor: a
shoemaker's son, 'but a good scholar, as is common with the
Scotch'. Another 'rigid Presbyterian'. Again we hear the
thunder-tones—in Latin. Later still, he attends Aberdeen
Grammar School (he adds the note: *Scotice* 'Schule'—*Aberdonice*
'Squeel').

Byron's letter to James Hogg, the 'Ettrick Shepherd', dated
'Albany, March 24' (1814) is another indication of the acute-
ness of his ear for the long 'ee' vowel so characteristic of
Aberdonian Scots—think only of the Aberdonian greeting 'Ane
Gweed New Yeir!'. He playfully chides Hogg for his Scots
rhymes:

> My dear sir, you may depend upon it, you never had *name* yet,
> without making it rhyme to *theme*. I overlook that sort of
> thing, however, and so must you, in your turn, pass over my
> real or supposed ruggedness. The fact is, that I have a theory
> on the subject, but that I have not time at present for explain-
> ing it.

There he puts an Aberdonian vowel—'neem' for 'name'—into
the mouth of Hogg the Borderer. For Byron, Scots was
Aberdonian.

Byron: Wrath and Rhyme

Anatole France, in a conversation published with his approval in 1922, opines on the subject of rhyme:

> Rhyme is not a difficulty to true poets. As they think in metaphors, they have at their disposal a much more extensive vocabulary than prose-writers and can easily find all their rhymes therein.
>
> What is a metaphor? A comparison. Now, one can compare everything to anything: the moon to a cheese and a bruised heart to a cracked pot. The metaphors therefore furnish an almost unlimited provision of words and rhymes.
>
> Better still, the rhyme draws attention to the metaphor as though by the tinkling of a bell.
>
> Add that each poet has his own metaphors, his own variegated epithets and, consequently, an immense reserve of rhymes which is the peculiar quality of his genius.
>
> Corneille rhymes by means of heroic words: *front, affront, outrage, rage.* . . .
>
> Racine rhymes by means of tender and sorrowful adjectives: *déplorable, misérable.* . . .
>
> La Fontaine's rhymes are satirical. Those of Molière jovial, etc.
>
> In fact, every great poet discovers a new region. In the case of one it is the land of heroism; in that of another, of burning passion; in that of a third, of jeering and banter; in that of a fourth, of generous gaiety.
>
> Rhymes full of imagery are, as it were, the flowers of those mysterious shores. They abound under the steps of the explorer. He has but to stoop to choose those whose colours blend.
>
> The bouquet of rhymes is the perfume, the adornment of the shores on which each dreamer has landed. It is the shade of his imagination.
>
> And, truth to tell, with excellent poets, imagination and sensibility make up for everything, even intelligence.[7]

How does this apply to Byron? He is a virtuoso of rhyme, perhaps the most brilliant virtuoso in the English language. He has a most un-English, a most Scottish, *bravura*. Proof of those asseverations is found in his *Don Juan*. Whereas other poets may have a specific resonance, Byron's poetry has multiple resonances.

But that Aberdonian 'ee' is intrusive in his poetry: a residual element from his Scottish childhood. Take a few examples from his shorter poems. From *Stanzas for Music*:

> I speak not, I trace not, I breathe not thy name,
> There is grief in the sound, there is guilt in the fame:
> But the tear which now burns on my cheek may impart
> The deep thoughts that dwell in that silence of heart.

The 'ee' sound occurs twice in line 1 and twice in line 3; once each in lines 2 and 4. (Note the musical symmetry.) It recurs like a sullen bell-stroke. But if we infer the Aberdonian 'ee' sound in the words 'trace', 'name', 'fame' (remembering the letter to James Hogg), the bell strikes nine times. Another case:

> There be none of Beauty's daughters
>   With a magic like thee;
> And like music on the waters
>   Is thy sweet voice to me:
> When, as if its sound were causing
> The charmèd ocean's pausing,
> The waves lie still and gleaming
> And the lull'd winds seem dreaming. . . .

Observe the 'ee' sound in lines 2 and 4, in the penultimate line and its double, consecutive employment in the last line.

What is the emotional significance of that 'ee' sound? Well, it's a very *closed* sound. It's the sound of a sneer. Maybe a sneer that can curl into a smile, but still a sneer. It is the cipher of the Luciferic in Byron. It is *worlds* away from the *open* sound of Blake's poetry, which is full of the 'ah' sounds of wonderment, the sounds of glad day (to borrow the title of one of his designs).

Byron's sound-world as lyricist is different, too, from say that of Wilfred Owen. I once wrote an article in *The Listener* [8] in which I took Owen's poem 'Strange Meeting' and explored its vowel sounds and their emotional content. The poem, you will recall, describes a soldier's nightmare, meeting in hell the enemy he killed. This enemy tells what he might have done with his life. Here Owen's words are woven out of the sound of pain:

> It seemed that out of battle I escaped
> Down some profound dull tunnel, long since scooped
> Through granites which titanic wars had groined.

Notice particularly the vowel sounds of the second line: ow—ugh—ow—ugh—ugh—oo!

Byron: Wrath and Rhyme

Back to Byron. (But we can only define the sonics of his poetry by comparison with other poets.) Like Corneille, Byron too can employ heroic rhymes, as in *The Destruction of Sennacherib*:

> The Assyrian came down like the wolf on the fold,
> And his cohorts were gleaming in purple and gold;
> And the sheen of their spears was like stars on the sea,
> When the blue wave rolls nightly on deep Galilee.

The Corneillesque rhyme 'fold/gold' is trumpet-toned; but observe again the three 'ee' sounds in the penultimate line and the two 'ee' sounds in the last line.

The trumpet sounds again in Byron's castigation of Sassenach arrogance in the early lyric 'I would I were a careless child':

> The cumbrous pomp of Saxon pride
> Accords not with the freeborn soul,
> Which loves the mountain's craggy side,
> And seeks the rocks where billows roll.

There's a group of the early lyrics in which Byron not only writes nostalgically of Scotland but fancies himself a Gael:

> When I roved a young Highlander o'er the dark heath,
> And climb'd thy steep summit, oh Morven of snow!
> To gaze on the torrent that thunder'd beneath,
> Or the mist of the tempest that gather'd below. . . .

Allowing for adolescent hyperbole, we must at least credit him with acknowledging the Scots Gaelic language in his *Lachin y Gair*, when so many others were (indeed, still are) ignorant of the treasures of this most ancient of Western European languages that is even yet still (just about) living.

Of course, he loved 'dressing-up', both poetically and sartorially—remember Thomas Phillips's portrait of him in Albanian dress[9] and the portrait of him wearing the Homeric helmet he ordered for his Greek adventure.[10]

The sonal palette of his poetry is bituminous and oriole: the tone-colours of a brooding hero, a hero *manqué*; his heroic aspirations frustrated by a deeply troubled, complex psyche; his helmet gleaming Rembrandtesquely from out of the enveloping darkness.

Perhaps Gabriele D'Annunzio is the poet nearest to Byron

84

in artistic type and also as a lyric poet with aspirations to be a playwright and a man of action. Cast a cold eye on them, and both sometimes may seem rather rididulous. But however that may be, the lines in *Don Juan* (X, xvi–xix), addressed to Jeffrey, were palpably written with a sincerity that shines through even the wish to be clever and funny. It is this section that contains the oft-quoted words

> But I am half a Scot by birth, and bred
> A whole one, and my heart flies to my head. . . .

And, in the tradition of well-travelled Scots, Byron was also an internationalist whose works take account of other European literatures—far more than does the poetry of any of his British contemporaries. Already at Harrow, at the Chattertonian age of 16, he was making creditable translations from the Greek of Aeschylus and Anacreon and from the Latin of Catullus and Horace. His love of Italian spurs him to commemorate Tasso in a lament; to translate from the Florentine of Luigi Pulci; and to emulate Dante's *terza rima* in translating the Francesca of Rimini episode (Canto V of *L'Inferno*); to translate two *terze rime* from *Il Purgatorio* (Canto VIII) in *Don Juan* (III, cviii); and to compose the extended *The Prophecy of Dante* in *terza rima*—perhaps the most successfully sustained example of its use in English apart from Elizabeth Barrett Browning's *Casa Guidi Windows*; though maybe lacking the mastery of *terza rima* exemplified by Goethe in 'Ariels Gesang' at the beginning of *Faust*, Part II.

Byron's *The Bride of Abydos* opens:

> Know ye the land where the cypress and myrtle
> Are emblems of deeds that are done in their clime?

—echoing Goethe's

> *Kennst du das Land, wo die Zitronen blühn,*
> . . .   .
> *Kennst du es wohl?*

Goethe (who also essayed English poetry) returned Byron's feelings for him 'with something of the tenderness of a father discovering in a prodigal the exuberance of his own youth'.[11]

Byron is the Poet of the Grand Tour, the anticipator of Karl Baedecker, the publisher of guide-books covering the greater part of the civilized world. Contemporaneously with his friend Moore's *Lalla Rookh*, Byron's Turkish Tales, *The Giaour* and *The Bride of Abydos* opened magic casements on to 'the gorgeous East'. His poetic feet were shod with Napoleon's 'seven-league boots'. He was in some ways Buonaparte's *Doppelgänger*, casting a saturnine shadow across the map of Europe. Few avoided his influence: his themes are taken up in the work of Victor Hugo, Pushkin, Mickiewicz and George Sand; and the tone-colours of his poetry were translated on to the canvases of Delacroix and Turner.[12]

In America, Edgar Allan Poe recited Byron in his lecture *The Poetic Principle*, choosing a minor poem:

> Though the day of my destiny's over,
>   And the star of my fate hath declined,
> Thy soft heart refused to discover
>   The faults which so many could find;
> Though thy soul with my grief was acquainted,
>   It shrunk not to share it with me,
> And the love which my spirit hath painted
>   It never hath found but in *thee*.

Poe comments: 'Although the rhythm, here, is one of the most difficult, the versification could scarcely be improved. No nobler *theme* ever engaged the pen of a poet.' Poe avers that this poem captures the Poetic Principle itself, which is 'strictly and simply, the Human Aspiration for Supernal Beauty'; the Principle always being found in

> *an elevating excitement of the Soul*—quite independent of that passion which is the intoxication of the Heart—or of that Truth which is the satisfaction of the Reason. For, in regard to Passion, alas! its tendency is to degrade, rather than to elevate the Soul. Love, on the contrary—Love—the true, the divine Eros—the Uranian, as distinguished from the Dionaean Venus—is unquestionably the purest and truest of all poetic themes. And in regard to Truth—if, to be sure, through the attainment of a truth, we are led to perceive a harmony where none was apparent before, we experience, at once, the true poetical effect—but this effect is referable to the harmony alone, and not in the least degree to the truth which merely served to render the harmony manifest.[13]

Byron as Lyricist: The Poet Among the Musicians

Those words of Poe's are, in my view, worth re-reading. By now, there should surely be the possibility of perspective on such romantic prose; unless the bigotry of a self-consciously modern aesthetic should allow distaste for the style to obscure understanding of its content. Poe knew a thing or two about what constitutes a true lyric—and wrote some outstanding examples himself.

So did James Joyce, though we all know that his greatest poetry was written in his prose. In *Portrait of the Artist as a Young Man*, Stephen is asked by a fellow-student: 'And who is the best poet?' Stephen (Joyce) names Byron. Ellmann's footnote tells us Joyce held to this opinion in later life. Joyce's character Leopold Bloom in *Ulysses* shares his creator's admiration for Byron's poetry: Bloom gave Molly a copy of his works during their courtship. Joyce unsuccessfully attempted to persuade the American composer George Antheil (Ezra Pound's protégé) to write an opera based on Byron's *Cain* and had no more success in trying to interest the Swiss composer Othmar Schoeck in the same idea.[14]

Earlier composers had based operas on libretti *d'après* Byron: Donizetti, *Parisina*; Verdi, *The Two Foscari*. Neither was a success.

What of Byron's own interest in music? We no more look to him than to Charles Lamb for anything more than superficial comments on it. Such sporadic impressions of music as occur in Byron's *The Waltz* indicate that his attitude to the opera house and the fashionable salons, with their baubles and glitter, meant no more to him than did the atmosphere of the *beau monde*, the casino and the prize-ring: all purlieus of scandal. It is true that volume 8 (1821) of Leslie A. Marchand's monumental edition of *Byron's Letters & Journals* (Murray, London), covering the idyllic period with the Countess Teresa Guiccioli in Italy, include more references to music (though fragmentary) than do any of the other volumes.

Byron's *Hebrew Melodies* were set to music by his friend the Canterbury-born Jewish composer Isaac Nathan, with the assistance of his fellow Jewish London-born composer and singer John Braham. They were published in fascicles between 1815 and 1822 and were well received. Nathan studied Hebrew at Cambridge but abandoned theology for music and

87

was articled to Domenico Corri in London. He specialized in the Hebrew cantillations of the synagogue, but there is no significant influence of this in his Byron settings. Nathan's music is like diluted Mendelssohn, although it antedates the appearance of the German master's works (Exx. 5 and 6). In 1829 Nathan published *Fugitive Pieces & Reminiscences of Lord Byron*. He died in Australia in 1864.

In 1884 there appeared *2 Hebrew Melodies* of Byron set to music by the 18-year-old Busoni, settings of the same poems as quoted in the Nathan examples. Unlike Nathan, Busoni (who was not Jewish) *did* attempt to infuse something of Hebrew cantillation in the piano introduction to 'I saw thee weep' (Exx. 7 and 7a). And Busoni set *By the rivers of Babylon* as a chorale (Ex. 8).

Busoni, a Tuscan pacifist, began, in the very month in which the Great War was declared (August 1914), a song-cycle with orchestra, conceived as 'a political panel', presenting poems by Victor Hugo, Carducci, Goethe and Byron: each set to music in its original language: *quattro grandi poeti, interpreti dell'anima di quattro grandi nazioni* ('four great poets interpreted in the spirit of four great nations') in the composer's own words.[15] The work was never completed. Busoni died, a victim of the war though not a combatant: heart-broken by the carnage and waste and the crack-up of culture. He was the heir to Liszt as pianist and to the Berlioz of *La Damnation de Faust* in his opera *Doktor Faust*.

Liszt's *oeuvre* demonstrates a near-obsession with Byron's *Mazeppa*. His Study Op. 1, No. 5 (composed at 16) is the *fons et origo* of music he re-worked sixteen years later in his *Transcendental Study* for piano, which itself became the basis of his symphonic poem *Mazeppa*, after a further twelve years, orchestrated with the assistance of Joachim Raff (Exx. 9, 10, and 11).

The Mazeppa legend is based on the life of a historical Polish nobleman Ivan Mazeppa (1644–1709), page to King John Casimir of Poland. His mistress was the young bride of a Podolian count who had Mazeppa tied naked to a wild horse which was driven into the Ukraine. The horse collapsed after careering for many miles. Mazeppa was rescued by Cossacks and eventually was elected their chief. Liszt's full score quotes a motto from Byron: 'Away! Away!' and the whole of Victor

Hugo's Byron-influenced poem on the same subject, as introduction. Liszt appears himself to have been tied to this wild horse of his imagination and borne with it over a creative career of nearly a quarter of a century.

In 1834, in response to a commission from Paganini, the 30-year-old Berlioz composed *Harold en Italie*, his second symphony. An unusual feature was the *concertante* viola part. This casting of the sombre-toned viola in the role of Byron's brooding hero is a masterstroke (Ex. 12). Berlioz's *Lélio* is also based on Byron, but his *Le Corsair*, which is not, takes its programme from Fenimore Cooper.

Byron acknowledged Goethe's *Faust* as an influence, together with Alpine scenery, on his semi-lyrical romantic drama *Manfred*. Schumann set to music scenes from Goethe's *Faust* and from Byron's drama. When he was composing his *Manfred*, Schumann was entering the final stage in his mental breakdown and identified his interior struggle with that of Byron's hero. Schumann's wife Clara wrote a diary-note: 'Byron's *Manfred* inspired Robert to an extraordinary degree.' Schumann himself declared: 'Never before have I devoted myself with such love and outlay of force to any work as to that of *Manfred*.' It is unusual in form: largely a *mélodrame*, that is, most of the text is spoken to orchestral accompaniment and sung only at the lyric peaks. It comprises an overture and fifteen numbers. Schumann edited and abridged Byron's text in German translation and added a concluding *Requiem aeternam dona eis*. The best moments are the sciomantic scenes. Perhaps the most beautiful is the luminous scene between Manfred and Astarte, which takes the unusual form of a song without words for orchestra (Ex. 13) while the reciter speaks the text: '*Gerufen hab' ich dich in stiller Nacht, aus Busch und Schlummer . . .*' ('For I have call'd on thee in the still night,/ Startled the slumbering birds from the hush'd boughs . . .').

Perhaps the genre of *mélodrame* is the ideal way of setting to music Byron's Sonnets, also—or any sonnets. Sonnet-form has its own structured music and is generally too concentrated and rich in content and thought-forms to bear setting melodically. There is no great song-setting of Shakespeare's Sonnets, unless (just possibly) it be Bernard Van Dieren's. Byron as sonneteer is not on the same altitude as Shakespeare—who is?—but the same observation applies.

Tchaikovsky was urged by Balakirev to compose a symphonic-poem-cycle in four movements on Byron's *Manfred*. (Incidentally, Tchaikovsky's opera *Mazeppa* is based on Pushkin's text, which only indirectly derives from Byron.) Manfred, the 'accursed wanderer', could have been Tchaikovsky the secret homosexual, the 'victim of fate'. Tchaikovsky composed his *Manfred* in 1885, eight years before his death. Its four movements depict the hero's wanderings in the Bernese Alps; the apparition of the Rainbow Sprite above the Staubbach waterfall; a *Pastorale*—the life of the mountain-dwellers; and a witches' sabbath in the gothic, subterranean palace of Ariman, ending with Manfred's pardon and death. It is scored for a large orchestra. It is a masterpiece, yet seldom performed.

Like Schumann in his *Manfred*, Schoenberg in his 1942 setting of Byron's *Ode to Napoleon Buonaparte* chooses the form of spoken, rather than sung, text (the original English), this time with string quartet and piano. Schoenberg, a Viennese Jew exiled in the U.S.A. from Nazi Germany, certainly saw a parallel between Napoleon and Hitler. Byron's blistering denunciation of Buonaparte provided Schoenberg with the opportunity of expressing, with all the force of his pentateuchal passion, his loathing of Nazism. He set the final stanza (excised by Byron from the published text), referring to Washington, 'the Cincinnatus of the West', as a tribute to the composer's adopted country. Structurally, Schoenberg's dissonant 12-note idiom here comes to terms with traditional, triadic harmony. The work ends in E flat major, the tonality of Beethoven's *Eroica*, which was originally intended to be dedicated to Napoleon (Ex. 14). During its course it alludes to another Beethoven work, the 'Fifth', and its Morse-code 'V for Victory' motive (Ex. 15).

The English composer, Alan Bush, in 1961 composed his *Byron Symphony*, Op. 53, his third symphony. It has four movements: Introduction and *allegro* (Newstead Abbey: Byron's youth); ceremonial march-theme and variations (Westminster: Byron in the House of Lords); *andante tranquillo* (Il Palazzo Savioli: a love idyll); introduction and choral finale to a Greek text by Solomos (Missolonghi: Byron's death in the cause of Greek freedom). The first movement's first subject embodies

Byron's ardent youth (Ex. 16). This theme is the basis for the sustained, periodized melody of the last variation in the second movement. Here Bush has a unique conception: to set to music the imagined intonation and gestures of Byron's speech to the Lords, against capital punishment for machine-breakers in the Industrial Revolution (Ex. 17).

Another exceptional procedure of Bush's is to repeat a development section in the finale which was heard in the first movement, when Byron is imagined as hearing the Greek trumpets from afar, responding with the intense vitality of his youth.

Again and again, one hears Byron, in his poetry, calling, 'Away! Away!': he is impatient for action. He pants after freedom for mankind and for himself. He would gladly exchange his quill for a brace of pistols. He is the brother-across-the-centuries of Garibaldi and Che Guevara. With him the struggle is the thing. One senses that he would rather be a brigand in the mountains than a victor in the metropolis. He is for eternal opposition, not a new Establishment. His spiritual brothers are such brigands as Fra Diavolo, the Spanish brigand Francisco Esteben El Guapo (Francis Stephen the Buck or Dandy) and Don José Maria, called *El Tempranillo* ('the early bird') who was the historical prototype of Merimée's and Bizet's smuggler and *bandolero* in *Carmen*. He would have had a fellow-feeling for Benedetto Mangone, of whom it is recorded that, having ambushed a party of travellers that included Torquato Tasso, he allowed them to pass unharmed out of his reverence for poets and poetry. Mangone was finally taken and bastinadoed to death in Naples. But he lived on in popular verse (in *ottava rima*—Byron's favourite verse-form!): '*Io canto li ricatti, il fiero ardire/ Del gran' Pietro Mancino fuoruscita . . .*' ('Of Pietro Mancino, that great outlawed man/ I sing, and all his rage . . .'). Byron is a brigand of the spirit, not so much among the poets as standing apart from them. His final action—training liberation fighters in Greece—materialized the spirit of his poetry. That he died in the Missolonghi marshes, not in action but in fever, was the final irony.

He was a lyric poet with aspirations to the epic. The frustration of his striving produced his mordant satire and the sprawling, reckless form of his *Don Juan*, which has more in common with Fielding's *Tom Jones* than with his contemporaries, and yet contains some of his finest lyric strains in the Haidée episode. Byron the satirist was at daggers drawn with his *alter ego*, the lyricist; for satire spits sibillants and plosives and clenches the teeth in consonants, whereas lyric poetry sings with open vowels and an open mouth. The bromine of Byron's satire flows like a red liquid through his verse. Like bromine itself, when the satire is laid in thick layers, it becomes black and a stench to delicate nostrils. Mixed with the only other liquid element—the mercury of the lyric—in the chemistry of his psyche, it produces a unique mercurous bromide of poetry: a compound of satire and lyricism; a strange unity of *olla podrida* and the perfumes of Araby.

Re-reading this essay, taking stock, I am a little surprised by its *Jugendstil*. Perhaps, like Alan Bush, I have imagined the trumpets of youth sounding over the years. Or maybe I am recapturing something of my boyhood response to 'So we'll go no more a-roving', which itself was a response to a folksong Byron heard when young. Perhaps the reader may grant that, to some temperaments, Byron's flamboyance is excited in others. Naturally, those who do not respond in this way may wish that others didn't. Byron, for all his heroic aspirations, had elements of cynicism. But we may also, if we choose, prefer to regard some of his cynicism and some of his heroics as play-acting. He tells us he 'will go no more a-roving' with us—but he *does*! His poetry has survived so late into the night. If mankind does not destroy itself—(he wrote 'Let there be light!' said God, and there was light!/ 'Let there be blood!' says man, and there's a sea!)—who knows but that Byron may go a-roving with those as yet unborn, in a new dawn.

NOTES

1. Andrew Rutherford, *Byron: A Critical Study* (Oliver & Boyd, Edinburgh & London, 1961).
2. John D. Jump, *Byron* (Routledge & Kegan Paul, London & Boston, 1972).

3. Bertrand Harris Bronson, *The Traditional Tunes of the Child Ballads* (Princeton, N.J., 1959). (Ref. Child No. 279, pp. 478ff.)
4. James Alison (ed.), *Poetry of Northeast Scotland* (Heinemann, London & Edinburgh, 1976).
5. Bronson, op. cit.
6. In his Foreword to his piano transcription of Gershwin's *The Man I Love* (New World Music Corp. Harms Inc., N.Y., 1944) Grainger includes the Maude Valérie White setting of Byron among his idiosyncratic list of 'the finest love-songs' from Dowland to Gershwin.
7. Paul Gsell, translated from the French by F. Lees, *Anatole France & his Circle* (John Lane/The Bodley Head, London, 1922).
8. Ronald Stevenson, *Britten's War Requiem* in *The Listener*, B.B.C. Publications, London, 2 November 1967.
9. The Thomas Phillips portrait, from which the illustration on the front cover of this volume is reproduced, hangs in the National Portrait Gallery, London.
10. Byron's Greek helmet is on display at Newstead Abbey. The portrait of him wearing it is reproduced in Peter Brent, *Lord Byron* (Weidenfeld & Nicolson, London, 1974).
11. Jeanne Ancelet-Hustache, *Goethe* (Grove Press, Inc., N.Y.; Calder, London, 1960).
12. Turner made designs for Byron's Poems published by Murray (London, 1834). Turner's literary work *Fallacies of Hope*, while a reply to Campbell's *Pleasures of Hope*, owes something to Byron.
13. Edgar Allan Poe, *The Poetical Works* (Sampson Low, London, 1858).
14. Richard Ellmann, *James Joyce* (O.U.P., N.Y., 1959).
15. Guido M. Gatti (ed.), *La Rassegna Musicale* (Firenze (Florence), Gennaio (January) 1940).

Byron: Wrath and Rhyme

Ex. 1

Ex. 2

Ex. 3

Byron

Ronald Stevenson

So, we'll go no more a - ro - ving, So late in - to —— the night, Though the heart be still as lo - ving, And the moon be still as bright.

Ex. 4

Maude Valérie White

So we'll go no more a ro - ving So

late in - to the night.

Ex. 5

Isaac Nathan

I saw thee weep, the big bright tear Came o'er that eye of blue:

Ex. 6

Isaac Nathan

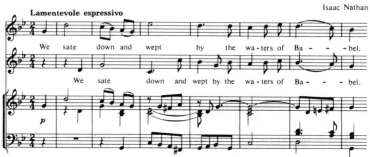

We sate down and wept by the wa - ters of Ba - - bel.

We sate down and wept by the wa - ters of Ba - - bel.

Ex. 7

Ex. 7a

Ich sah' die Thrä-ne gross und schwer in dei-nes Au-ges Blau.

Ex. 8

An Ba-by-lons Was-sern wir wein — — ten und

dach-ten des Ta-ges in Leid

Ex. 9

Ex. 10

Ex. 11

Ex. 12

Ex. 13

Ex. 13 (continued)

Ex. 14

Schoenberg

Ex. 15

Schoenberg

Ex. 16

Ex. 17

Part Two:
LITERATURE AND LIFE

5

The Hero as Lover: Byron and Women

by JENNI CALDER

Byron's reputation in his lifetime owed a great deal to the response of women, to himself and to his poetry. He lived at a time when sexual competitiveness and success, at least amongst the upper classes, occupied a place at the forefront of social relations. It was an environment responsive to sexuality and conducive to sexual adventuring. It was also a time when women were making some impact beyond the sexual, domestic and symbolic roles. Byron's emotional life was lived dangerously; this may have been as much due to the fact that he encountered some challenging women as to his own adventurousness and compulsion to take risks. He came across women who were not afraid to be clever, as well as women who were apparently not afraid of their own sexuality or its consequences.

Yet it was also a time when conventions of behaviour weighed heavily. Byron's life and personality were full of tensions and dislocations. His aristocratic inheritance conflicted with his constrained and Calvinist early years. His radical leanings did not quite tune in with his enjoyment of privilege. Whatever his scorn of the mores of upper-class society the ambience of Harrow, Cambridge and the London social scene offered possibilities which Byron was not going to ignore, and this ambience clung to him throughout his life.

103

Opportunities for good wine, compliant women and stimulating discourse were unquestioned: these were all high priorities. The conventions, as Byron saw them, were essentially those of a hypocritical society. The rules that were publicly acknowledged were not privately obeyed. Yet Byron needed the conventions. He needed them for his poetry, his public stance and his private satisfaction, for convention, hypocritical or not, gave him a structure to rebel against. Anarchy means nothing, except in terms of a structured, ordered and consequently repressive society.

Anarchy is perhaps not quite the right word to use in Byron's case, although there are anarchic qualities in his actions and attitudes. His projection of himself as hero was very much the product of his education and his environment. His models were Classical and military: they almost had to be. The figures of his own time from whom he could not tear his eyes away were Napoleon and Wellington, and like most thinking people of his generation his attitude to Napoleon was ambivalent. His experience of the Levant and Islam was almost incidental, although it provided food for the nourishment of an exotic and individualist hero. But whatever the models and the influences, heroic endeavour in a benign and concurring society had little point, whether that endeavour was expressed in writing or in action. He needed to believe that what he saw as the fateful satanity of the Byrons was not just a more colourful version of what everyone was like. Amongst the many strands of irony that are woven into his life one of the most piquant is that *Childe Harold* and the group of 'heroic' poems written around the same time, with their hints of extremes of feeling and behaviour, brought him such public approval, or rather, and even more pleasurable, a kind of disapproving adulation. Perhaps he left England not because England would not accept him, but because he became too popular, and thus the ground for rebellion was whipped away from beneath his feet.

In tackling the subject of Byron and women there are a multitude of questions which must be asked, but to which there seem to be no very satisfactory answers. Was he merely a sexual adventurer? Were his marriage, his relationship with his sister Augusta, his penchant for boys, prostitutes and married women, calculated exploits, intended primarily to shock, or the enactment of some genuine need—if such a thing can be defined? Were women his victims? If so, some of them were clearly willing. Can his sexual ethic, if looked at objectively, be seen as anything other than an ideology of oppression and exploitation—in contrast to his political ethic? And are his attitudes to love and sex as expressed in his poetry genuine, or merely fashionable, or the work of a rebellious poseur?

I can't attempt to answer these questions, only to explore some of the possible responses and to pursue some of the more tantalizing avenues that are opened up. Like all the more satisfactory heroic figures Byron is both individual and representative, and thus contains the quintessential challenge and attraction of the hero. The individualism includes those elements of anarchy, the representativeness, the embodiment of collective need. He is contradictory, yet emblematic in his contradictions. He was representative in the tensions he contained. It wasn't only that his early upbringing was humble and democratic and he then embraced the new horizons of aristocracy. He grew up at a time when the entrenched power and privilege of the landowning class was being challenged, when established values were being threatened, when both class and the subservience of women were beginning to look as if they were no longer the absolutes that they had seemed to be. As an aristocrat he both capitalized on his privileged status and suffered from all the difficulties of a landowner who could no longer be dependent on the land. He did not choose the route of the reforming landowner, which might have calmed his uneasy conscience. His ambiguous relationship with Newstead Abbey plagued him. He could not make it work for him; he could only make money out of it by selling it; yet he was reluctant to relinquish such a splendid symbol. He did not accept the responsibilities of privilege, for he despised privilege. Yet there are indications of paternalism.

Similarly, he both acknowledged the conventions of upper-class society and learned to work the system that they represented, and he mocked them and threatened them in a way that thrilled that society itself. His flamboyance was aristocratic rather than bohemian, as much the product of having learnt the ways of the wealthy as a reaction against them, or a reaction against the austerity and Calvinism of his early background. However, austerity, and the guilt that was the inevitable child of Calvinism, were ingredients that had to be preserved in his existence. The austerity was all the more demanding for being self-imposed: his strict regimes of diet and exercise, for example. The guilt was the more dramatic for being a. reaction to extremes that one senses were pursued precisely in order to generate guilt. The obvious examples are his relationship with Augusta, and possibly also that with his wife. Both austerity and extremes had to be present so that he could react against them.

Writing was an ideal occupation for a man of feeling who was distinctly not destined for a profession. Byron's letters alone are evidence enough that he lived and wrote with intensity, in fact more impressive evidence than much of his poetry, which is distinguished more by its magnificent exceptions than by a consistent quality. Inevitably much of the content of both his letters and his poetry concerns his relations with women. At the same time there is underlying much of his writing a feeling that this was not what life really should be all about, that although affairs with women were quite fun—and inevitable—they were not fundamentally serious. Yet relations with women were to dominate his life. In a society of men and women without professions, and whose daily objectives were often sexual when they were not political, most often in a rather trivial sense, the moves in the games of sexual competition were scrutinized with perhaps undue attention. It was hardly possible for Byron to escape this, given that he was an attractive man and soon discovered that he could play the game very well. The sexual game, as a game, features in his early poetry, overlaid with the conventions that made it palatable.

He of course made an issue of not accepting the rules at face value. But in his poetry even as he takes up an anti-romantic stance:

> Away with your fictions of flimsy romance;
> Those tissues of falsehood which folly has wove![1]

he is borrowing the language and rhythms of conventionalized verse—though in this case love song rather than poetry.

The Hero as Lover: Byron and Women

Give me the mild beam of the soul-breathing glance,
    Or the rapture which dwells on the first kiss of love.[1]

There is something of the lightness and a hint of the irony of
John Gay here, just as there is a touch of Macheath in the
Byronic pose. Byron condemns 'romance' because he sees it as
artificial; it does not stem from true experience. Conventional
love poems are 'cold compositions'.[2] He prefers the 'effusions
that spring from the heart'. He implies that verse itself is a cold
calculation of language, yet uses it, does not depart from its
conventions, and if he is a little playful he is not satirical. The
hallmark of this particular convention is not coldness, but
lightness. It certainly has little to do with depth of feeling.
Byron was always going to have a problem when it came to
conveying depth of feeling. He was never very good at it in his
poetry.

This is of course an early poem, and most writers will serve
their apprenticeship by making use of accepted forms, and
indeed there is no reason not to. Yet Byron's readiness to make
use of the conventional is much more present than one might
have imagined. The language, the form, the cultural parameters,
in particular the Classical ambience, that were available to
Byron were in many ways those of an earlier generation. This
is not to suggest that they were not those of his own generation
also, but does imply a continuity with the eighteenth century
which we tend to think the Romantic poets broke. The
cultural environment with which early nineteenth-century
writers were familiar would remain essentially the same, until
the balance of education itself shifted under pressure from a
changing society. Byron's writing right through his lifetime is
stamped with the features of the eighteenth century and a
privileged classical education much more strongly than that
of, say, Wordsworth, who was much more exposed to other
cultural currents.

Part of the 'romance' which Byron might have been expected
to rebel against was the idealization of women, especially as
there were some notable eighteenth-century examples to
encourage him. He met and seems to have been somewhat
alarmed by Madame de Stael—'she is frightful as a precipice',
he comically proclaimed, referring to her looks.[3] He made fun

of the 'blues', or bluestockings—there was a lot of it—fun-making—about. He seems to have genuinely respected the talents and intelligence of the woman who became his wife, Annabella Milbanke. But more conspicuous and more sugges-tive than the presence of clever women in fashionable society was a dramatic change in the appearance of women which had come as a direct result of the French Revolution. The stiff, cumbersome, elaborate hooped skirts of an opulent and elaborate French Court that was totally out of touch with real life but yet led the way in European fashion, disappeared. At the time the young Byron was embarking on experiences with the opposite sex, women were wearing soft, clinging, figure-enhancing garments that were in every sense unrestricting. It was one of the most dramatic fashion changes ever, and was full of social and sexual implications. It is debatable whether it is artificiality or naturalness that most encourages the view of women as sex objects. Whichever it is, Byron was not able to depart from that most conventional of reactions. He satirizes female behaviour, and criticizes it, but the ideal of female beauty and of feminine character, and the acceptance of the belief that females ought to be beautiful, is maintained. Don Juan is not indiscriminate in his loves. His women are always good-looking, in a conventionally feminine way, and although they may be cuckolding their husbands, they have all the appropriate female attributes.

If we look at a better known poem, one that has been safely anthologized, we see the idealization process in operation. 'She walks in beauty' was written about Byron's cousin Mrs. Wilmot, whom he met at a party wearing a black spangled dress.

> She walks in beauty, like the night
>   Of cloudless climes and starry skies;
> And all that's best of dark and bright
>   Meet in her aspect and her eyes:
> Thus mellow'd to that tender light
>   Which heaven to gaudy day denies.
>
> One shade the more, one ray the less,
>   Had half impair'd the nameless grace
> Which waves in every raven tress,
>   Or softly lightens o'er her face;

Where thoughts serenely sweet express
How pure, how dear their dwelling-place.

And on that cheek, and o'er that brow,
    So soft, so calm, yet eloquent,
The smiles that win, the tints that glow,
    But tell of days in goodness spent,
A mind at peace with all below,
A heart whose love is innocent![4]

The poem is finely written, with a lilting emotional conviction
that makes it all the more interesting. If the central image is
slightly unusual (less so if we remember the black spangled
dress), the attitude of reverence towards female beauty is not
in the least out of the ordinary. Neither language nor sentiments are in any way unconventional. The description of
beauty and the implication of personality tell us a great deal
about a very important part of Byron's attitude to women.
Unlike the earlier poem, quite different in tone, there is a
measured seriousness here, a consideredness, a current of calm
assessment. And 'calm' is a word that features, along with
others that contribute to the male conventionalization of the
female: 'tender', 'grace', 'softly', 'serenely sweet', 'eloquent'
(of looks, not words), 'smiles', 'glow', 'goodness', 'peace',
'pure', 'innocent'.

It would not be very helpful to take a doctrinaire feminist
line on this kind of thing, to condemn Byron for doing very
well what many poets have done indifferently, and for operating
within a conventional attitude to women which would persist
for a good deal longer and still underlies a great many
assumptions about human relations. The poem transcends the
stereotype—one way of defining a successful piece of writing.
The problem with Byron is that we know too much about him
to accept writing of this kind without question. Did a man for
whom fornication was so significant an activity really set such
store by purity and innocence? Or who apparently enjoyed
sexual conflict and all the excitements of intrigue and the
challenges of rebellion really value sweetness and serenity?
The answer is probably yes, and the affirmative still keeps us
rooted within a convention—the convention of the male double
standard. 'She walks in beauty' has the ring of conviction: the

poet, as a poet, believed in what he was setting down. Elsewhere the impression is that women were less important to Byron as soothing angels than as providing opportunities for living life more intensely, and intensity of living was essential to him. But the evidence suggests, and particularly the evidence of his relationship with Augusta, that like so many men Byron wanted women to be both angel and temptress. Poetically, the problem was to bring the two together. He solved that problem in *Don Juan.*

Of course Byron could as readily satirize as idealize, and the double bluff of mockery can be pointed and amusing. He can address a lady on the infelicities of keeping an outdoor December assignation:

> But here our climate is so rigid,
> That love itself is rather frigid:[5]

— and acknowledge the irony of the trappings of, presumably, illicit love: the exchange of locks of hair and the formalized expectations of the wooer and the wooed. The indications are, though, that Byron *enjoyed* courtship rituals, in spite of this youthful opinion of what he considered essentially trivial formalities which was expressed in a letter to Augusta:

> ... I feel inclined to laugh at you, for love in my humble opinion, is utter nonsense, a mere jargon of compliments, romance, and deceit; now for my part had I fifty mistresses, I should in the course of a fortnight, forget them all, and if by any chance I ever recollected one, should laugh at it as a dream, and bless my stars, for delivering me from the hands of the little mischievous Blind God.[6]

He not only enjoyed the rituals of courtship, but proved to be very good at just the kind of thing he mocks. He was able to make the conventions work to his advantage, often at the same time as he outrageously flouted them. Yet he was perhaps never quite as outrageous as he made himself out to be, or as the Victorian generation made him out to be. Certainly he slept with boys and had adulterous affairs, but that was not uncustomary for young men of his status and education. Public school and university fostered the former, while the latter was tacitly accepted as an appropriate way for young men to gain sexual experience. Married women were safer and possibly friendlier than prostitutes.

As in most aspects of Byron's life the contradictions are monumental. He scorns the 'mere jargon of compliments', yet masters the accepted modes of seduction. He scorns love, enjoys conquest, and demands passion. And woven into all this is a tangle of double standards. 'I am buried in an abyss of sensuality,' he writes to John Cam Hobhouse in February 1808, '. . . I am given to Harlots, and live in a state of Concubinage, I am at this moment under a course of restoration by Pearson's prescription, for a debility occasioned by too frequent connection.'[7] A little over a year later he is full of righteous indignation, admittedly in a letter to his mother, at the behaviour of his manservant Fletcher for associating with prostitutes, yet the moral stance is genuine. Fletcher had also been guilty of introducing a young lad to a 'woman of the town'. Byron writes of the 'machinations of a scoundrel who has not only been guilty of adultery, but of depraving the mind of an innocent stripling, for no other motive, but that which actuates the devil himself, namely, to plunge another in equal infamy . . .'.[8] Byron accepts his own action as being inevitable, compelled by the curse of the Byrons, and accepts also the consequences with a certain sanguinity—the 'debility' he refers to. His own involvements in adultery, or with prostitutes are, in some moods, *really* driven by the devil himself. The 'infamy' of his own behaviour is if possible to be avoided by others.

The double standards are detectable everywhere, partly a product of social attitudes, partly of Byron's own genius for self-delusion. He is decent—he sees that his illegitimate children are properly cared for. Yet there is something almost dismissive in his decency. 'I cannot have the girl on the parish',[9] he writes to his agent John Hanson, of a maid at Newstead who is pregnant by him, yet there is no examination of the convention that accepts the inevitability of maids bearing the children of young gentlemen, no scrutiny of values, and no curiosity in the child he had fathered. It is of course not a simple case of self-delusion, nor of a sensitive man at odds with both himself and society. One of the reasons why Byron is so intriguing— and attractive—a figure is precisely because he writes large, exposes both deliberately and inadvertently so much of what a sponge-like society absorbs and neutralizes. When the exposure is as glittering, trenchant and enjoyable as it is in *Don Juan* it is hard not to forgive him everything.

It is perhaps not unhelpfully simplistic to see the young Byron facing a choice between two areas of action, sex or politics, and to see the two as offering similar possibilities. Byron was clearly not going to fit into the established political life of early nineteenth-century Britain, although he flirted with the idea. His talents didn't really lie in that direction. Until he found his feet as a writer, sexual relations gave him the possibilities of social attack that he needed. But it was not a period that was conducive to sexual politics. Too much was acceptable, however tacit the acceptance. And however exploitative Byron's relations with women may have been, he was probably not ruthless enough to use sex in this aggressive way.

Byron's restlessness was partly the result of not knowing quite what his target should be, or what cause he should mobilize. He could attack hypocrisy, injustice, specious government, but that wasn't particularly difficult or challenging. What was difficult was to find in England an embraceable cause. The objects of his fragmented attacks were often too close to what sustained him for comfort, and this further complicated matters. Hence the need to create the Childe Harold persona, the noble outcast, and to leave vague exactly the reasons for his disquiet. Childe Harold and his kin are at the same time, it is implied, the victims of women and the objects of their sympathy. The other side of Byron's manipulation of sexual politics, the use of unorthodox sexual relations as a means of attacking society, was the rationalization. Byron quite genuinely saw himself at times as victim, of his own sexuality as well as of women. And the vehicle of sympathetic understanding has always been one of the classic ways of women presenting in acceptable fashion their own sexuality.

To attack government and royalty was easy—which is not to suggest that Byron didn't do it very well. *The Vision of Judgment* surely still makes the reader wince on behalf of its victims. To mount an attack on society as a whole was altogether trickier, and in a sense out of Byron's time, in spite of reason and revolution. A comprehensive analysis of social

ills and the structure of exploitation was yet to come. Action
was the problem, and it was there that relations with women
came to the rescue: in that area action, for Byron, was not a
problem. It was a very easy way to demonstrate his prowess.
Deformity may have made the need for this particularly
strong; his unhappy relationship with his mother may have
contributed. The fact that he was fond of boys, and of one in
particular, John Edleston, whom he had known at Cambridge—'I certainly *love* him more than any human being'[10]—
may have reinforced a need to prove that he was successful
with women. This is speculation, however interesting. Whatever the reasons, there can be no doubt that Byron made use
of sex and women in a number of ways.

To what extent can we trust his poetry, or trust his letters?
'The great object of my life is sensation—to feel that we
exist—even though in pain—it is this "craving void" which
drives us to Gaming—to Battle—to Travel—to intemperate
but keenly felt pursuits of every description whose principal
attraction is the agitation inseparable from their accomplish-
ment. . . .'[11] In this letter to Annabella Milbanke he begins
with 'I', and then generalizes—all men are the same. It could
be part of his attempt to make himself acceptable to the
fastidious Miss Milbanke. On the other hand, he enjoyed
shocking her. And is he describing here a fictive Byron (Childe
Harold) or the real man? The question is complicated by the
fact that Byron's reality was itself partly his own invention. If
sex and gender were to be manipulated as weapons against
society, it required Byron's mediating interpretation—a
public relations job—to make the most of it. This is what his
poetry was doing. He wrote in a letter to Thomas Moore 'I can
never get people to understand that poetry is the expression of
excited passion[12]; but it was also a way of making passion
acceptable. Once it had been put into words it became interpretation, not actuality. Passion described, even implied, is
passion tamed. Language, particularly written language, has a
defusing effect often at the same time as it has an inflating,
self-enhancing tendency. If it is written down in sentences,
even—or especially—rhymed, metred sentences, it becomes
in a sense respectable, or at least safe. Even *Don Juan* is safe, as
is Mozart's *Don Giovanni*. In both cases the limits of form and

convention control both the emotion and the threat.

Without poetry it was very difficult to know what strong feeling was for, unless it was to be experienced simply for its own sake. With Byron there is always the suggestion that passion was escape. 'I am totally absorbed in this passion', he wrote to Lady Melbourne of his affair with Frances Webster.[13] There is always a tension between the inward and the outgoing effects of profound feeling. For Byron 'love' was often self-absorbing. Did passion also make him more compassionate, sensitive, generous towards human frailties? *Don Juan* suggests an answer in the affirmative. Absorption in the love of women was certainly a major objective in Byron's existence, and the feeling was heightened if it was dangerous. For anyone but Byron there would have been enough danger in adultery; Byron experimented with incest. 'I am much afraid that perverse passion was my deepest after all', he wrote,[14] a month or so after his remark about Frances Webster, and again to Lady Melbourne, to whom he wrote with an honesty which often seems doubtful elsewhere. His friendship with her was a cardinal factor in his life for several years. He wrote often to his sister Augusta, and often insisted that he could love no other woman as he loved her. It was partly the fatal bond of the Byrons that he saw drawing them together, partly the fact that she seemed to understand him as no one else could—or that he believed this.

Certainly his wife did not understand him. Again, Byron's courtship and marriage were totally compatible with the society in which he lived. Byron chose a woman who had money and talents, a woman whom society might have chosen for him, but whom he could never have loved. He conducted with her a careful correspondence in which he protested his admiration and respect and his belief that she would be good for him, encouraging her to believe that she could reform him. That in itself amounted to cruelty, and the cruelties would be compounded after their marriage. He appeared to be accepting the conventional view of women, and conducting the courtship rituals as society demanded. 'I am good-humoured to women, and docile; and if I did not fall in love with her, which I should try to prevent, we should be a very comfortable couple', he wrote in his journal.[15] Byron may have genuinely felt that Annabella Milbanke could be his salvation, or genuinely *wanted* to believe it.

I yet wish to be good—with you I cannot but be happy—but I never shall be what I would have been—luckily I do not wish to be so now—reflection & experience have taught me that all pursuits which are not founded on self-esteem & the good of others—lead out to the same result. . . . I am thankful that the wildness of my imaginations has not altogether prevented me from recovering the path of peace.[16]

Part of him may have felt a profound need for 'peace', but that path would be closed to him, and he almost willed its closure. Peace implied a retiral from the sexual battleground, and it seemed highly unlikely that Byron could have convinced himself that that was what he needed, or indeed that it was possible.

He made every attempt to rationalize his proposed marriage with Annabella. 'There is something to me very softening in the presence of a woman,—some strange influence, even if one is not in love with them,—which I cannot at all account for, having no very high opinion of the sex. But yet,—I always feel in better humour with myself and everything else, if there is a woman within ken.'[17] The problem was that the acceptance of marriage was the acceptance of an institution shaped and supported by just the hypocritical values that Byron detested, and no amount of wry comment on Byron's part could disguise that. Marriage would make him respectable; indeed that was why he wanted it, in so far as he really did want it. For a while it seemed that he was prepared to pay that price for what he hoped would prove to be an escape from the self-torture that his sexual liaisons seemed to lead to. His association with Caroline Lamb, for example, had proved a disaster and an embarrassment, maybe because she out-Byroned Byron, and marriage could perhaps be a way of laying that ghost. Then there was Augusta; but he was never going to be able to escape the anguish of that relationship. In *Don Juan* Byron successfully describes sexual activity as innocent fun, in spite of the irritations of subterfuge and deceit. There is very little hint of that in his life.

Some years after his marriage, in a letter to his close friend Thomas Moore—there is a quality of honesty in Byron's letters to Moore as there is in those to Lady Melbourne—in the same letter in which he talks of poetry as 'the expression of *excited passion*', he added 'there is no such thing as a life of passion any more than a continuous earthquake, or an eternal feaver. Besides, who could ever *shave* themselves in such a state?'[18] Life could not have the continuous intensity of opera, although a later Byronic figure Robert Louis Stevenson would wish wistfully that it could, but nevertheless there had to be arias and high notes. If the earthquake could not be ever-lasting it had to be repeated, and if the repeats would not come naturally they would have to be artificially, or artfully, gener-ated. For someone who was so fond of the idea of love, it was extraordinary that Byron could contemplate marriage, which he looked at coolly as a union of convenience in which love would be an irrelevance. Although he uses the word in con-nection with his marriage, it is quite clear that by it he does not mean passion, precisely because passion was eruptive, not an even tenor of existence.

It is difficult to know to what extent Byron was self-deluded, to what extent he was rather desperately trying to manipulate what society offered into something that might be genuinely 'good' for him. His reaction against the failure of his marriage suggests self-delusion. Whatever else it damaged, it damaged his pride. Lady Byron outmanoeuvred him, in quite a different way from Caroline Lamb, but the effect was similar. A broken marriage, or a broken love affair, is a reasonable justification for strong feeling and self-pity. Byron probably experienced more intensity with the breaking than with the making of his marriage.

> . . . she—or rather—the separation—has broken my heart—I feel as if an Elephant had trodden on it—I am convinced I shall never get over it—but I try. . . . I breathe lead.[19]

This was in a letter to Augusta, on whom he could count for sympathy. Later he wrote '*that woman* has destroyed me.'[20] Caroline Lamb he claimed to hate, when she was being at her most aggravating, following and pestering him. The tone of his comments on Annabella is also full of hatred, so that we react with suspicion at something like this, written to her:

> . . . do not destroy whatever slender or remote hope I may still cling to—but believe me when I tell you with the most sincere & solemn truth to you and before God—that if there were a means of becoming reunited to you I would embrace it.[21]

116

Sixteen days later he is confiding to Thomas Moore that he has fallen in love—he is in Italy now—and indeed is involved in a Mozartian incident which he describes with insouciant good humour. 'I have fallen in love with a very pretty Venetian of two and twenty . . . we have found and sworn an eternal attachment—which has already lasted a lunar month', he wrote to Augusta.[22] There were also, of course, the episode with Claire Clairmont, which produced a daughter, and numerous Venetian ladies.

It was at this stage in his life, in 1819, that Byron met Teresa Guiccioli, who would dominate his emotional existence until his death. It was a tangled and tortuous affair, plagued by jealousies and misunderstandings and interferences. If Byron in some ways rather enjoyed the intrigue and the risks—the Contessa was married to a man forty years older than herself—the negotiating of the minefield of Guiccioli connections and Italian conventions soon became tedious and at times almost unbearable. However, Byron had lost none of his masterly touch at the manoeuvrings of the love affair, and protested eternal love, in spite of all difficulties, to the object of his affections. That he was still expert at declarations of love we can see in his letters to Teresa, but his talent is within the conventional, although the fact that he was writing in a language not his own may have been a limiting factor. He was able to write to her as 'my only and last love', 'you shall be my last passion.'[23] It was indeed his last love, but it did not stand in the way of other sexual relationships. And at the same time as he was elaborating on his love for Teresa he was writing to Augusta. 'I have never ceased nor can cease to feel for a moment that perfect and boundless attachment which bound & binds me to you—which renders me utterly incapable of *real* love for any other human being—what could they be to me after *you*?'[24] He was thinking seriously of marriage with Teresa, if both of them were free, but the pull of Augusta was as strong as ever. 'I always loved you better than any earthly existence, and I always shall unless I go mad.'[25] It is possible that Byron himself was surprised at how important his relationship with Teresa had become, and possible also that he could continue to express confidently the depth of his feelings for Augusta because there was nothing that could be done about it. It was

117

a safe commitment, a safe passion, now confined to letters.

Teresa was a strong personality. Initially the conventions of Venice appealed to Byron greatly. It was accepted that married women would have lovers, as there was no pretence that marriage was anything but a union of convenience. But there were nevertheless certain rules: high standards of fidelity and constancy were exacted in these extra-marital relationships, and a degree of discretion. Byron wrote at some length about these arrangements to John Murray:

> Their system has its rules—and its fitnesses—and decorums—so as to be reduced to a kind of discipline—or game at hearts—which admits few deviations unless you wish to lose it.—They are extremely tenacious and jealous as furies—not permitting their Lovers even to marry if they can help it—and keeping them always close to them in public as in private whenever they can.—In short they transfer marriage to adultery—and strike the *not* out of that commandment.—The reason is that they marry for their parents and love for themselves.—They exact fidelity from a lover as a debt of honour—while they pay the husband as a tradesman—that is not at all.—You hear a person's character—male or female—canvassed—not as depending on their conduct to their husbands or wives—but to their mistress or their lover.[26]

If Byron thought at first that the acceptance of extra-marital liaisons were a sign of a sexually easy-going society, he soon learnt differently. A difficulty for him was that in fact he found the system hard to accept, for it was a labyrinth that presented obstacle after obstacle to the progress of true love. In the end he became bored with trying to negotiate it, although his feelings for Teresa remained strong.

Other powerful feelings were growing more insistent. They had always been there but had never found an appropriate objective correlative. In a letter to John Cam Hobhouse of October 1819, Byron wrote:

> My taste for revolution is abated—with my other passions.—Yet I want a country—and a home—and if possible—a free one—I am not yet thirty two years of age—and I might still be a decent citizen and found a *house* and a family. . . .[27]

The abatement was temporary. Decent citizenship within the limits of a hypocritical society was not acceptable. Freedom had to be fought for before paternalism, in both its senses, was possible. The journey to Missolonghi was in a way the first necessary step in the process of settling down, as well as providing the literary hero at last with an opportunity to break out into action, and to escape from tedious and sterile social demands.

What is Byron's status as a heroic figure, and how can we assess the hero as lover? There is no doubt that Byron took advantage of women and exploited the opportunities that his personal and his literary magnetism gave him. Teresa reacted to both, which flattered his vanity and spurred his own feelings. Yet he saw himself as the victim of strong passions. He wanted to live life with intensity, and relished the danger and the damage that he exposed himself to, but he was exposing others at the same time. In his writing he created characters who were simultaneously intensely involved and aloof, and this suggests a need to protect himself. In the group of tales that followed *Childe Harold* the love of women is woven into accounts of heroic action and an atmosphere of diffuse exoticism. Passion is transplanted from the intrigues of the drawing room to a heroic, even epic, canvas. It is a translation in quality as well as in environment, although the latter has a great deal to do with the former. In *The Giaour*, for instance, love is given a heroic dimension by action:

> Yet death I have not fear'd to meet;
> And in the field it had been sweet,
> Had danger woo'd me on to move
> The slave of glory, not of love,
> I've braved it—not for honour's boast;
> I smile at laurels won or lost;
> To such let others carve their way,
> For high renown, or hireling pay:
> But place again before my eyes
> Aught that I deem a worthy prize—
> The maid I love, the man I hate—
> And I will hunt the steps of fate
> To save or slay. . . .[28]

Love is a passion to die for or to kill for. It demands sacrifice, risk, courage on the part of both man and woman, and with all this it is sanctified—'love indeed is light from heaven.' The feeling itself, and the commitment, raises it above the sordidness of the adulterous intrigue or the exploitativeness of the harem. However, although love is a major theme, or pivot of action, in this group of poems, most of the language—and they are long—is taken up with the communication of ambience rather than with specific feeling.

Love may be an active passion in these poems, enhanced by blood and daring, but the women are on the whole passive. They are there to be admired by men, to be, in fact, pivots of action rather than to act. This is Zuleika, in *The Bride of Abydos*:

> The light of love, the purity of grace,
> The mind, the Music breathing from her face,
> The heart whose softness harmonized the whole,
> And oh! that eye was in itself a Soul!
> Her graceful arms in meekness bending
>   Across her gently-budding breast. . . .[29]

And so on: purity, grace, meekness, Music, harmony, Soul— language like this defuses the sensuality of female beauty. The more beautiful the woman the more likely she is to be not only the victim of man's lust but the pawn of man's ambition. It is not surprising that the women tend to die. Given too much substance, too much life, they become dangerous. The heroes bear the burden of the victimization of women with a heavy heart, yet they carry on. Just as the language of heroic romantic love diverts the reader's attention from sex, so the hero's fierce and solitary courage, the 'loneliness and mystery',[30] divert enquiry away from the possible responsibility for the heroine's fate. Women, in other words, enhance the hero, but are expendable. When Byron went to Greece he did not take Teresa, but he felt guilty about leaving her behind.

It is of course the classic tendency. Byron did not invent it, and it would have a long and flourishing tradition after him— although partly thanks to him. It may be built into the heroic tradition. It may not be possible for the hero to be lover without at best exploiting women, at worst destroying them. But only a step away from the heroic tradition is *Don Juan*. With *Don Juan* Byron looked at the contemporary scene, and cast away the escapist possibilities of exotic climes, heroic traditions, and conventional poetic language. 'How I do delight in observing life as it really is!' he exclaimed in his journal.[31] In *Don Juan* he wrote about the life he observed and life as he would have wished to experience it. And suddenly he has a poem peopled with flesh and blood men and women.

The men and women are flesh and blood, but of course the life is not real, or rather the hero's existence is not real. Much of what Byron described was society as he had tangled with it, the mores he had encountered on his early visit to Spain, and with which he was more directly involved in Italy. Donna Julia of Canto I, the attractive young woman married to an older man, could have been Teresa Guiccioli. The double standards he exposed he had both experienced and participated in. The devout puritanism of Juan's mother and his education devoid of 'natural history'[32] were also very close to home. But in Juan Byron projected not what he himself was, but what he might have wanted to be: genuinely innocent and genuinely liberated from the false constraints and specious ambitions and conquests of society. In spite of the freewheeling stanza, the manipulation of rhyme, the deliberately fractured versification—or perhaps because of these things—Byron's sixteen-canto, profoundly serious romp is full of a delicate and deadly irony, wry, controlled, but above all generous—and most noticeably generous to women.

Don Juan is both idealistic and realistic. Byron sidesteps the whole problem of sexual conquest by presenting women as equal players in the game, and at the same time avoids the characterization of the female as calculating temptress—a tendency that surfaced rather often in his life, where he fluctuated between interpreting himself as sexual victim and sexual conqueror. But if the ladies in *Don Juan* are real (they are no less attractive than the Leilas and Zuleikas, but their looks are substantive, and their presence physical rather than sentimental), what about the sex? It is surely ideal. Juan innocently succumbs to innocent female beauty (not wiles) aided and abetted by the time of year, the moon, the climate. There are, Byron disingenuously argues, as we all know, forces at work which will bring a man and a woman together in spite of all their rational and moral inclinations, and it could not possibly be Juan's fault, or Julia's, and besides, when we are talking about a natural and mutual attraction blame is not a part of things. In other words, Byron creates an environment in which there is no need for sexual responsibility. *Social* conventions may be flouted but *human* feelings are not damaged. In Mozart's *Don Giovanni* we have an exposure of human vulnerability and a real tension between the romantic temptations of seduction (for both seducer and seduced) and suffering. This is not a part of Byron's creation. He is interested in exploring the possibilities of freedom in the three great arenas of love, war and politics. His celebration of man's relations with woman is beyond the persuasive arts of Don Giovanni because in *Don Juan* men and women are simply doing what comes naturally. It is the difference between liberation and libertinism. But there is a problem. Sex is and is not natural, and cannot be stripped of the layers with which religion, culture and social organization have coated it. Byron implies that guilt and pain in sexual relations are the result of artificial constraints and interpretations, and with this the twentieth-century reader might be inclined to agree. Nevertheless, as soon as there are communities of men and women there are controls, and therefore artificialities. The fact that Byron uses *Don Juan* to expose these artificialities, and the hypocrisies they breed, and that this is done with such vivacity, is in itself seductive. However, it is part of the idealism. The environment in which Byron's Juan operates is not amoral but ideal, gorgeously and irresistibly—and self-consciously—ignoring certain of the realities of human relations.

Juan moves through relations with women, political situations, battlefields, fluidly and harmlessly. He learns as he goes, absorbs, responds. He is the genuinely liberated hero, who reminds us that the older and more persistent heroic tradition, which seems to demand if not the victimization of women at least an inability to accept them as active and equal participants in experience, need not dominate. Somehow the critical gaiety of Byron's writing carries him through all kinds of treacherous areas. He could do it in verse. He could not do it in his own life. His own experience demonstrated just how idealized *Don Juan* was. Whether Byron liked it or not, and however hard he rebelled against it, he was buffeted by conventions of morality which he may have despised but with which he had to find a way of operating. Love, passion, the embracing of experience for its own sake, intensity of living could not of themselves create the momentum that would carry him past the shoals of prejudiced and hypocritical attitudes.

When it came to the point freedom was not really about love for women. He felt compelled to abandon the Contessa Guiccioli in the cause of the liberation of Greece. Both heroism and freedom had to go beyond commitment to an individual human being. As Juan moved from the liberties of love to the liberties of humankind so Byron endeavoured. Teresa might have accompanied him, as she wished to, in the capacity of angel; hardly in the capacity of comrade. 'A mistress never is nor can be a friend', Byron had said revealingly some years earlier.[33] Perhaps his only female friend had been Lady Melbourne. Freely expressed sexuality imposes its own burdens and restrictions.

The questions remain unanswered. One of the problems is that Byron himself invites high expectations. His awareness and self-awareness are such that the reader, like the deluded Miss Milbanke, is anxious to believe the best of him, and is then perhaps doubly disappointed to find that for all his generosity of spirit he could never quite pull himself out of the morass of mutually damaging relations between the sexes. If we accept Byron's heroism, his genuine commitment to a creative liberation, we may also have to accept that the painless world of Juan's loves is both a delightful fiction and a conscious apology for the harsher realities of sexual exploitation.

NOTES

All quotations from Byron's letters and journals are taken from *Byron's Letters and Journals*, edited by Leslie A. Marchand (John Murray, 1973–82). Quotations from Byron's poetry are taken from *The Poetical Works of Lord Byron* (Oxford University Press, 1945).

1. 'The First Kiss of Love', *Poetical Works*, p. 8.
2. Ibid.
3. Quoted in Leslie A. Marchand, *Byron: A Portrait* (John Murray, 1971), p. 169.

4. 'She walks in beauty', op. cit., p. 77.
5. 'To a Lady', op. cit., p. 15.
6. Letter to Augusta Byron, 25 October 1804. *Letters and Journals*, Vol. I, p. 52.
7. Letter to John Cam Hobhouse, 27 February 1808, ibid., p. 158.
8. Letter to Mrs. Catherine Gordon Byron, 19 May 1809, ibid., pp. 203–4.
9. Letter to John Hanson, 17 January 1809, ibid., p. 189.
10. Letter to Elizabeth Bridget Pigot, 5 July 1807, ibid., pp. 124–25.
11. Letter to Annabella Milbanke, 6 September 1813, *Letters and Journals*, Vol. II, p. 109.
12. Letter to Thomas Moore, 5 July 1821, *Letters and Journals*, Vol. VIII, p. 146.
13. Letter to Lady Melbourne, 11 October 1813, *Letters and Journals*, Vol. II, p. 143.
14. Letter to Lady Melbourne, 25 November 1813, ibid., p. 174.
15. Ibid., p. 241.
16. Letter to Annabella Milbanke, 26 September 1814, *Letters and Journals*, Vol. IV, pp. 183–84.
17. *Letters and Journals*, Vol. II, p. 246.
18. Op. cit.
19. Letter to Augusta Leigh, 8 September 1816, *Letters and Journals*, Vol. V, p. 91.
20. Letter to Augusta Leigh, 28 October 1816, ibid., p. 120.
21. Letter to Lady Byron, 1 November 1816, ibid., pp. 120–21.
22. Letter to Augusta Leigh, 17 November 1816, ibid., p. 129.
23. Letter to Teresa Guiccioli, 22 April 1819, *Letters and Journals*, Vol. VI, p. 112.
24. Letter to Augusta Leigh, 17 May 1819, ibid., p. 129.
25. Letter to Augusta Leigh, 19 August 1820, *Letters and Journals*, Vol. VII, p. 159.
26. Letter to John Murray, 21 February 1820, ibid., p. 43.
27. Letter to John Cam Hobhouse, 3 October 1819, *Letters and Journals*, Vol. VI, p. 226.
28. *The Giaour, Poetical Works*, p. 261.
29. *The Bride of Abydos*, ibid., p. 266.
30. *The Corsair*, ibid., p. 302.
31. *Letters and Journals*, Vol. II, p. 240.
32. *Don Juan, Poetical Works*, p. 641.
33. *Letters and Journals*, Vol. II, p. 219.

6

Byron as Unacknowledged Legislator

by GEOFFREY CARNALL

'Who would write,' asked Byron in his Journal on 24 November 1813, 'who had anything better to do?' He was reflecting on a report that William Windham, who had died some three years earlier, regretted having not devoted himself entirely to literature and the sciences, instead of involving himself so much in politics. Byron dismissed Windham's regret as the weakness brought on by a painful terminal illness. In a more robust condition, Windham would surely not have countenanced cant of this kind. He had been 'one of those who governed nations'—not always, one should add, to the taste of Byron's political associates, but with independence and competence. Why should he have wanted to be a metaphysician, a rhymer, a scribbler? 'I do think,' said Byron, 'the preference of *writers* to *agents*—the mighty stir made about scribbling and scribes, by themselves and others—a sign of effeminacy, degeneracy, and weakness.'[1]

In writing thus, Byron was consciously setting himself against a prevailing sentiment at a time when much was said of the March of Intellect towards the Reign of Mind. Friend and foe to the French Revolution were alike willing to agree that writers like Voltaire and Rousseau had played a major part in the subversion of the old régime, and of traditional institutions everywhere; and if these institutions were not altogether in jeopardy, then some credit would have to be given to David Hume, whose religious scepticism had been less influential than his cogent presentation, in essay and history, of an enlightened conservatism in politics. If trade and manufactures were expanding with unprecedented speed, it was Adam Smith who had laid the foundations of a more intelligent management of the economy in *The Wealth of Nations*. For a year or two, at least, Godwin's *Political Justice* seemed to have based a utopian polity on irresistible reasoning; after that, Malthus's *Essay on Population* threatened to annihilate Godwin's reasoning with all the force that mathematical demonstration could supply. Burke aroused effective opposition to the revolutionary cause by bringing the rationalizing thinkers into disrepute with his vindication of Prejudice. With the exception of Burke, these were all thinkers who made their mark primarily through their impact on the *reading public*: another term which came in with the March of the Mind and the Spirit of the Age. One might complain, as Coleridge did in *The Statesman's Manual*, about the multiplication of readers whose heads and hearts were dieted at the circulating libraries and the periodical press; but of the weight and importance of that phenomenon there could be no doubt.

A special place was occupied by the new kind of journal of opinion, the *Edinburgh Review* in particular, and its Tory counterpart the *Quarterly*. Their characteristic anonymity exalted the opinions of an individual contributor at least into the views of a great party in the state (or faction, according to one's sympathies), at best into an utterance of the spirit of the age. To be a reviewer was probably the most efficient way of getting one's ideas into circulation and influencing decision-makers. It is amusing to watch the excitement with which Robert Southey and John Rickman planned to transform the whole climate of political thinking with the review that they wrote in 1811 for the *Quarterly* on Charles Pasley's *Military Policy*. It was to put an end to vacillating war-policies that suited only the appeasers of Bonaparte. Southey in his remote study in Keswick, Rickman sardonically observing the political process at close quarters, had neither of them any direct political role; but as reviewers their pretensions were unlimited. On this occasion, unfortunately, they had tried to do too much: the editor was alarmed, assistance was sought at the highest level, J. W. Croker softened the effect sufficiently to make Southey disclaim all interest in the article. The uncompromising ruthlessness of the men of ideas was tempered by the exigencies of practical politics.[2]

In spite of such mishaps, Southey valued his role as guardian of sound values in the *Quarterly*. An even wider field of opportunity opened to him (or so it seemed) when in 1813 he was offered the post of Poet Laureate. He saw it, in a way that none of his predecessors had done, as the office of National Bard, serving the best interests of the people, panegyrizing merit and condemning wickedness, strengthening religion and government. His appointment is a landmark in the history of attitudes towards poetry: not a secure landmark, because the reform party regarded the office as a ludicrous anachronism, and Southey's acceptance of it as a sad apostasy, but still significant, because the Prince Regent evidently saw it as something more than a mere court appointment, and allowed the new Laureate to choose his own occasions for launching into verse. His Royal Highness almost certainly got more than he bargained for: no previous Laureate had ventured to remind his employer that 'the Poet's fame' endures.

> when the Monarch's name
> Is but an empty sound, the Conqueror's bust
> Moulders and is forgotten in the dust.

Hazlitt remarked on the uncourtliness of such sentiments,[3] but Southey would have been quite unconscious of impropriety: they had become part of the commonplace of criticism. Poets were recognized as an important contingent in the March of Intellect. Back in 1759 Samuel Johnson was probably only playing with the idea when he made Imlac in *Rasselas* claim that the poet 'must write as the interpreter of nature, and the legislator of mankind'. Rasselas, after all, interrupted his 'enthusiastick fit' with the remark that Imlac had persuaded him that 'no human being can ever be a poet.'[4] But in the 1760s, men like John Brown and Thomas Percy were beginning to yearn for the time when the bard was a weighty figure in the commonwealth, and the immensely popular poetry of 'Ossian', as reconstructed by James Macpherson, established the notion of the bard as the enduring voice of his society.[5] By the time that Wordsworth composed his preface to *Lyrical Ballads*, he was able to take for granted that 'the Poet binds together by passion and knowledge the vast empire of human society, as it is spread over the whole earth, and over all time.'[6] With the emergence of Walter Scott and of Byron himself, the pre-eminence of the poet as a social power was manifest. In an extravagantly enthusiastic review of the fourth canto of *Childe Harold* in the *Edinburgh Review*, John Wilson spoke of 'the warm, life-flushed and life-breathing' poetry of his time, so superior to the 'languid, faint, cold' delineations which sufficed for readers a hundred years earlier.

> This literature of ours, pregnant as it is with living impressions,— gathered from Nature in all her varieties of awfulness and beauty,—gathered too from those high and dread Passions of men, which our ordinary life scarcely shows, and indeed could scarcely bear, but which, nevertheless, have belonged, and do belong, to our human life,—and held up in the powerful representations of the poets to our consciousness at times, when the deadening pressure of the days that are going by might bereave us of all genial hope and all dignified pride,—we say it is impossible for us to resist the belief that such pregnant, glowing, powerful poetry, must carry influences into the heart of this generation, even like those which are breathed from the heart of Nature herself. . . .[7]

It is implicit in Wilson's rhapsody that the welfare of society is threatened by the 'deadening pressure' of routine, and the point is made more explicitly by Shelley two years later in his *Defence of Poetry*, when he actually recalls Johnson's amused speculation, and invests it with a passionate sense of conviction. Speaking of the 'electric life' which burns in the work of his contemporaries— 'less their spirit than the spirit of the age'—he concludes:

> Poets are the hierophants of an unapprehended inspiration; the mirrors of the gigantic shadows which futurity casts upon the present; the words which express what they understand not; the trumpets which sing to battle, and feel not what they inspire; the influence which is moved not, but moves. Poets are the unacknowledged legislators of the world.[8]

In the preface to *Prometheus Unbound*, Shelley spoke of contemporary writers as 'forerunners of some unimagined change in our social condition or the opinions which cement it'.[9] The cloud of mind was about to discharge its collected lightning, the cementing opinions would disintegrate, with consequences which Shelley presents symbolically in the downfall of Jupiter. Or, as Hazlitt expresses it in his summary history of the effects of the French Revolution in the third chapter of the *Life of Napoleon*, it was the printing press itself which had eventually generated an enlightened public opinion, whose operation had shattered 'strongholds of pride and prejudice to atoms, as the pent-up air shatters whatever resists its expansive force'.[10]

No writer of the time was felt to have had more shattering force, more 'electric life', than Byron. As Francis Jeffrey put it in the *Edinburgh*, he surpassed all his contemporaries 'in force of diction, and inextinguishable energy of sentiment'.[11] This power had been generally acknowledged from the time of the appearance of the first two cantos of *Childe Harold* in 1812, and it was the security he felt in the public's recognition of it that emboldened him to be so disdainful of his own achievement. Hazlitt thought this a conscious attempt to procure additional admiration: 'Whatever he does, he must do in a more decided and daring manner than any one else; he lounges with extravagance, and yawns so as to alarm the reader!'[12] But the disdain for scribbling that he expressed in November 1813 was at least partly the effect of disappointment with his own abortive parliamentary career. At least a part of himself would have enjoyed being an acknowledged legislator.

The main outline of his career in the House of Lords is well known. His maiden speech almost exactly coincided with the first publication of *Childe Harold*, and had been almost as successful. He had attacked the proposal to introduce the death-penalty for frame-breaking, speaking from his own knowledge of those parts of Nottinghamshire where the Luddite rioters had been most active. His conclusion has something of the force of his most powerful poetry, and leaps out of the dreary columns of the parliamentary report like a flash of lightning. He imagines a victim of this new law dragged into a court for trial.

> Still, there are two things wanting to convict and condemn him; and these are, in my opinion,—Twelve Butchers for a Jury, and a Jefferies for a Judge![13]

He made a second speech in support of a measure directed towards Catholic emancipation, and had presented a petition on behalf of the veteran advocate for parliamentary reform, Major Cartwright. He had voted with the Whigs, but had evidently not been over-diligent in his attendance at the House of Lords. In one of the debates on Catholic emancipation, he had been fetched from a ball to take part in a division. He stood for a moment on entering the chamber, waiting behind the Woolsack. Eldon, the Lord Chancellor, turned round,

> and, catching my eye—immediately said to a peer (who had come to him for a few minutes on the Woolsack as is the custom of his friends) 'Damn them! they'll have it now, by G-d!—the vote that is just come in will give it them.'[14]

If Byron had been reluctant to leave 'the sound of revelry by night', at least on this occasion he could feel that he had made some contribution to the emancipation of five millions of his fellow-citizens.

His faltering interest in what he called his 'senatorial duties' was challenged in the autumn of 1813 by an approach to him from a debtor imprisoned in the King's Bench gaol, one W. J. Baldwin. Baldwin wanted Byron to present a petition relating to Lord Redesdale's Insolvent Debtors' Bill, and informed him of the bad conditions in which prisoners were kept. Presenting such a petition would have given him an opportunity to speak about reform both of the law and of prisons: issues which offered some scope for his eloquence. The main object of the Redesdale Bill was to remove from creditors the power to keep debtors in prison indefinitely. Sir Samuel Romilly had described it as an important innovation, 'which, as such, would have to encounter every species of obstruction from those who are, on all occasions, the defenders of long-prevailing abuses'.[15] Lord Ellenborough the Lord Chief Justice thought that Redesdale ought to have been put in a straitjacket, and November 1813 saw a good deal of manoeuvring going on to delay the application of the Act, now passed by both Houses of Parliament. As for prisons, their evil state had emerged as one of the current topics for reformers. Coldbath-Fields Prison had been investigated in 1808–9; James Neild's large survey of the state of the prisons had been published in 1812, and prominently reviewed in the *Edinburgh* by Francis Jeffrey himself; while in 1813 Elizabeth Fry was making her first visits to Newgate. At the end of November 1813, the Grand Jury of London inspected Newgate and found it to be grotesquely overcrowded and inadequate. The Commons discussed the matter on the 7 December, and Alderman Atkins of the City of London earned some notoriety for his remark that when the prison had been freshly cleaned in the morning, he would not be ashamed to compare it with any dairy in the country. It was the prisoners themselves who made the prison foul, particularly the women. Of course, there were too many of them![16] Atkins was felt to be particularly outrageous, and it is only fair to that generation to add that 1813 was also the year in which the new model prison at Millbank was begun.

It would not have been difficult for Byron to brief himself on the subject, but he refused to take the matter up, explaining to Baldwin that he did not wish to injure the cause 'by a premature and precipitate pressure of the question upon the legislature'. His letter is written with an evident and increasing embarrassment, and at the end he averts his gaze from the painful subject with something approaching incoherence:

> I have read your address—and I have read it with a hope almost for the sake of those to whom it is uttered—that their situation is less grievous than it would lead me to believe—not that I have any reason to doubt the statement—except the wish that in this—or in any country—such oppression had never existed.[17]

And so he pushed the matter out of his mind. Baldwin continued to 'bore' him with the petition a little longer, but Byron felt he had neither head nor nerves for the business. In the privacy of his Journal he acknowledged that he was shirking an evident duty. He was like Sterne, who preferred 'whining over a "dead ass to relieving a living mother"'. Lady Oxford might have persuaded him, if she had been there, with 'three words and half a smile': she always encouraged him to take his responsibilities as a peer seriously, especially on behalf of the weak, but without her he could not stimulate himself into making a speech. He was sick of 'parliamentary mummeries', and doubtful of his capacity to become an orator. Not, he added, that he had ever set out to do this *con amore*. Identifying himself for the moment with Falstaff, he claimed that 'company, villainous company, hath been the spoil of me', and that he had 'drunk medicines', if not to make him love others, then at any rate to hate himself. He was sinking into the condition of people like Scott and Moore, who might have been 'agents and leaders', but had become mere spectators. He had no ambition; at least (in a curious reservation) 'if any, it would be "aut Caesar aut nihil".'[18] He had, one infers, no taste for becoming a secondary actor in the parliamentary opposition, with a dubious prospect of future pre-eminence—certainly not the pre-eminence of a Caesar. On the other hand, as a man of letters his standing was little short of imperial. *The Giaour*, *The Bride of Abydos*, and in 1814 *The Corsair* conjured up in the public mind a spirit which could hardly find adequate expression in the lobbies of Westminster.

It was easy enough to speak in general terms of the cloud of mind discharging its collected lightning. The actual process of improvement was apt to be advanced by temperaments less overtly tempestuous than Byron's and less exalted than Shelley's. To enter into the diligent perseverance of Romilly in his penal reforms, or the tireless philanthropic committee-work of people like William Allen and Fowell Buxton, or the patient combination of shrewd industrial management and social propaganda engaged in by Robert Owen, is to feel that Byron is indeed a detached and dilettante figure. These fore-runners of the Victorian cult of earnest endeavour developed in themselves the character appropriate to sustain the volun-tary philanthropic organizations that proliferated so abundantly in the first decades of the nineteenth century. They find their poetic celebration in the revised version of Keats's *Hyperion*, written in 1819, but not published until 1867, in which he speaks of the 'thousands'

> Who love their fellows even to the death,
> Who feel the giant agony of the world,
> And more, like slaves to poor humanity,
> Labour for mortal good.

In this poem, Keats probably had Byron in mind when he dismissed the 'careless Hectorers in proud bad verse'.[19] All the same, Byron was not entirely irrelevant to this earnest endeavour.

The relevance lay in the exemplary dramatization in much of Byron's work of a quality indispensable to the effective reformer: relentless tenacity. The fact that he did not display this quality in the context of Parliament is nothing to the purpose. He created a myth, and it was the myth to which people responded. When Romilly recognized that any useful reform could expect to encounter obstruction by powerful defenders of long-prevailing abuses, his words suggest the strength of his own will, and his half-repressed exasperation with attitudes that make his strength of will necessary. A character-sketch in *The Examiner* of 14 November 1813 remarks that Romilly has a reputation for being easily irritated, and that his speeches have the air of someone whose feelings have been wounded. He could afford to be more sparing in his reproaches, and might even try a little flattery. But, the writer goes on, this unconciliatory temper is very understandable. A benevolent man will constantly encounter things that will 'disturb and agonize his feelings'. If he is also a contemplative man,

> he finds it impossible to disengage the painful idea from his mind: it haunts his dreams and even his pleasures: distresses upon distresses accumulate before his recollection or his imagination, till he is irritated into a state of torture only equalled by those sufferings of others from which it results. . . . May not this sensation of uneasiness be the best security for the exercise of active benevolence?[20]

While the mind of the Giaour or of Conrad the Corsair may be irritated into a state of torture by misadventures that are too theatrical to be taken seriously by most modern readers, one can readily see how a reformer of the barbarous penal code, thwarted again and again by an obstinate Lord Chief Justice, might find some relief to his feelings in a passage such as this:

> Dark and unearthly is the scowl
> That glares beneath his dusky cowl.
> The flash of that dilating eye
> Reveals too much of times gone by;
> Though varying, indistinct its hue,

Oft will his glance the gazer rue,
For in it lurks that nameless spell,
Which speaks, itself unspeakable,
A spirit yet unquell'd and high,
That claims and keeps ascendency. . . .[21]

That would have put Lord Ellenborough in his place! The frustrations and uneasiness and insecurity inevitable in a society subjected to the kind of changes that Regency England was enduring are caught up in a sense of guilt so generalized that it does not interfere with fantasies of dominance and self-vindication—perhaps even stimulates and enhances their effect. As Jeffrey remarked of Conrad, he may be spoken of as a ruffian, but he shows himself to be 'a perfect pattern of tenderness and humanity', carrying his generosity to Quixotic lengths.[22]

Earnest Victorians were apt to despise Byron's self-indulgent heroics. Carlyle came to dismiss the whining, theatrical dandy, but even he, in his earlier manhood, had spoken of him as 'the noblest spirit in Europe . . . full of fire and generous passion, and proud purposes'.[23] It was Matthew Arnold who attempted to clarify the received view most carefully. He conceded that Byron did not see the true way out of the state of things that enraged him, 'the slow and laborious way upward; he had not the patience, knowledge, self-discipline, virtue, requisite for seeing it.' But Arnold warmed to him as a 'passionate and dauntless soldier of a forlorn hope', waging battle against the old impossible world with incomparable sincerity and strength.[24]

The fire, the passion, the purposefulness were essential qualities of character for anyone with an ambition to improve society, and they could be seen as valuable even in a perverted state. Just as eighteenth-century devotees of sensibility had admired even the weaknesses of an amiable character, so there was something of a consensus in the early nineteenth century that even the wickedness of a potent spirit should not distract one—*could* not distract one—from the admirable energies manifested. The 'unconquerable will' of Milton's Satan was felt to be particularly stirring, and even an evangelical moralist like John Foster, the Baptist essayist, speaks of the temptation to say 'What a noble being this would have been, if goodness had been his destiny!' (Admittedly he adds that, if so, Milton committed a very serious error.)[25] Foster's observation occurs in the course of his essay 'On Decision of Character', one of a set of four *Essays* that first appeared in 1805, and enjoyed a considerable reputation well on into the middle of the century. The painter Benjamin Robert Haydon particularly valued the 'Decision of Character' essay, and constantly re-read it and recommended it to friends and correspondents.

Foster argues that people of irresolute character are made for subjection, passing like slaves from owner to owner. The heart is fretted and exhausted by an alternation of contrary motives, and Foster points out that long-wavering deliberation can actually cost more to feeling than 'some bold action of difficult virtue'.[26] It is a mark of the decisive character that it consumes little energy in dubious musings and abortive resolutions. It is also encouraged by the deference that resolution spontaneously engenders. 'When a firm decisive spirit is recognised', he says, 'it is curious to see how the space clears around a man, and leaves him room and freedom.'[27] Foster enlarges on the various traits of a decisive character, and lays particular emphasis on the strenuous will that must accompany the confident judgement.

> The intellect must be invested, if I may so describe it, with a glowing atmosphere of passion, under which the cold dictates of reason take fire, and spring into active powers.[28]

Foster quickly perceives that all this may have little to do with virtuous conduct. He points out the 'seductive and pernicious dignity' that the untameable soul has in cases where every moral principle is offended.

> Often in the narrations of history and fiction, an agent of the most dreadful designs compels a sentiment of deep respect for the unconquerable mind displayed in their execution.[29]

It is at this point that he recalls Milton's Satan; but not all unconquerable minds, of course, are Satanic. Foster finds a virtuous example in John Howard the prison-reformer: but even he paid a price for his single-mindedness. He had no leisure-feeling to spare for the variety of the scenes in which he travelled. He could even visit Rome without a glance at the ruins.

Such a sin against taste is very far beyond the reach of common saintship to commit. It implied an inconceivable severity of conviction, that he had *one thing to do*, and that he who would do some great thing in this short life, must apply himself to the work with such a concentration of his forces, as, to idle spectators, who live only to amuse themselves, looks like insanity.[30]

Another unpleasing trait of the decisive character is that it is with difficulty combined with the Christian virtues of mildness and patience. Firmness may result from overcoming feeling, but it is more likely to be the effect of not having the feeling at all.

To be tremblingly alive to gentle impressions, and yet to be able to preserve, when the prosecution of a design requires it, an immovable heart, amidst even the most imperious causes of subduing emotion, is perhaps not an impossible constitution of mind, but it must be the rarest endowment of humanity.[31]

Foster ends his essay with a regret that the illustrations he has been able to give of the decisive character are conspicuous not so much for goodness as for power. 'I attribute it', he says engagingly, 'to defect of memory.' But as it is, too many of those capable of achieving objects of the grandest utility, and of intimidating the collective vices of the age, have been 'themselves the very centres and volcanoes of those vices'.[32]

The dashing heroes of the Turkish tales provide a picturesque commentary on Foster's analysis. They are evidently meant to display the utmost energy of character, including an intense capacity for feeling, which, as Foster's essay suggests, throws the energy itself into even stronger relief. In his later work, Byron enlarges on the feelings of guilt that paralyse the decisive powers, but the element of stubborn resistance to oppression remains, rejecting the sense of enslavement as intolerable. At the end of his essay, Foster speculates on the ultimate fate of those great and wicked decisive characters before the Supreme Tribunal where their adamantine resolution must melt away. But Byron's Manfred shows no signs of melting. He re-enacts the situation of Dr. Faustus—the demonic spirits rise up to summon him to perdition—he defies them, and—they disappear.

I have not been thy dupe, nor am thy prey—
But was my own destroyer, and will be
My own hereafter.—Back, ye baffled fiends!—
The hand of death is on me—but not yours![33]

What Marlowe would have made of this is uncertain, and
Foster would certainly have shaken his head in disapproval:
but it is an audacious illustration of the space that clears
around a confident man, leaving him room and freedom.

The decisive character generates an atmosphere of success,
but may not always succeed. For many years Napoleon was a
symbol of energetic mastery, so that John Foster could speak
casually of the need for 'a Buonaparte in morals', and his
friend Joseph Hughes could speak of Foster's own 'Napoleonic
energy' as a writer.[34] But in due course Napoleon's power
failed him, to the consternation of his admirers. Byron, for one,
was 'utterly bewildered and confounded' by his abdication in
1814. Like Hazlitt, Byron wished that his hero had decided to
fight to the end. He did not have the sound feeling (said
Byron) that Macbeth had in not wishing to 'kiss the ground
before young Malcolm's feet'. Sylla managed things better,
revenging and resigning in the height of his sway, 'red with the
slaughter of his foes—the finest instance of glorious contempt
of the rascals upon record'.[35] Hazlitt quoted Shakespeare too,
invoking the elder Percy in *Henry IV*, who had a juster idea of
war, where all order died, and—

each heart being set
On bloody courses, the rude scene may end,
And darkness be the burier of the dead!

Napoleon should have staked his success on the revolutionary
ardour of the people; but he would not unleash popular fury
because it might have overwhelmed him as well as the
Bourbons and their allies.[36] Byron was quick enough to forgive
Napoleon when he returned from Elba, but the bloody conflict
of Waterloo sufficed even to satisfy the taste of a Sylla or a
Percy—'the crowning carnage' as Byron called it in *The Vision
of Judgment*, when the recording angels

threw their pens down in divine disgust—
The page was so besmear'd with blood and dust.[37]

137

Byron's immediate reaction to both abdication and final
defeat of his hero is expressed in rather a commonplace way
in the poems explicitly devoted to the subject, and his deeper
feelings emerge more effectively in a poem not directly concerned with Napoleon at all: *The Siege of Corinth*. He was
writing this through much of 1815. Its catastrophe is of a
kind that strains the imagination of all-encompassing destruction to the limit: at least, in the terms possible to a writer in the
early nineteenth century. He took the incident of an accidental
explosion in a gunpowder magazine, and turned it into the
deliberate mining of the church where old Minotti made his
last stand. The conquering Turks surge into the church and
see the high altar with the consecrated cup still on it.

> Brightly it sparkles to plunderers' eyes:
> That morn it held the holy wine,
> Converted by Christ to his blood so divine,
> Which his worshippers drank at the break of day,
> To shrive their souls ere they join'd in the fray.
> Still a few drops within it lay:
> And round the sacred table glow
> Twelve lofty lamps, in splendid row,
> From the purest metal cast;
> A spoil—the richest and the last.
>
> So near they came, the nearest stretch'd
> To grasp the spoil he almost reach'd,
>   When old Minotti's hand
> Touch'd with the torch the train—
>   'T is fired!
> Spire, vaults, the shrine, the spoil, the slain,
>   The turban'd victors, the Christian band,
> All that of living or dead remain,
> Hurl'd on high with the shiver'd fane,
>   In one wild roar expired![38]

The explosion takes many further lines to describe, and Byron
enters into the business with enthusiasm. Minotti carries
decision of character as far as it will go: several hundred feet in
the air, in fact.

Thereafter Byron was more concerned to explore the stoical
endurance developed in the third and fourth cantos of *Childe*

Harold, and with particularly powerful effect in *The Prisoner of Chillon*. Although the latter poem appears to describe the utter desolation and subjection of Bonnivard, that effect is belied by the vigorous rhythms which intimate the reckless willpower that has never given in, sustaining itself in an apparently hopeless situation. In fact, as Byron points out in his 'advertisement', he wrote the poem before he knew the full story of Bonnivard, and the edifying sequel to his imprisonment, when he was honoured by his fellow-citizens of Geneva, and served the cause of religious toleration. Taken together, the Advertisement and the poem form a composition of considerable political impact: showing the contrast between the subjective impression and the historical process. The unconquerable will may or may not win the day, but there is never ground for absolute despair.

In suggesting that there is a political relevance in poems where the chief ingredient might seem to be a self-indulgent egotism, I do not forget the caustic self-mockery that is so evident in Byron's letters and journals. Byron is never sure of the status of any of the feelings that he articulates so eloquently, and the chief difference between the poems mainly considered here and the satirical poems in *ottava rima* on which his modern reputation is based is that in the latter this uncertainty is freely expressed. But even the dashing manner in which the intrepid passion of Conrad and Minotti astounds the reader has the poise of an accomplished performer rather than the dedication of a single-minded zealot. Byron repudiates altogether the pretensions of the National Bard like Southey, whose 'grand heroics' are exploded in *The Vision of Judgment* with an effectiveness almost equal to the explosion at the end of *The Siege of Corinth*. His conversational manner is offhanded in a way completely appropriate to a writer who attached so little importance to his own art, and valued those who governed nations far more highly than he did the tribe of scribblers.

He discovered in the cause of Greek independence an active career that he missed in the House of Lords. His patient statesmanship among the Greek rebels has often been praised, and it is curious that he once described his role in terms of a dedicated philanthropy from which both in 1813 and the last years of his life he seemed so comically remote. In his Journal in September 1823 he remarks that

> whoever goes into Greece at present should do it as Mrs. Fry went into Newgate—not in the expectation of meeting with any especial indication of existing probity, but in the hope that time and better treatment will reclaim the present burglarious and larcenous tendencies which have followed this General Gaol delivery.[39]

The engaging persona of the author of *Don Juan* may hardly seem more analogous to Elizabeth Fry than the Giaour himself. But just as the implacable obstinacy of the latter may be taken as an oblique and highly coloured representation of the stamina necessary for the practical reformer, so the relaxed and equable acceptance of adultery, shipwreck, harem, war, and intrigue implies a tenacity that the practical legislator needs if he is not to explode in a spasm of self-destructive fury.

NOTES

1. *Letters and Journals*, ed. Leslie A. Marchand (1973–82), Vol. 3, pp. 219–20. Hereafter referred to as *LJ*.
2. There is an account of this episode in my *Robert Southey and his Age* (Oxford, 1960), pp. 123–30.
3. W. Hazlitt, *Complete Works*, ed. P. P. Howe (1930–34), Vol. 7, p. 88. Hereafter referred to as *Hazlitt*.
4. S. Johnson, *Rasselas*, Chapters 10 and 11.
5. See J. Brown, *Dissertation on Poetry and Music* (1763), T. Percy, 'Essay on the Ancient Minstrels of England', in *Reliques of Ancient English Poetry* (1765). The influence of Macpherson's work has been usefully assessed in an as yet unpublished study by Alexander French.
6. *Wordsworth's Literary Criticism*, ed. W. J. B. Owen (1974), p. 81. This passage was first published in 1802.
7. *Edinburgh Review*, 30 (June 1818), 118–19.
8. *Shelley's Prose*, ed. D. L. Clark (Albuquerque, 1954), p. 297.
9. Ibid., p. 328.
10. *Hazlitt*, Vol. 13, p. 40.
11. *Edinburgh Review*, 27 (December 1816), 277.
12. *Hazlitt*, Vol. 11, p. 70.
13. *Cobbett's Parliamentary Debates*, 21 (1812), 972. 27 February 1812.
14. *LJ*, Vol. 9, p. 28.

Byron as Unacknowledged Legislator

15. S. Romilly, *Memoirs* (1840), Vol. 3, p. 111.
16. *Examiner*, 12 December 1813, 790.
17. *LJ*, Vol. 3, p. 165 (14 November 1813).
18. *LJ*, Vol. 3, pp. 228–29, 206, 217.
19. *The Fall of Hyperion*, I, lines 156–59, 208.
20. *Examiner*, 14 November 1813, 734.
21. *The Giaour*, lines 832–41.
22. *Edinburgh Review*, 23 (April 1814), 220.
23. *Collected Letters of Thomas and Jane Carlyle*, ed. C. R. Sanders and K. J. Fielding (Durham N.C., 1970–), Vol. 3, p. 68. 19 May 1824.
24. M. Arnold, *Complete Prose Works*, ed. R. H. Super (Ann Arbor, 1960–77), Vol. 9, p. 236.
25. J. Foster, *Essays in a series of Letters*, 4th ed. (Oxford, 1811), p. 119.
26. Ibid., p. 99.
27. Ibid., p. 100.
28. Ibid., p. 115.
29. Ibid., p. 118.
30. Ibid., p. 124.
31. Ibid., p. 143.
32. Ibid., p. 165.
33. *Manfred*, Act 3, sc. 4, lines 138–41.
34. J. E. Ryland, *Life and Correspondence of John Foster* (1852), Vol. 1, pp. 198, 337n.
35. *LJ*, Vol. 3, p. 256; Vol. 4, p. 93.
36. *Hazlitt*, Vol. 15, p. 185.
37. *The Vision of Judgment*, stanza 5.
38. *The Siege of Corinth*, xxxii–xxxiii, lines 1001–20.
39. *LJ*, Vol. 11, p. 32.

7

The Byronic Philosophy

by WALTER PERRIE

Byron's death at Missolonghi contributed to the final achievement of Greek independence. The pedestrian circumstances of
his death did not tarnish its glamour. Byron was to be a hero
in the cause of Liberty. His death was not his own but
belonged, as Byron may have intended, to the European
imagination. In France he became an icon for the post-Bourbon
Romantics. His admirers and imitators included most of the
major writers: Hugo, Gautier, de Musset, Lamartine, de
Vigny and de Nerval. Perhaps because the course of French
Romanticism had been so deflected by the obligatory neo-
classicism of the First Empire, Byronism was to remain an
active force in French literature throughout the nineteenth
century. In Germany, though admired by Goethe and Heine
(Byron was the model for *Euphorion* in *Faust* II), his most
momentous influence was on the young Nietzsche who, in *Ecce
Homo*, recorded: 'I must be profoundly related to Byron's
Manfred; of all the dark abysses in this work I found the
counterparts in my own soul—at the age of thirteen I was ripe
for this book', and compared it favourably to *Faust*. It was
largely Byron's influence on Nietzsche—and the Byronic hero
as prototype for the *Übermensch*—that led Bertrand Russell to
devote a chapter in his *History of Western Philosophy* to the
subject of Byronism and its influence on the history of ideas.
Despite the cursory nature of his comments, Russell does state
the main point when he says that Byron '. . . was more
important as a myth than as he really was'.[1]

142

In short, Byron attracted enthusiastic attention from writers as remote from each other in time and space as Pushkin, Ibsen and Leopardi. Nor was his influence confined to the *literati*. As Andrew Rutherford has observed:

> Byron became an ideal, an almost mythical figure in the minds of Continental liberals for whom Mazzini acts as spokesman: '. . . The holy alliance of poetry with the cause of the peoples; the union—still so rare—of thought and action—which alone completes the human Word, and is destined to emancipate the world; . . . all that is now the religion and hope of the party of progress throughout Europe, is gloriously typified in this image . . . [of Byron at Missolonghi]. The day will come when Democracy will remember what it owes to Byron.'[2]

In Britain Byronism was the fashion of a few years, but not much more than a decade after his death its influence had already waned. For the rest of the century his reputation was eclipsed by those of Keats, Shelley and Wordsworth. Below the surface a Byronic influence was still at work and emerged, briefly, among the aesthetes of the 1890s and again in some of the 'public' poetry of the 1930s, most notably in the work of W. H. Auden. By and large though, Byron has been out of favour with mainstream Anglo-American critics. His public postures, his rhetoric, and his discursiveness have been anathema to most contemporary opinion. Russell remarks that 'To most of us, his verse seems often poor and his sentiment often tawdry . . .',[3] and T. S. Eliot described it as '. . . nothing but sonorous affirmations of the commonplace'.[4] How such 'tawdry' sentiment and 'poor' verse came to exercise such profound and lasting influence, as they evidently have, is a matter to which we must return, having looked at the contents of the Byronic philosophy.

The closest Byron ever came to enunciating a set of intellectual or aesthetic arguments outwith his poetry was in his letters 'On the Rev. W. L. Bowles's Strictures on the Life and Writings of Pope' (1821) in which he claimed that '. . . poetry is in itself passion, and does not systematize. It assails, but does not argue; it may be wrong, but it does not assume pretensions to Optimism.'[5] Byronism is not to be found in any manifesto. Nor was it exclusively the property of Lord Byron.

Friends, lovers, enemies, commentators and biographers all contributed to its manufacture. While Mary Shelley laboured to create of her dead husband the feeble angel of Victorian hagiography, Lady Byron was equally assiduous in creating the depraved monster she needed to justify her own moral purity.[6] Byronism was, therefore, a curious schist of rumour and malice, fact and fancy, as well as of texts. It was as much a set of attitudes towards Byron and his texts as it was of any argument embedded in them. To be a supporter or opponent of Byronism was to say something, not just about Lord Byron's poems, but about one's attitudes to the world at large.

The outline which follows of the main components of the Byronic philosophy concentrates on *Childe Harold* I/II, and on *The Bride of Abydos* as typical of the Turkish tales. I take the view that all the main elements of Byronism were already present in these early works (1812–13) and that Byron's later writings and career were poured into a mould of understanding established by the early works and their reception. So much so, indeed, that Byron's later life has something of the quality of a self-fulfilling prophecy about it; his early fame having made him a victim of his own inventions so that, as the myth developed, it became increasingly unlikely that Byron himself could escape its confines.

The focal point of Byron's work is invariably the feelings and actions of a male hero-figure. Those feelings and actions are a product of (a) personality and (b) circumstance or fate. Since the former is also understood to be, in great measure, a product of the latter, the Byronic hero is, essentially, a victim. His character is acutely sensual and sensitive: passionate to a greater degree than that of other men. He is, above all, energetic.

Circumstance, having marked out the Byronic hero as different from other men, has endowed him not only with more vitality and more intense appetites, but with greater abilities. His is a 'great soul' and he is an aristocrat and leader of men. In youth he has suffered some disappointment of his affections and has committed some crime against established morality, the nature of which is not generally specified. This disappointment and/or crime has produced in him a strong sense of a loss of innocence so that he sees himself as both fallen from grace and as alienated from ordinary society. His energetic disillusion makes him deeply restless, compelling him to seek ever fresh sensations and new experiences to whet his jaded appetites and assuage his self-conscious suffering. He is profoundly aware of being a prisoner of his own nature.

Melancholy and lonely, the Byronic hero hides his true feelings behind a mask of aristocratic pride and hauteur. His alienation from society, often imaged as an exile, is not merely passive but shades over into a deliberate defiance of conventions: political, moral and religious. He questions the sincerity of social ideals thereby making of himself a sceptic and iconoclast. In his unhoused condition he finds allies in a revolutionary or libertarian counter-world, but his pronounced individualism and sense of aristocratic difference preclude any espousal of egalitarianism. His are the chivalric and heroic ideals of nobility, courage and personal honour.

At the heart of the Byronic hero's motivations is a thwarted idealism. He cannot reconcile his awareness of the actuality of innocence (the wholly fallen could not know themselves to be so), with the cynicisms and pragmatic evasions of social life. He is, therefore, a naïf whose primary value is a redemptive, romantic love which he associates with purity and, hence, with truth and beauty. In defiant mood, that idealism easily merges into a Promethean fixation on moral absolutes. Implacably hostile to utilitarian principles, he denounces society for its cant and hypocrisy, seeing it as corrupt: the product of a decline and fall built into the nature of the human condition. Finally, he feels more akin to nature than to human society, finding in nature an image of his own stormy, elemental character and of that pre-lapsarian naturalness which he and the social world have forfeited.

Childe Harold I/II was published in 1812. By then Byron was already known to the literary world as the author of *English Bards and Scotch Reviewers* (1809) which had had all the benefits of a succès de scandale as a powerful satire on the literary establishment. Only a few weeks before the publication of *Childe Harold* Byron had come to the attention of the political establishment with a successful maiden speech in the Lords on the Frame-Work Bill. *Childe Harold* was an immediate, spectacular success and Byron was lionized by fashionable society. He consolidated that success with the Turkish tales: *The Giaour, The*

Bride of Abydos, Lara and *The Corsair*, the last of which sold 10,000 copies on publication day and went through seven editions within a month.[7]

Childe Harold I/II was largely composed during Byron's travels in Portugal, Spain, Albania, Greece and Turkey in 1809–11. It is a rambling account of similar travels by the Childe who is little more than a peg on which Byron can hang his observations. Although Byron protested in the 'Addition to the Preface' (1813) that he should not be identified with the Childe, the protest was half-hearted and ineffective. Byron undercuts his own protest by interrupting the poem from time to time to speak *in propria persona* (e.g. at I, xciii and II, xvii). This early use of a digressive narration linking different episodes loosely together, sometimes *in propria persona*, is significant for the later works. As Jerome McGann points out:

> The key to the form of *Don Juan*, then, is the episodic method, where fortuitousness, not probability is sought, and where plans and designs operate only in restricted ways.[8]

What begins in *Childe Harold* I/II as an only partly self-conscious accent on circumstance and personality becomes in *Don Juan* the stylistic cornerstone of the work. By the time of *Childe Harold* III/IV, Byron's intrusion into the poem has become its central feature.

In the same 'Addition to the Preface' Byron set out his aim as:

> . . . to show, that early perversion of mind and morals leads to satiety of past pleasures and disappointment in new ones, and that even the beauties of nature, and the stimulus of travel (except ambition, the most powerful of all excitements) are lost on a soul so constituted, or rather misdirected.

The melancholy Childe goes on a sort of exotic Grand Tour to escape his own feelings of disappointment and self disgust. Unable to secure the favours of an idealized love, he has taken to debauch:

> Few earthly things found favour in his sight
> Save concubines and carnal companie. . . .   (I, ii)

These pleasures, however, have soon palled:

> Worse than adversity the Childe befell;
> He felt the fulness of satiety:
> Then loathed he in his native land to dwell. . . .   (I, iv)

Some crime of debauch is hinted at (I, iii) but not specified. The Childe, however, is no mere tourist. As with virtually all the Byronic heroes, his restlessness is linked to his fatality through the figure of Cain:

> Pleasure's pall'd victim! life-abhorring gloom
> Wrote on his faded brow curst Cain's unresting doom.
>
>   (I, lxxxiii)

and the association is reinforced in the stanzas 'To Inez' (I, lxxxiv-v). The Childe, however, conceals his true feelings:

> For his was not that open, artless soul
> That feels relief by bidding sorrow flow,
> Nor sought he friend to counsel or condole,
> Whate'er this grief mote be, which he could not control.
>
>   (I, viii)

Like Lara and Manfred, the Childe prefers to retain an aura of mystery.

Political themes surface briefly in Canto I when Byron laments the loss of Spanish liberty under the Napoleonic conquest (I, xlii–iv), but are much more in evidence in Canto II. Byron sees Greece, in which the canto is largely set, as fallen from its former glories:

> They won, and pass'd away—is this the whole?
> A schoolboy's tale, the wonder of an hour!
> The warrior's weapon and the sophist's stole
> Are sought in vain, and o'er each mouldering tower,
> Dim with the mist of years, gray flits the shade of power.
>
>   (II, ii)

Nostalgia for glories past colours Byron's view of history as deeply as it does the characters of his Byronic heroes, and the theme is soon repeated on a personal note:

> Who with the weight of years would wish to bend,
> When Youth itself survives young Love and Joy?
> Alas! when mingling souls forget to blend,
> Death hath but little left him to destroy!
> Ah! happy years! once more who would not be a boy?
>
>   (II, xxiii)

Byron urges the Greeks to action:

> Hereditary bondsmen! know ye not
> Who would be free themselves must strike the blow?
>
> (II, lxxvi)

Despite the gloomy Childe, Cantos I/II are highly readable. The pace seldom flags and many of the descriptions are racy and interesting in their own right. Nor were Byron's travels particularly gloomy, and in later years he looked back on the visit to Greece as one of the happiest times of his life. Part of the reason for that happiness, especially after the departure of his English companion Hobhouse for home, was that he was then free to indulge his homosexual tastes without restraint. As he wrote to Hobhouse in August 1810:

> In short, what with the *women*, and the *boys*, and the *suite*, we are very disorderly. But I am vastly happy and childish, and shall have a world of anecdotes for you. . . .[9]

Byron was never again quite so carefree. Within a few weeks of his return to England, he was plunged in grief and it is from this period that some of the gloomiest stanzas in *Childe Harold* date. Not only did his mother die, but several close friends, and he learned then of the death of John Edleston, the Trinity chorister whom he had idealistically loved and of whom he wrote the Thyrza poems. One of these late additions to *Childe Harold* is sadly prophetic:

> What is my being? thou has ceased to be!
> Nor staid to welcome here thy wanderer home,
> Who mourns o'er hours which we no more shall see—
> Would they had never been, or were to come!
> Would he had ne'er return'd to find fresh cause to roam!
>
> (II, xcv)

From 1812–15 Byron, despite his tremendous popularity, was increasingly troubled. He believed that his political ambitions had failed, though he hadn't tried very hard, realizing perhaps that a discipline of compromise was beyond him. He conducted numerous love affairs, none of which satisfied him, and got into increasing financial difficulties, partly on account of a riotously indulgent social life. His reputation as a rake grew considerably, not least on account of his very public

148

pursuit by the lunatic Lady Caroline Lamb. More serious than any of these, however, was his tormenting affair with his half-sister Augusta Leigh, and it was perhaps his sense of guilt on that score which induced him to marry. It is from this period that the Turkish tales date. As he wrote to Tom Moore in November 1813:

> ... All convulsions end with me in rhyme; and to solace my midnights, I have scribbled another Turkish story. ... I have written this, and published it, for the sake of the *employment*, to wring my thoughts from reality. ...[10]

The tale in question was *The Bride of Abydos* in which he treated obliquely of his involvement with Augusta, as in *Lara* he was to treat obliquely of a homosexual attachment, though these facts were not, of course, known to his public.

For intellectual content the Turkish tales are all but inter-changeable. The story of *The Bride* is set at the court of Giaffir, a pasha whose daughter, Zuleika, is shortly to be married off to a powerful magnate whom she does not love. The hero of the tale is her apparently effeminate brother Selim (I, iv). The sensitive Selim is not, however, what he appears (II, x). He is in love with Zuleika and she with him. They arrange to meet secretly by night in a cave in the palace grounds. There, Selim tells her of his love and of his true character. As in *Hamlet*, Selim's real father has been murdered by his uncle (Giaffir) for political power. Giaffir is an ambitious tyrant. Selim has been preserved by some whim of fate:

> Why me the stern usurper spared,
> Why thus with me his palace shared,
> I know not. Shame, regret, remorse,
> And little fear from infant's force;
> Besides, adoption as a son
> By him whom Heaven accorded none,
> Or some unknown cabal, caprice,
> Preserved me thus. ...   (II, xv)

In the first version Byron had intended Selim and Zuleika to be brother and sister but thought better of it. Later, in *Cain*, he did treat openly of the incest theme. Zuleika is an image of innocence and purity, associated, as all such figures were for Byron, with childhood, though, ambiguously, she is compared with Eve before the Fall:

> Fair, as the first that fell of womankind . . .
> Soft, as the memory of buried love;
> Pure, as the prayer which Childhood wafts above. . . .
>
> (I, vi)

Selim, who learned his true parentage from a slave (Haroun), has effectively been a prisoner at court:

> He rear'd me, not with tender help,
> But like the nephew of a Cain. . . .   (II, xii)

Like Cain and the Childe, Selim is restless in his captivity:

> What could I be? Proscribed at home,
> And taunted to a wish to roam;
> And listless left—for Giaffir's fear
> Denied the courser and the spear. . . .   (II, xviii)

Selim's true nature is stormy and virile, associated, like those of Conrad, Manfred, Lara, the Childe, Cain and Sardanapalus, with lightning (I, xii).

While Giaffir has been absent on a military campaign, Selim has taken his chance for freedom and gone wandering through the Greek islands:

> 'Tis vain—my tongue can not impart
> My almost drunkenness of heart,
> When first this liberated eye
> Survey'd Earth, Ocean, Sun, and Sky. . . .   (II, xviii)

In the course of his wanderings he has become the leader of a band of free corsairs. This community of fellow-outcasts is more, however, than merely an assemblage of bandits. Some at least are political exiles:

> And some to higher thoughts aspire,
>   The last of Lambro's patriots there
> Anticipated freedom share. . . .   (II, xx)

Selim is no egalitarian:

> So let them ease their hearts with prate
> Of equal rights, which man ne'er knew;
> I have a love for freedom too.   (II, xx)

Byron's favourite epithet of abuse was 'vulgar'. He did not believe in an equality of rights because he did not believe in an equality of powers.

Selim invites Zuleika to share his life as a free-roaming outcast, and the imagery at this point is consistently natural rather than social, for social life is both corrupt and corrupting:

> . . . in time deceit may come
> When cities cage us in a social home:
> There ev'n thy soul might err—how oft the heart
> Corruption shakes which peril could not part!   (II, xx)

Selim's corsairs are waiting offshore, but the lovers are disturbed by Giaffir and his soldiers before they can escape. Selim goes out to defend himself. As Eve to Adam, however, Zuleika is the cause of Selim's fall. Turning at the shore for a last glimpse of her, he is killed (II, xxv), as are all the comrades who have come to his aid. Zuleika dies of grief in terms which Byron thought rather applied to himself:

> Ah! happy! But of life to lose the worst!
> That grief—though deep—though fatal—was thy first!
>   (II, xxvii)

Giaffir is driven mad with grief for the death of his daughter, and so the tale ends, not just with the death of the lovers, but with the destruction of both communities, court and corsairs. Byron was to repeat the theme in the Haidee episode of *Don Juan* (IV, lxx–ii).

The cluster of related themes we have traced through *Childe Harold* I/II and *The Bride* continued to figure in Byron's mature works, though their treatment became vastly more powerful; their exploration deepened and generalized. There were no sudden thematic shifts in Byron's development, though there were, of course, important turning points in his career, the most crucial of which was his exile of 1816. Before turning to Byron's later career, however, it will be instructive to disentangle from the Byronic complex those elements which can be directly related to Byron's personal history before 1816. To do so will not tell us why Byronism caught the imagination of the age, but it will help to explain something of how Byron's personal experience fitted him for the mythic role he was later to play.

The central fact of Byron's biography is his overwhelming sense of insecurity and of the capriciousness of fate. As he recorded in a notebook of 1821: '. . . I have always believed that all things depend upon Fortune, and nothing upon ourselves.'[11] Born with a clubbed foot, he remained sensitive about the fact throughout his life and once attempted to have it amputated. As Marchand says, it 'probably did more to shape his character than it will ever be possible to calculate'.[12] He was a plump, pretty child but a fat adolescent; a fact which mortified him and he made violent efforts to control his weight.[13]

Byron senior vanished from his life when Byron was 2, leaving him in the care of a highly strung mother who alternated between extremes of rage and affection with extraordinary capriciousness. Even Byron's social position can have done nothing for his sense of security for it too came capriciously, through the sudden death of the old Lord's heir. Byron was, at the age of 10, removed from the relatively poor, middle-class life of Aberdeen to an alien world of rank and privilege without, at first, the financial means to sustain that position. As if these circumstances were not of themselves sufficient to provide Byron with a series of complexes which would keep any competent Freudian in a career for a lifetime, his early experience was odd in a further, crucial respect.

Byron's maternal grandmother had been a devout, illiterate Calvinist who had left her mark on Byron's mother. Whatever of Calvinism Byron imbibed from his mother and from the general ambience of Aberdeen in the 1790s was deeply coloured by his nurse, May Gray, between his eighth and eleventh years. In due course it was discovered that while May Gray had been inculcating him with Old Testament Calvinism, reinforced with frequent beatings, she had also been subjecting him to some form of masturbatory sex-play. Miss Gray, it appears, was also not averse to a regular 'small refreshment'. As Gilbert Phelps has noted: 'The Bible myth became for Byron, in consequence, a particularly apt parable for his own imagined expulsion from an Eden of innocence and security.'[14] Those experiences are clearly the source for Byron's lifelong detestation of cant and hypocrisy and his insistence on sincerity as the decisive virtue.[15] As Nietzsche remarks, we never stress one particular virtue until we notice its absence in our opponents. Here, too, Marchand has located the source for some of the

The Byronic Philosophy

key Byronic imperatives. On the one hand, Byron took refuge in a sentimental ideal of unsullied love. As Marchand says, his early devotion to Mary Duff and Margaret Parker

> . . . stimulated him to a 'dash into poetry' and became the constant symbol to him of the ideally beautiful unpossessed love, the sort of image that usually blossoms in adolescence but that in Byron was a dominating vision between the ages of eight and twelve. It had numerous embodiments male and female during the rest of his life.[16]

On the other hand, Byron's '. . . premature sexual awakening, caused disillusionment, the melancholy which springs from physical disgust and the failure of the real experience to measure up to the ideal'.[17] Byron was driven by the desperation of his emotional needs not just into poetry and risky situations—one imagines that what Augusta provided was, above all, a symbolic, if illusory, security—but into the creation of the Byronic myth.

Byron compensated for his insecurities with a cool public persona and a driving ambition. There can be few doctrines more clearly designed to produce a sense of insecurity than Calvinism with its notion of *Election* and, as McGann says, 'Filled with a desire for greatness, Byron looks to *fama* as a sign of his election.'[18] It is a simple transition from a sense of difference originating in insecurities to a defiant sense of personal destiny. Hugh MacDiarmid, another Scottish poet with a presbyterian background, made the same transition. Byron identified himself obsessively with Napoleon and in a journal entry for November 1813 we find the revealing disclaimer, 'But I have no ambition; at least, if any, it would be *aut Caesar aut nihil*',[19] and we may recall his aside on the subject in the 'Addition to the Preface' to *Childe Harold*.

As for his public life, that too was coloured by insecurity:

> . . . his shyness had caused him to play his own hero, the aloof and melancholy Childe Harold. They did not realize how much his studied politeness and his cynical pose were a mask to hide his lack of ease in an aristocratic society to which he had been a stranger most of his life.[20]

Byron's psychological difficulties are only of concern to us here to the extent that they account for certain elements in Byronism.

For some understanding of the excitement Byron engendered in society, we have to look beyond Byron to the milieu in which he moved.

Some measure of Byron's early fame can clearly be attributed to his rank. In the last days of the reign of George III a Peer of the Realm, as well as being a remote and romantic figure, might still exercise a degree of influence on the machinery of power inconceivable today. Byron's friends in the tory and Holland House circles in which he moved were, quite simply, the ruling class. Something of the shocking quality of *Childe Harold* and the Turkish tales for his contemporaries arose from the fact that Byron was a member of that class. More significant, however, was the mood of that class in Byron's lifetime.

That Jeffrey, in a sympathetic notice in the *Edinburgh Review* (1812), could describe the inoffensive Childe as 'this Satanic personage' strikes rather oddly on the modern ear but Jeffrey's attitude was that of the establishment. Until about 1790–91, when alarm bells began to ring loudly in British tory circles, a degree of liberal sentiment had been tolerated by the ruling classes. By the panic year of 1797, any such toleration had entirely evaporated as they felt themselves threatened with anarchy and revolution: 'Political fear meant religious revival, an enormous boost in the growth of Evangelicalism and its ascetic view of sex.'[21] Up until the early years of the Regency, the ruling classes themselves were, to some extent, exempt from this 'moral revolution', but not for long:

> Fear of sex, fear of conspiracy lurking in every corner, fear of the masses who were both morally and politically inflammable were forming a nexus of anxiety that was to last for several decades.[22]

By the time of Peterloo (1819) and the publication of the first Cantos of *Don Juan*, that nexus had sufficiently infected the ruling classes for Byron's friends to urge him against publication. As Eric Trudgill observes:

> In the nervous years after the Napoleonic wars there was still enough conspiracy hysteria in existence, like that of 1797, to promote the fear that political sedition might be affected through moral subversion, and this subversion affected through immoral literature.[23]

It is only in such a context that we can understand how the 'deliciously shocking character of his heroes, the daring scepticism of his metaphysics, and the unconventionality of his political reflections . . .'[24] in 1812, could have turned by 1819 into the hysterical denunciation of a 'cool unconcerned fiend, laughing with detestable glee over the whole of the better and worse elements of which human life is composed'.[25] Byron was unfortunate enough to fall victim to the growing power of middle-class moralism at a time when the ruling classes could no longer escape its censure. It is but a short step from a Byron urging the Greeks to liberate themselves from tyranny to a Byron, as an influential member of the ruling class, urging Britons to throw off a similar tyranny, and several commentators have suggested that the government may have encouraged the public campaign against Byron as a means of being rid of someone of whom they were nervous.[26]

Had Byron's literary career ended in 1815, he would now be a minor curiosity in the history of the Romantics, for while he had achieved an unusual measure of public attention, he had not fundamentally modified that tradition in which he worked. Many of the elements we have considered from a Byronic perspective were, in fact, the commonplaces of the Romantic/Gothic tradition. The cult of personality, a concern for the exotic, the criminal, the marginally scandalous, for nature and for history, were all well-trodden paths since about 1780. Shelley was far more of a radical than Byron. The turning point in Byron's career did not come until 1816.

Byron married Annabella Milbanke in 1815. As was obvious from the beginning to Byron's friends, the marriage was a foolish one. It would be difficult to find two characters less compatible than Byron and Lady Byron. In any case, Byron seemed determined to drive the marriage on to the rocks if it would not float there of its own accord. The marriage collapsed in 1816 in bitterness and exaggeration and Byron, in the midst of an extraordinary public uproar, fed by the malicious Caroline Lamb, left the country. He never returned. He left in a state verging on emotional collapse, convinced of persecution and believing that all his hopes, political and emotional, had been irretrievably crushed. This exile, in stark contrast to the literariness of his pretended exile of 1809–11, presented him with an unpleasantly harsh reality.

This catastrophe seemed to unlock Byron's literary powers, perhaps because it realized his own fantasies. Within two years he had composed *Childe Harold* III/IV, *Manfred*, and the opening Cantos of *Don Juan*. Though the themes are much as before, their treatment is so much more powerful as to transform Byron from a minor exponent of Gothic *Weltschmerz* into one of the two or three leading figures of European Romanticism. There is no space here to follow Byron's development in detail, but it is necessary to look at one or two strands in *Childe Harold*.

Keeping to the rough form of a travelogue, *Childe Harold* III (1817) takes us from Waterloo, across the Rhine and Alps, to Italy where, with the exception of his expedition to Greece, Byron lived for the rest of his life. As the Canto progresses Byron increasingly forgets about the Childe and speaks *in propria persona*. He tells us that he has resumed the poem:

> So that it wean me from the weary dream
> Of selfish grief or gladness—so it fling
> Forgetfulness around me. . . .   (III, iv)

That, and stoicism, must enable him:

> In strength to bear what time cannot abate,
> And feed on bitter fruits without accusing Fate.   (III, vii)

The theme is reiterated at IV, xxi.

On the site of Waterloo he reflects on the political reaction which has followed on the defeat of Napoleon:

> What! shall reviving Thraldom again be
> The patch'd-up idol of enlighten'd days?   (III, xix)

and, identifying Napoleon as a kindred spirit, states the Byronic dilemma:

> But quiet to quick bosoms is a hell,
> And *there* hath been thy bane; there is a fire
> And motion of the soul which will not dwell
> In its own narrow being, but aspire
> Beyond the fitting medium of desire;
> And, but once kindled, quenchless evermore,
> Preys upon high adventure, nor can tire
> Of aught but rest; a fever at the core,
> Fatal to him who bears, to all who ever bore.   (III, xlii)

For Byron, such figures as Napoleon, Milton's *Satan*, the Lucifer of *Cain* and, of course, himself, were marked out by destiny to suffer: suffering being the price of a difference marked by hybris:

> . . . One breast laid open were a school
> Which would unteach mankind the lust to shine or rule. . . .
>
> (III, xliii)

For such 'wanderers o'er Eternity' (III, lxx), there can be no peace.

Byron now sees his own alienation as an instance of something proper to particular types of soul, inherent in their constitution. Rousseau, the 'apostle of affliction' (III, lxxvii), is another such soul. Byron sees him as one of the moving forces behind the Revolution and, hence, ultimately, behind the Napoleonic catastrophe. In a curiously Burkeian passage he makes clear the links between his politics, his view of history, and the Byronic spirit:

> They made themselves a fearful monument!
> The wreck of old opinions—things which grew,
> Breathed from the birth of time: the veil they rent
> And what behind it lay, all earth shall view.
> But good with ill they also overthrew,
> Leaving but ruins, wherewith to rebuild
> Upon the same foundation, and renew
> Dungeons and thrones, which the same hour refill'd,
> As heretofore, because ambition was self-will'd. (III, lxxxii)

The crucial line is the last one. He returned to the theme in *Childe Harold* IV to make the link with personal history fully evident:

> And vile Ambition, that built up between
> Man and his hopes an adamantine wall,
> And the base pageant last upon the scene,
> Are grown the pretext for the eternal thrall
> Which nips life's tree, and dooms man's worst—his second fall.
>
> (IV, xcvii)

The concept of the Fall as both political/historical and personal catastrophe is at the centre of Byronism. In opposition to the hybris/ambition which leads to disaster, Byron sets the concept of the brotherly band, such as was foreshadowed by Selim's corsairs:

> While Waterloo with Cannae's carnage vies,
> Morat and Marathon twin names shall stand;
> They were true Glory's stainless victories,
> Won by the unambitious heart and hand
> Of a proud, brotherly, and civic band. . . . (III, lxiv)

Byron's only partly explicit ideal is that of the heroic self-sacrifice of the lover-warrior band such as, under Leonidas, faced the Persians at Thermopylae.

Canto IV is set in Italy and opens in Venice which, with the decay of its former might and its many literary associations, made an ideal locus for the Byronic spirit. For the first time, Byron credits literature with some redemptive power:

> The beings of the mind are not of clay;
> Essentially immortal, they create
> And multiply in us a brighter ray
> And more beloved existence: that which Fate
> Prohibits to dull life, in this our state
> Of mortal bondage, by these spirits supplied,
> First exiles, then replaces what we hate;
> Watering the heart whose early flowers have died,
> And with a fresher growth replenishing the void. (IV, v)

The imagery of the young heart as a rank garden—prompted by Venice's Shakespearian associations perhaps—is taken up again and powerfully elaborated in IV, x. Only now can Byron acknowledge:

> My hopes of being remember'd in my line
> With my land's language. . . . (IV, ix)

This is in the strongest contrast to his earlier denunciations of literature as, for example, in a journal entry for November 1813:

> —but I do think the preference of *writers* to *agents*—the mighty stir made about scribbling and scribes, by themselves and others—a sign of effeminacy, degeneracy, and weakness. Who would write, who had any better thing to do? 'Action—action—action'—said Demosthenes: '*Actions*—*actions*' I say, and not writing,—least of all, rhyme.[27]

This marks a fundamental change for Byron and much of the rest of the Canto is given over to a comparison and analysis of power in its various forms, literary and political. In a lengthy passage on Tasso and his patron, Alfonso of Este, Byron compares political and literary power directly and concludes that, in the long run, the latter is more effective (IV, xxxv–ix).

Linked with Byron's discussion of power are his reflections on love, for that is the basis of the self-sacrificial heroism which alone is redemptive in history. For Byron, beauty, liberty and love are ideal in the philosophical sense—that is, they are products of mind. Byron, however, is no Berkeleian as his attack on Berkeleian views in *Don Juan* makes clear (XI, i–ii et seq.). Byron places a high value on the actual, on what is, and continually stresses the factualness of his poetry and its truthfulness. Byron never wholly lost his religious beliefs and in his *Detached Thoughts* (1821) concludes that Mind is probably eternal. He was very insistent that his daughter Allegra be educated as a Christian and thought the Shelleys a bad influence on the child. His accent on fact is clearly seen in his defence of *Don Juan* to his friend Kinnaird: 'It may be profligate but is it not *life*, is it not *the thing*? Could any man have written it who has not lived in the world?'[28] The Byronic dilemma is precisely that the world of fact seems so intractable to the ideal. There is in Byronism a powerful element of mind/body, is/ought dualism:

> Oh, Love! no habitant of earth thou art—
> An unseen seraph, we believe in thee,—
> A faith whose martyrs are the broken heart,—
> But never yet hath seen, nor e'er shall see
> The naked eye, they form, as it should be;
> The mind hath made thee, as it peopled heaven,
> Even with its own desiring phantasy,
> And to a thought such shape and image given,
> As haunts the unquench'd soul—parch'd, wearied, wrung, and riven.
>
> Of its own beauty is the mind diseased,
> And fevers into false creation:—where,
> Where are the forms the sculptor's soul hath seiz'd?
> In him alone.

(IV, cxxi–ii)

The clearest statement of this complex of themes comes in Byron's final confrontation with Napoleon in *Childe Harold* which he concludes:

> What from this barren being do we reap?
> Our senses narrow, and our reason frail,
> Life short, and truth a gem which loves the deep,
> And all things weigh'd in custom's falsest scale;
> Opinion an omnipotence,—whose veil
> Mantles the earth with darkness, until right
> And wrong are accidents, and men grow pale
> Lest their own judgments should become too bright,
> And their free thoughts be crimes, and earth have too
>   much light. (IV, xciii)

The criminality of Byron's own ideals, of his political ideals of liberty and of his emotional ideals of homosexual or incestuous attachments, is obviously at the root of this duality of good and bad power. On the one hand, the ideal is represented by good power—that is, that achieved through self-sacrificial love or the ideality of art—and, on the other, the actual is represented by bad power, which springs from ambition. Since heroic self-sacrifice is called forth only by extreme circumstances, history is inevitably a decline:

> There is the moral of all human tales;
> 'Tis but the same rehearsal of the past,
> First Freedom, and then Glory—when that fails,
> Wealth, vice, corruption,—barbarism at last. (IV, cviii)

But Byron, for all his grim stoicism, does not abandon hope but sees it as made possible by a sort of perversity of spirit, a view closely akin to that of the later Dostoyevsky:

> Yet, Freedom! yet thy banner, torn, but flying,
> Streams like a thunder-storm *against* the wind. . . .
>   (IV, xcviii)

The inevitable conclusion is that there is something out of joint in the very conditions of existence and this leads Byron to one of his most powerful statements of the Byronic philosophy:

> Few—none—find what they love or could have loved,
> Though accident, blind contact, and the strong
> Necessity of loving, have removed

160

The Byronic Philosophy

Antipathies—but to recur, ere long,
Envenom'd with irrevocable wrong;
And Circumstance, that unspiritual god
And miscreator, makes and helps along
Our coming evils with a crutch-like rod,
Whose touch turns Hope to dust,—the dust we all have trod.

Our life is a false nature: 'tis not in
The harmony of things,—this hard decree,
This uneradicable taint of sin,
This boundless upas, this all-blasting tree,
Whose root is earth, whose leaves and branches be
The skies which rain their plagues on men like dew—
Disease, death, bondage—all the woes we see,
And worse, the woes we see not—which throb through
The immedicable soul, with heart-aches ever new.

Yet let us ponder boldly—'tis a base
Abandonment of reason to resign
Our right of thought—our last and only place
Of refuge; this, at least, shall still be mine:
Though from our birth the faculty divine
Is chain'd and tortured—cabin'd, cribb'd, confined,
And bred in darkness, lest the truth should shine
Too brightly on the unprepared mind,
The beam pours in, for time and skill will couch the blind.

(IV, cxxv–vii)

In this curious combination of Calvinism and modernity, is
the core of Byronism.

For most of Canto IV Byron has spoken *in propria persona*,
forgetting the Childe. As he does so, his identification with his
own heroes becomes complete. This becomes hair-raisingly
clear when, towards the end of the Canto, Byron lets his sense
of destiny be seen at full stretch in the great Forgiveness Curse
(IV, cxxxi–viii) when he summons Nemesis to avenge him on
his detractors:

But I have lived, and have not lived in vain:
My mind may lose its force, my blood its fire,
And my frame perish even in conquering pain;
But there is that within me which shall tire
Torture and Time, and breathe when I expire;

161

Something unearthly, which they deem not of,
Like the remember'd tone of a mute lyre,
Shall on their soften'd spirits sink, and move
In hearts all rocky now the late remorse of love.

(IV, cxxxvii)

Byron can now take it for granted that his audience will identify him as the speaker and be familiar enough with the circumstances of his career not to require further information about it. No other Romantic poet could reasonably have made that assumption. From 1818 onwards, as his explorations of the Byronic complex deepened through *Cain*, *Don Juan* and *Sardanapalus*, Byron could build on that capacity to speak *in propria persona* and, as he did so, the myth of Byron as Satanic misanthrope or libertarian Prometheus gained in power and resonance. In Italy, he supported the nationalists who wanted Austria out and, finally, the image was consummated at Missolonghi. By then, 1824, Byron had achieved a unique identity between his literary works and his public image as a man of action, as the Byronic hero. The enthusiasm of the liberals is readily understood. It is only with these facts in mind that we can finally see what gave the Byronic philosophy its power.

Byron's attacks on his contemporaries, and on the Lake poets in particular, were notorious. As McGann points out:

> According to Byron, the Lakers, by teaching theories of 'Imagination' as a basic principle of poetry, have revoked altogether the poet's teaching function. They have literally lost their minds, and Coleridge's 'metaphysics'—an explanation of poetry needing its own explanation—typifies the situation.[29]

For Byron poetry was only of value if it had a moral force. As he wrote in the letter on Bowles, 'In my mind, the highest of all poetry is ethical poetry, as the highest of all earthly subjects must be moral truth . . .',[30] and 'If the essence of poetry must be a *lie*, throw it to the dogs, or banish it from your republic, as Plato would have done. . . .'[31] Hence, his defence of *Don Juan* rests on its ethical intent: '. . . *Don Juan* will be known by and bye, for what it is intended,—a *Satire* on *abuses* of the present states of Society, and not an eulogy of vice. . . .'[32]

Byron's dislike of the Lake poets stemmed from his rather

Calvinistic view that they were failing in their duty, that 'Stern Daughter of the voice of God', and his defence of Pope springs from similar considerations. The underlying reason for Byron's difference in view is the fact that, quite simply, in one central respect, his experience of the world was wholly different from theirs. One of the factors which most sharply distinguishes the Augustans from the Romantics is the difference in their respective audiences.[33] By 1800 the directly accessible audience of Augustan patrons had given way to the 'public' which was at one and the same time an idealized abstraction only nominally related to the people who bought and read books, and the general mass of such people. Between about 1780 and 1820 the phenomenal growth of the circulating libraries had brought about basic changes in the nature of the writer's public. As the nineteenth century developed, and reading became increasingly a middle-class leisure occupation, the divergence between the actual and ideal publics widened enormously so that, increasingly, writers wrote for a non-existent abstraction or simply became suppliers of the raw materials for the distraction of the middle-classes—that is, producers whose function was simply to write, not to act. That dislocation between the writer and actual social conditions rendered the writer impotent to affect those conditions directly through his writings. It is a dislocation with which contemporary literature still struggles. As early as Keats and Wordsworth, however, the retreat by poets from a sense of their capacity to change actual conditions directly is clearly evident. There is nothing disreputable about an introspective or symbolist poetry if nothing else is possible, and, as McGann says, 'To know by symbols is to make up for what Wordsworth calls "the sad incompetence of human speech" ' (*Prelude*, IV, 592). Byron opposes a discourse ruled by symbols, which drive into silence and ecstatic revelation, with a discourse of 'conversational facility' (*Don Juan*, XV, xx).[34]

Alone among the Romantics, Byron did not accept—because he did not perceive—that dislocation. Byron's social position had given him a sense, not wholly illusory, of the real possibility of power, of changing the lives and conditions of men. When he changed political for literary ambitions, he carried over that sense of congruence—albeit only as a possibility—between the real (actuality and action) and the ideal (liberty, truth and beauty). It is for this reason that Byron was so insistent on the truthfulness of poetry and on its ethical task: 'History, tradition, and facts are Byron's ground not because Byron is a materialist, but because, for him, use and act are logically, and humanly, prior to ideas.'[35]

We have already seen how Byron's personal life contributed to shaping his literary imperatives. Ironically, it was precisely that marriage of personal circumstance to literary form which enabled Byron—however fleetingly and precariously—to resolve in his life and work the core dilemma of Romanticism, which is the impotence of the artist to reconcile the desired with the actual, action with talk. Romantic discontent with actual conditions—with the effects of urbanization, loss of an immediate audience, the growth of revolutionary hopes and the continued power of ancient, despotic structures—is the central thread binding together Goethe and Beethoven, Byron and Wordsworth. It was Byron's unique combination of chivalric and heroic ideals, a powerful sense of social and personal corruption, *and of the actuality of power*, which gave the Byronic myth its vitality and appeal. Only Byron was in a position to live out the congruence, in Mazzini's phrase, 'of thought and action'. It was that public role too which made him a mediator between two ages, casting a long shadow forward into the nineteenth and even twentieth centuries, and with a long look backwards to the vanished Augustan wholeness (so he thought) of deed and word. Byron summed it up in a memorandum in his journal of 1821: 'What is Poetry?—The feeling of a Former world and Future.'[36]

NOTES

1. B. Russell, *A History of Western Philosophy* (London, 1946), p. 780.
2. A. Rutherford (ed.), *Byron: The Critical Heritage* (London, 1970), pp. 21–2.
3. B. Russell, op. cit., p. 774.
4. J. D. Jump (ed.), *Byron: A Symposium* (London, 1975), quoted by F. Berry in his article, *The Poet of Childe Harold*, p. 36.
5. P. Gunn (ed.), *Byron: Selected Prose* (Middlesex, 1972), p. 420.

The Byronic Philosophy

6. The best account of Byron's fate at the hands of his biographers and friends is to be found in Mrs. D. L. Moore's *The Late Lord Byron* (London, 1961).
7. L. A. Marchand, *Byron: A Portrait* (London, 1971), p. 162.
8. J. J. McGann, (1) *Don Juan in Context* (London, 1976), p. 103.
9. P. Gunn, op. cit., p. 77.
10. Ibid., p. 158.
11. Ibid., p. 447.
12. L. A. Marchand, op. cit., p. 9.
13. Wilma Paterson, in an article in *World Medicine* (May 1982), examines the evidence of Byron's attitudes to his weight and his associated behaviour patterns and concludes, I think convincingly, that Byron was an anorexic (pp. 35–8).
14. G. Phelps, *The Byronic Byron*, in J. D. Jump, op. cit., p. 67.
15. The most detailed account of this issue can be found in B. Grebanier, *The Uninhibited Byron* (London, 1971), pp. 22–4, et. seq.
16. L. A. Marchand, op. cit., p. 21.
17. Ibid.
18. J. J. McGann, (2) *Fiery Dust: Byron's Poetic Development* (Chicago, 1968), p. 16.
19. P. Gunn, op. cit., p. 168.
20. L. A. Marchand, op cit., pp. 118–19.
21. E. Trudgill, *Madonnas and Magdalens: The Origins and Development of Victorian Sexual Attitudes* (London, 1976), p. 30.
22. E. Trudgill, op. cit., p. 32.
23. Ibid., p. 144.
24. A. Rutherford, op. cit., p. 8.
25. 'Remarks on *Don Juan*', in *Blackwood's Magazine*, August 1819. Given in A. Rutherford, op. cit., pp. 166–73.
26. A view suggested, for example, by G. Wilson Knight in his *Byron and Shakespeare* (London, 1966), p. 101.
27. P. Gunn, op. cit., p. 171.
28. Ibid., p. 322.
29. J. J. McGann, (1) op. cit., p. 77.
30. P. Gunn, op. cit., p. 403.
31. Ibid., p. 407.
32. Ibid., p. 489.
33. R. Williams, *Culture and Society 1780–1950* (Middlesex, 1963), pp. 48–64.
34. J. J. McGann, (1) op. cit., p. 111.
35. Ibid., p. 114.
36. P. Gunn, op. cit., p. 379.

8

The Rhetoric of Freedom

by J. DRUMMOND BONE

Byron's enthusiasm for freedoms of different kinds needs little underscoring. In practical matters his concept of freedom was most often negatively defined—it was freedom *from* political, social or economic oppression, freedom *from* convention, freedom *from* hypocrisy, cant, humbug. He ignored any anatomy of the state of freedom itself, and in the case of the Greek War of Independence actively scorned any projected anatomy of the free state—he would have nothing to do with Stanhope's Utopias—and there is little trace of the nineteenth century's *idée fixe*, the organic nation-state, in his pragmatic help for the Italian Carabinieri—if unity is necessary for freedom it is as a practical prerequisite:

> To break the chain, yet . . .
> What is there wanting then to set thee free,
>   And show thy beauty in its fullest light?
>   To make the Alps impassable; and we,
> Her sons, may do this with *one* deed—Unite.
>
> (*The Prophecy of Dante*, II, 139, 142–45)[1]

The same could be said for his Lords' speeches on the 'Frame-Work Bill', the 'Catholic Claims' motion, and his presentation of Major Cartwright's Petition:

> . . . the town and country were burthened with large detach-ments of the military; the police was in motion, the magistrates assembled . . . the police, however useless, were by no means idle: several notorious delinquents had been detected;—men,

liable to conviction, on the clearest evidence, of the capital crime of poverty. . . . When a proposal is made to emancipate or relieve, you hesitate, you deliberate for years, you temporise and tamper with the minds of men; but a death-bill must be passed offhand, without a thought of the consequences.

. . . [of the Catholics] it might as well be said, that the negroes did not desire to be emancipated, but this is an unfortunate comparison, for you have already delivered them out of the house of bondage, without any petition on their part. . . .

The petitioner, my lords, is a man whose long life has been spent in one unceasing struggle for the liberty of the subject, against that undue influence which has increased, is increasing, and ought to be diminished; and whatever difference of opinion may exist as to his political tenets, few will be found to question the integrity of his intentions.[2]

The accent is on freedom as the opposite of actual limitation, physical, economic, or mental. It is not a question of what the content of the freedom once attained might be, but of the removal of palpable restriction. This is partly a necessary consequence of the political tact involved, all the more so if we believe that Byron's speech on the Frame-Work Bill was conditioned by Party tactics rather than prompted wholly by a personal feeling of outrage.[3] It also however suggests the central problem of the ontology of the state of freedom, a somewhat different matter from the problem of the 'free state' in the political sense, which latter for Byron remained a strictly pragmatic business of standing still by pushing against encroachment from all points of the compass (in which metaphor the poles might be characterized as 'tyranny by the throne' and 'tyranny by the people').[4] However to define the state of freedom itself by negation is even simply on the face of it unsatisfactory, a process treating a substance of acceptance in terms of denial. The concept and contradictions of the inner structure of freedom became more and more important philosophically, at least on the Continent, as existentialism grew from Kierkegaard to Husserl. The first manifest signs of the difficulty, if not actually its roots, can be seen in the literary character of the Romantic Rebel who fills his existence with

the rejection of social and religious convention. 'Byronic Hero'
and 'Romantic Rebel' have become virtually synonymous. But
Byron's concept of the free hero (or rather the hero seeking
freedom) is not monolithic—it has both development and
inconsistency, and these are both produced by and help to
condition the rhetoric of his poetry. Moreover 'freedom' in the
poetry is not simply a matter of a central character's struggle
(in the Turkish Tales it might approximate to this, though
recent developments suggest otherwise[5]), but of explicit and
implicit examination of historical and other fictional examples
of its existence, or more often its failure to exist. Indeed the
very structure and *modus operandi* of some poems are discourses
on the difficult nature of freedom. It is these interactions of
form and content in his varying idea of individual freedom
which I wish to examine.

The notion of freedom as the rejection of restraint produces
the image of the hero as a social rebel *or* social outcast, for
perhaps curiously the two work interchangeably. The point is
worth labouring, for Byron's own heroes have a habit of
equating the two, as do the texts of the poems in which these
heroes exist, but this is not a necessary equation, nor one made
by all or even most of his contemporaries. The rebel has a
particular cause, even if that particularity is of huge scope (one
could scarcely imagine one larger than that of Shelley's
Prometheus), which may or may not result in his being cast
out, depending both on the scale of the rebellion and on its
success or failure. In the case of the 'Byronic hero' the process
is put into reverse, and the hero becomes a rebel or associated
with rebellion through being made an outcast, or indeed casting
himself as an outcast. Whereas for Wordsworth (in say 'Lines
. . . in a Yew Tree' in *Lyrical Ballads*) or Shelley (notably in
Alastor) the move into social detachment is seen negatively, in
Childe Harold Cantos I and II, or *The Giaour*, or *The Corsair*,
or even *Don Juan*, social exile is virtually a precondition of
rebelliousness or rebellious social criticism. Shelley's comments on incest as an act of social rebellion are illuminating:

> Incest is like many other *incorrect* things a very poetical cir-
> cumstance. It may be the excess of love or of hate. It may be
> that defiance of every thing for the sake of another which

clothes itself in the glory of the highest heroism, or it may be that cynical rage which confounding the good & bad in existing opinions breaks through them for the purpose of rioting in selfishness & antipathy.[6]

The first case has a particular purpose, but the second at best only a general one (for Shelley implicitly *too* general). Casting oneself as an outcast, while masquerading as a freeing of oneself from restriction, is in Shelley's view an act of self-definition, in which the self is bounded by the rules it refuses to obey—its freedom, its selfhood, is in other words defined: it is that which is not bound by the incest taboo. Leaving aside the obvious relevance to *Manfred* for the moment, it is usually true that the being outcast, or the self outcasting, of the Byronic hero is associated with particular social or metaphysical criticism, either in the hero himself, or in the texture of the poem as a whole, or in both (as in *Childe Harold*, where it is of course difficult to distinguish the eponymous hero in his 'own' poem). But the blurring of the rebel/outcast distinction and the prominence of outcast imagery help to emphasize the isolation, and through the isolation the importance, of the hero-figure. Following McGann's recent collation of the latent political references in the Turkish Tales in his new edition of the poetical works much will no doubt be written about the anti-establishment implications of these works, and the social point of *Childe Harold* has been more or less always obvious, even with the toned-down stanzas and omitted notes. Yet at the time, despite or because of Byron's protestations to the contrary, the centre of attention in all these poems—indeed the very *raison d'être* of the 'follow-up' Tales—was the outcast hero. In so far as the hero dominates the poems the thrust against repression is realized then most importantly as an 'outcast from', not a 'freedom for', and the process of realization is not a breaking down of restriction but a limiting of itself by contrast and conflict.

The free-spirit's becoming is thus paradoxically involved with its limitation. No news this of course to existential philosophy, but the practical consequences of this in Byron's rhetoric, or more strictly the *causes* of this paradox in his rhetoric, have not I think been explored. Harold's existence

169

outside of conventional society is established (and even the word 'established' might already hint at contradiction) at the beginning of the poem—'Few earthly things found favour in his sight. . . . Then loath'd he in his native land to dwell . . . Nor sought he friend to counsel or condole. . . . If friends he had, he bade adieu to none' (I, ii, 7; iv, 8; viii, 8; x, 5). The sense of the free space in which he moves beyond our control is carried by the mystery surrounding him—'whence his name/ And lineage long, it suits me not to say . . . As if the Memory of some deadly feud/ Or disappointed passion lurk'd below'— and in terms of the 'plot' by his setting sail from his 'native home' to 'traverse Paynim shores, and pass Earth's central line' (I, iii, 1–2; viii, 3–4; xi, 9). But at the same time there is an opposite movement towards definition, counterbalancing the detaching of Harold from his context by fixing him as uniquely definable, though undefined: 'one sad losel soils a name for aye. . . . Nor deem'd before his little day was done/ One blast might chill him into misery. . . ./ [he] Had sigh'd to many though he lov'd but one,/ And that lov'd one, alas! could ne'er be his . . .' (I, iii, 5; iv, 3–4; v, 3–4). Clearly the reader is being invited to have and to eat his cake. Harold is presented as an outcast, both willingly and unwillingly, whose existence is a mystery to us, but at the same time it is implied that he does have an absolutely unique identity, and that the mystery has a definite solution. Mysteriously then this con- textless individual, who insists on the meaninglessness of his own life, carries with him the sense of an absolutely defining context, or in other words the dramatization of his sense of futility portrays that sense as full of meaning. It is no wonder that *Childe Harold* was a popular poem, for in identifying with the hero's sufferings, and then with the hero's *poem*, the reader finds a context for his own sense of contextlessness, and what is felt as isolation is transformed into heroic rejection. The manoeuvre however is essentially a simplistic one as literary devices go, a rhetorical sleight of hand rather than a serious realization of the problem. The two levels of text do not interact in themselves, they merely amalgamate in the reader's response (or, if one prefers, the text is unaware of itself; or from yet another critical angle the character of Harold shows no awareness of the complexity of his situation as *isolato*). This technique of surrounding the isolated outcast with the rhetoric of sharp definition became a mannerism in the Tales. In *The Giaour* for example the fragmented chronology actually aids the definition of character and scene rather than cutting it loose from context. It 'freezes' scenes, attaching them to an eternal moment by detaching them from the flow of time—one need look no further than the motto from Moore[7] or the total stillness of the poem's first six lines, in which the meaning of the question 'When shall such Hero live again?' (presumably paraphrasable as 'At what future time, if any . . .?', with the *question*, the uncertainty, part and parcel) is turned upside down in the sense by the *certainty*, the absolute and unchanging quality of the moment described:

> No breath of air to break the wave
> That rolls below the Athenian's grave,
> That tomb which, gleaming o'er the cliff,
> First greets the homeward-veering skiff,
> High o'er the land he saved in vain;
> When shall such hero live again?
>
> (*The Giaour*, 1–6)

Perhaps the most extreme example is the juxtaposition of the mystery of the Giaour's identity (which as in Harold places him—or displaces him—not only beyond the surrounding Moslem society but also beyond the reader's control) with the image of his reining in his horse for a dramatic pause. Here we have the sleight of hand of definition and mystery in rather embarrassing obviousness, a Mills and Boon prototype:

> One glance he snatch'd, as if his last,
> A moment check'd his wheeling steed,
> A moment breathed him from his speed,
> A moment on his stirrup stood—
> Why looks he o'er the olive wood?
>
> (*The Giaour*, 217–21)

Indeed this image lasts until line 250. Sometimes the device and the effect is more subtly handled, but it remains omnipresent in the Tales.[8]

The dramatization of loneliness thus begs the question of the meaning of the state of freedom in creating a seeming meaning for the individual who has rejected or has been rejected by society. Even in passages where a purpose is overtly described, most notably in terms of love of nature, the yoking of selfhood to larger context is seldom secure:

> More blest the life of godly eremite,
> Such as on lonely Athos may be seen,
> Watching at eve upon the giant height,
> Which looks o'er waves so blue, skies so serene,
> That he who there at such an hour hath been
> Will wistful linger on that hallow'd spot;
> Then slowly tear him from the 'witching scene,
> Sigh forth one wish that such had béen his lot,
> Then turn to hate a world he had almost forgot.
>
> (*Childe Harold*, II, xxvii)

This is not only insecure in the intentional sense that the outcast has to tear himself away from Nature once more (an image of Nature which of course includes the divine), but also in the obviousness of the situation and the rhetoric used to suggest the transcendent but carefully not imprisoning context. The word 'one' appears yet again to move us into the world of absolutes, and the loneliness of the 'eremite' is taken over by the loneliness of Athos, which dominates the scene of which it is a part—the individual remains of 'godly' stature while receiving the comfort of the 'skies so serene', just as the 'he who there hath been' receives the comfort of the identification with the 'eremite' while retaining his own status as outcast. It is well done certainly, but it is not deeply convincing.

Elsewhere in *Childe Harold* I and II the values of individual freedom are explicitly extolled in opposition to the values of religious and political reaction, surely enough, but my point is that the state of selfhood independent of limiting context is in the main realized as a finally unsatisfactory juggling of images of isolation and attendant futility on the one hand, and definition and dramatic (if mysterious) meaningfulness on the other.

It seems unarguable that Byron himself became increasingly aware that at least his literary conception of the free self was simplistic, a wallowing in its futility to the point where, in our modern terms of catastrophe theory, it flipped into a meaningful state of self-dramatization—and this while remaining quite detached from the practically valuable process of serving the *cause* of freedom by the rejection of oppression. It is not

172

possible however to trace a continuously progressive chronology for this and indeed it would be surprising if one could—why one should expect such rigour in art any more than in life is difficult to understand, unless one confuses the patterning of art with a teleological view of existence. This warning must serve by way of qualification of the general tendency I shall now try to trace.

The Byron of *Childe Harold* III picks up the theme of exile in a much more self-conscious way than his earlier narrator, scarcely surprisingly given his own exile:

> In my youth's summer I did sing of One,
> The wandering outlaw of his own dark mind. . . .
>
> (III, iii, 1–2)

>   . . . still uncompell'd,
> He would not yield dominion of his mind
> To spirits against whom his own rebell'd;
> Proud though in desolation; which could find
> A life within itself, to breathe without mankind.
>
> (III, xii, 5–9)

> Self-exiled Harold wanders forth again,
> With nought of hope left, but with less of gloom;
> The very knowledge that he lived in vain,
> That all was over on this side the tomb,
> Had made Despair a smilingness assume. . . .
>
> (III, xvi, 1–5)

The gradual merging of narrator and Harold in theory as well as in practice begins in III, vi, a stanza looked at in some detail below, but the effect is not to flatten the topography of the poem's point of view, but on the contrary to throw it into much sharper relief. As can be seen from the above quotations, the poem now shows an awareness of the contradictions handled surreptitiously by the preceding Cantos—freedom is a matter of self-exile, it entails 'desolation'; yet paradoxically this very desolation leads through pride to some sort of desperate 'smilingness'. A worrying over all this furnishes a deal of the matter of III. Moreover, in the crucial stanza vi just referred to, the process in which the desolation becomes meaningful in the poem is characterized. The effect of the narrator's question at the end of the preceding stanza has been 'Why do we write?' He now answers:

'Tis to create, and in creating live
A being more intense, that we endow
With form our fancy, gaining as we give
The life we image, even as I do now.
What am I? Nothing: but not so art thou,
Soul of my thought! with whom I traverse earth,
Invisible but gazing, as I glow
Mix'd with thy spirit, blended with thy birth,
And feeling still with thee in my crush'd feelings' dearth.

This describes the process of self-dramatization already noted. The act of realizing a fictional alter-ego, for author and for reader, turns the despair of author, reader, and alter-ego into intense feeling—we feel still in the life we have imaged, even if (this is implicit in the fact that the character in question is Harold) that image is one of despair and dearth of feeling. So III is not only more aware of some of the inherent tensions of I and II, it is also more aware of the reason for these Cantos' existence and success. But this does not mean that a resolution is reached formally, nor that a solution to the metaphysical problem of the free self is suggested in the content. What does happen is that contradiction and tension, rather than a transformation of tension into a transcendent *Angst* which is *Angst's* own contradiction, become the poem's most characteristic structure. Many 'solutions' and objections to these solutions are put forward, and in the putting forward the sense of the problem is genuinely created.

Like the Chaldean, he could watch the stars,
Till he had peopled them with beings bright
As their own beams; and earth, and earthborn jars,
And human frailties, were forgotten quite:
Could he have kept his spirit to that flight
He had been happy; but this clay will sink
Its spark immortal. . . .

(III, xiv, 1–7)

This passage perhaps bears at first sight some resemblance to the Nature-loving image of the monk on Mount Athos already quoted above (p. 172). It is in fact significantly different. There is no attempt to bring the 'he' into the world of the Chaldean; there is no attempt to identify either the 'he' or the Chaldean with the object of his gaze other than in the explicit statement that *he*, Harold, attempted such an identification; there is no 'one wish' that 'such had been his lot' because the failure to remain in this state is an internal failing, not one imposed by circumstance, unless in the sense that it is part of the inevitable condition of the self's existence; and the contradiction in clay sinking its own immortal spark is left simply as contradictory. This stanza ends

> . . . as if to break the link
> That keeps us from yon heaven which woos us to its brink.

and leaves the emphasis on the unresolved relationship between the individual and nature, where II, xxvii ends on 'a world he had almost forgot', and thus brings us despairingly but nevertheless definitely back to earth. In the next stanza of III we find Harold immediately discontented 'in Man's dwellings', and imaged as a falcon 'To whom the boundless air alone were home', and then again as a bird in a cage. The movements are abrupt and explicit. There are other differences too which are typical of the differences in the two Cantos—less emphasis in III, xiv on adjectives and adverbs avoids the surreptitious yet too obvious search for intensity in II, xxvii ('godly eremite . . . lonely Athos . . . giant height . . . waves so blue, skies so serene . . . such an hour . . . wistful linger . . . hallow'd spot . . . slowly tear . . . 'witching scene . . . one wish'), and its verse handles both enjambment and caesura with much greater freedom, at the same time this freedom creating the tension of which the stanza speaks by displacing the 'expected' regularity. In short the Canto II stanza presents the grandeur of Nature in individualist terms, and the individual's sense of loss transformed into drama, unaware that its form reverses its apparent content; the Canto III stanza creates the tension of the isolated self both in realization and in motive.

Occasionally, as I have said, the later work retreats to the manner of the former—a good example is xxiii where the Duke of Brunswick sits apart from 'the festival' in a 'window'd niche', his isolation in fact dramatizing his heroism, which has an inner, personal, motive—he is the type of isolation and of commitment at one and the same time. But more usually the values of individualism are left in their confusion. We move from the image of the futility of grief in xxxiii and xxxiv— 'There is a very life in our despair,/ Vitality of poison,—a quick root/ Which feeds these deadly branches' itself a marvellously disrupted and contradictory image of disruption and contradiction—to the balancing of the scales in the judgement of Napoleon, or rather to the impossibility of ever finding a balance. His spirit is 'antithetically mixt. . . . Conqueror and captive of the earth art thou! . . . Oh, more or less than man . . . quiet to quick bosoms is a hell,/ And *there* hath been thy bane; there is a fire/ And motion of the soul which will not dwell/ In its own narrow being. . . . This makes the madmen who have made men mad. . . . Away with these! true Wisdom's world will be/ Within its own creation, or in thine,/ Maternal Nature! . . .' (extracted from xxxvi–xlvi). The contradictions of the free individual, his greatness and futility, his power for evil and for good are realized in their agonizing contradictoriness; we then turn from them to the hope of peace within Maternal Nature. In fact the next few stanzas arguably find Byron returning to his old manner of suggesting loneliness and loss *and* transcending content at the same time, for in amongst the 'Fruit, foliage, crag, wood, cornfield, mountain, vine', we find 'chiefless castles breathing stern farewells/ From gray but leafy walls, where Ruin greenly dwells'. A more clear-cut example of union with Nature as an image of the content of life when it is withdrawn from other contexts is to be found in the 'Wordsworthian' stanzas lxviii–lxxv, though even here doubt creeps back in with the incessant phrasing of what should be affirmation as question:

> . . . shall I not
> Feel all I see, less dazzling, but more warm?
> The bodiless thought? the Spirit of each spot?
> Of which, even now, I share at times the immortal lot?
>
> Are not the mountains, waves, and skies, a part
> Of me and of my soul, as I of them?
>
> (lxxiv, 6–9; lxxv, 1–2)

And so on to the end of that stanza. That this is self-hectoring questioning rather than rhetorical reinforcement is clearly shown by the abrupt about-turn of the next stanza—we move from a transcendent vision to the grave:

> But this is not my theme; and I return
> To that which is immediate, and require
> Those who find contemplation in the urn,
> To look on One, whose dust was once all fire. . . .
>
> (lxxvi, 1–4)

—and dive into the contradictions of another free-spirit, Rousseau, who was a 'self-torturing sophist', but yet 'knew/ How to make Madness beautiful'.

Tension, contradiction, abrupt switches of subject and of tone are of the essence of *Childe Harold* III. The imponderables of the state of individual freedom which while apparently the subject were in fact spirited away, too easily dissolved, in the rhetoric of the early cantos, here shape both rhetoric and apparent content. But it could be argued still that they do so in despite of Byron's conscious direction, rather than because of it, at least after the introductory seven stanzas.[9] There can be little doubt of his self-awareness in the metaphysical mental theatre of *Manfred*.

The point has been made many times that *Manfred* traces the hero's rejection of all help and support on the grounds that they would demand some subordination of his self,[10] that self which at one and the same time is his pride and his agony. The problem of the state of freedom is at the centre of the drama— to seek freedom is to reject the contexts which give meaning to life. Manfred rejects the spirit's claims that they control his destiny, in particular the seventh spirit's ideas of predetermination; he is saved from casual suicide (that is, from a suicide based on the feeling that there is no value in life: 'If it be life to wear within myself/ This barrenness of spirit, and to be/ My own soul's sepulchre, for I have ceased/ To justify my deeds unto myself—/ The last infirmity of evil . . .' (I, ii, 25–9)) by the Chamois Hunter, the type of simple life, but simple life is not enough for Manfred; he rejects what one might call the 'Wordsworthian solution', the aid of the 'Spirit of the place', the love of the beauty of Nature; he refuses any pact with Arimanes, the 'Faustian solution'; and finally he rejects the solace of religion in the person of the Abbot. At each attempt to find a meaning for his soul's existence he feels the absolute freedom of his soul is to be in danger of being compromised. There is not the equivocation of *Childe Harold* I and II which seeks to insinuate a sense of significance into the feeling of futility, and the contradictions apparent in *Childe Harold* III are now directly addressed. To be free is to be isolated; isolation ,brings a sense of futility yet still one insists on freedom.[11] The only spectre in front of which Manfred is subdued is Astarte, his sister, his other self, and it is his guilty love for her which is the objective correlative of his withdrawal from, or his being outcast by, the rest of the world.[12] In the end Manfred appears almost to will his own death, but this is not a suicide in the face of an empty and valueless existence:

> ... I bear within
> A torture which could nothing gain from thine:
> The mind which is immortal makes itself
> Requital for its good or evil thoughts,—
> Is its own origin of ill and end—
> And its own place and time: its innate sense,
> When stripp'd of this mortality, derives
> No colour from the fleeting things without,
> But is absorb'd in sufferance or in joy,
> Born from the knowledge of its own desert. ...
> ... [I] was my own destroyer, and will be
> My own hereafter.

(III, iv, 127–40)

Manfred has rejected any transcendent reality, but what Elledge calls the 'vacuum of his selfhood'[13] is in fact filled with self-created meaning. His sense of value is no longer created by a reference to social, moral, or religious systems outside himself, but clearly this no longer leads inevitably to nihilism, for the mind 'makes itself/ Requital . . . Is its own origin of ill and end . . . its own place and time . . . own destroyer, and . . . own hereafter'. If freedom must reject, it can also create within itself. What ontological status this created value has is another problem, only hinted at in *Manfred* by the Abbot having the last, doubtful, words—*his* doubts remaining unaffected by Manfred's triumphant assertion. But the main effect at the end of the play is the revelation that meaning can be produced from within, and does not depend on inevitably restricting systems 'beyond' the individual.

However, though this is a major development in the depth of Byron's thinking about the problem of freedom, it is not reflected in a thorough-going way in the form of the play. Indeed *Manfred*, for all the hero's agonizing, is in many ways more sure of itself than *Childe Harold* III, and in so far as this is the case its form works against the intention of its content. It becomes obvious early that the pattern of Manfred seeking help and then rejecting it will be repeated throughout the play (no later than the rejection of the Chamois Hunter), and the sense of certainty in his episodic progress is not far removed from the world of the morality play. The 'set-pieces' of the sunset (III, ii) and the Coliseum by night (III, iv) return us to the 'frozen scene' method of the early *Harold* and the Tales. In the first the hero is in effect identified with the 'chief Star!/ Centre of many stars'. As the sun sets Manfred says: 'He is gone—/ I follow.' The reader through this identification translates Manfred into precisely that transcendent world he so steadfastly refuses. The same rather obvious use of a dramatizing context underlies the Coliseum passage. 'I linger yet with Nature . . . and in her starry shade/ Of dim and solitary loveliness,/ I learn'd the language of another world' says Manfred (III, iv, 3–7), and we find ourselves appreciating the comfort of the Universal context while still feeling that the hero has not compromised his isolation, for Nature has somehow become herself 'solitary'. Manfred remembers that it was 'such a night' as this—and he reminds us at the end of his recollection again "Twas such a night!' to drive home the particularlity of the moment which raises it out of time—'When I was wandering . . . I stood within the Coliseum's wall,/ 'Midst the chief relics of almighty Rome' (III, iv, 9–11), and magically his 'wandering' and the sense of time's irreversible passage in the decay of Rome is stopped in its tracks in this one night. Once again by defining a moment that moment is lifted out of time. It is the moon on which our attention is directed here, and as the speaker's consciousness is filled with the sense of that moon's transcendence so the reader identifies that consciousness with the moon—it becomes Manfred who is unchanging as he stands in the middle of the Coliseum, full of precisely that sense of

179

value in existence which in fact at this point in the drama he lacks. Even if one were to argue that this is the moment at which his sense of triumph begins, there would be an inconsistency in dramatizing that triumph *of the self* in terms of natural beauty.[14] The climax of the passage reads:

> And thou didst shine, thou rolling Moon, upon
> All this, and cast a wide and tender light,
> Which soften'd down the hoar austerity
> Of rugged desolation, and fill'd up,
> As 'twere anew, the gaps of centuries;
> Leaving that beautiful which still was so,
> And making that which was not, till the place
> Became a religion. . . .
>
> (III, iv, 31–8)

Not surprisingly 'Manfred' 'apologizes' for the digression— not only by way of self-defence from the reader's question 'What is this passage doing here?', but more seriously to present as random and free a scene which has been defining him through a carefully structured (melo-) dramatic context:

> 'Tis strange that I recall it at this time;
> But I have found our thoughts take wildest flight
> Even at the moment when they should array
> Themselves in pensive order.
>
> (III, iv, 42–5)

Manfred's last long speech, already quoted at some length above (p. 178), again uses a defining context to create a sense of significance and timelessness which does not exactly marry with the absolute freedom of which the text speaks, for of course he is 'quoting' Satan in *Paradise Lost* Book I, 252–55. True, the meaning has in some sense been freed from its previous Miltonic existence, since here we read it as truth. But clearly the reference has the effect of raising Manfred to Satan's existential level, if one can so speak, and thus of dramatizing his existence for the reader as the hero of a mythic structure. Far from remaining himself for the reader at the crucial moment when *he* realizes that he can only be himself, Manfred becomes identified with the super-human.

There are various features of *Manfred* then which make it less formally effective in rendering its central concern than the non-theatrical but in fact much more dramatically tense *Childe Harold* III, though again this latter has not the philosophical depth of *Manfred*. It is in *Beppo* that Byron manages finally both a subtle analysis of the state of freedom and a form with which to express it—as of course it is *Beppo* that marks the coming of his poetic maturity in general.

Beppo finds its characters free of the oppression of hypocritical morality and the Puritan social conventions of England, but there is no trace here of the emptiness or isolation Byron earlier associated with the free state. Nor is their freedom compromised by a commitment to some purpose larger than themselves. The content of their freedom is on the contrary a limited, relative, and artificial value, yet for all that a value. Not only has Manfred's lesson been learnt—meaning is created from within, not an effect of reference to some external system— but its relative, subjective, quality has been accepted; the poem *Beppo* is both Manfred and his observer, the Abbot, at the same time. In terms of the plot, Beppo's return can be accommodated within Laura's relationship to the Count, as his absence has been filled by the Count's presence: the 'freedom' of Beppo's absence does not empty Laura's life, but neither does her new 'commitment' usurp her freedom—she has no need to react against either in order to define her self. It is freedom, not commitment *or* rebellion, which fills her being. The ironic setting of the poem in the Carnival (for the etymology see stanza vi) underlines the freedom of the Venetian society, for this is anything but a farewell to the flesh, and yet the indulgence of the flesh is seen neither as hypocritical nor importantly as a self-dramatizing gesture of rebellion.

It is the texture of the poem, in Nabokov's sense,[15] that breaks quite new ground. To look first at an instance still partly connected with the flow of the plot, the treatment of the moment at which Beppo reveals his identity is almost the reverse of the treatment of such crucial moments in the Tales. If we say that this poem is 'comic', the earlier ones 'serious', and only that, we say the obvious and nothing of worth; if we say only that *Beppo* parodies Romantic melodrama we have said something certainly, but little to explain the quality of the effect produced. The Count and Laura, in particular Laura, refuse to allow the poem to stop, to lift itself out of the relativizing flow of time. There is no question here of a second's pause being inlaid with significance over the thirty-three lines that it took for the 'moment' in which the Giaour 'checked his wheeling steed'. On the contrary Laura's one wordless moment ('She said,—what could she say? Why, not a word') is covered by the Count's invitation to Beppo to enter his own house, from which point the irony of Laura's word-lessness is revealed in her continuous stream of questions over two and a half stanzas. Time does not stand still at the climax of the story—it speeds up:

> . . . 'Beppo! what's your pagan name?
> Bless me! your beard is of amazing growth!
> And how came you to keep away so long?
> Are you not sensible 'twas very wrong?
>
> 'And are you *really*, *truly*, now a Turk?
> With any other women did you wive?
> Is't true they use their fingers for a fork? . . .'
>
> (xci, 5–8; xcii, 1–3)

As Laura's freedom creates itself before the reader's eyes so the possibility of dramatic definition, the setting of limits to the significance of the moment, its elevation in Faulkner's phrase to a 'symmetry above the flesh',[16] dissolves. The rhetoric does not create significance by holding the moment static, it fills it with meaning by releasing it.

I have only space to consider two more examples of this rhetoric of freedom, but they are I believe typical of Byron's *ottava rima* method. Art itself, whether literary or plastic or, though less frequently, musical, becomes increasingly import-ant to Byron as a type of the creation of meaning—artificial certainly, but not the less meaningful for that (after *Manfred* what other kind of 'meaning' could there be?—the temptation of the absolute had finally been rejected). Both aspects must be present in his poems' experience of art. Thus the description of the reality of Italian female beauty gives way at the end of xlv to a description of it first in mythological terms and then in terms of Raphael's and Canova's art. This teaches us 'all we know of Heaven, or can desire' (and incidentally the passage claims that Canova's sculpture is superior to words in the description of beauty). For all the praise, the art is still earth-bound, and all the more so given the next stanza, which is presented as an annotation and ends:

> Since, as we all know, without the Sex, our Sonnets
> Would seem unfinished, like their untrimmed bonnets.

This reduces female beauty and the content of art to the level of a piece of ribbon, and in doing so also reinforces its artificiality, for it is as if a Sonnet could somehow exist independently of its subject. The point is that *Beppo* moves without tension from one view to the other, from art as the giver of significance to art as mere form, and in that movement creates its own meaning as freedom.[17] The state of freedom fills its own meaning with itself.

Finally Byron's presence in the poem in the guise of bewildered narrator, reminds us that as with Venetian society the poem is clearly an artifice, it makes no appeal to divine or any other transcendent authority, it spins meaning only out of itself, and for all that it is a poem not of desolation and nihilistic cynicism, but one which includes compassion and calm assurance of value:

> A certain lady went to see the show,
>   Her real name I know not, nor can guess,
> And so we'll call her Laura, if you please,
> Because it slips into my verse with ease.   (xxi, 5–8)

> The gentle reader, who may wax unkind,
>   And caring little for the author's ease,
> Insist on knowing what he means, a hard
> And hapless situation for a bard.   (l, 5–8)

> I've half a mind to tumble down to prose,
> But verse is more in fashion—so here goes.   (lii, 7–8)

The poem can see its own meaning as arbitrary, contextless, free, without being reduced to futility. Beppo makes friends in his old age by telling stories, even if the narrator does not 'believe half of them'. Byron's new rhetoric creates a freedom which is not futile, but which does not either lose itself in commitment. As time has been freed in this new freedom from

the compulsion to become eternity, so there is no absolute
moment for the ending of the poem:

> My pen is at the bottom of a page,
>   Which being finish'd, here the story ends;
> 'Tis to be wish'd it had been sooner done,
> But stories somehow lengthen when begun.

NOTES

1. Quotations are taken, for the sake of easy reference, from Ernest
   Hartley Coleridge (ed.), *The Poetical Works of Lord Byron* (1905; reprinted
   1958), except in the cases of poems published before April 1816, which are
   from Jerome J. McGann (ed.), *Lord Byron: The Complete Poetical Works*,
   Volumes I–III (1980–81).
2. Cobbett's *Political Register*, Vols. XXI (1812) p. 966ff., XXII (1812)
   p. 642ff., XXIII (1812) p. 480ff.
3. Kelvin Everest, 'Luddites, Catholics and Whigs: Byron in Parliament', a
   paper at the International Byron Seminar, University of Groningen,
   1982.
4. See *Don Juan*, IX, xxiv–xxvi, for example, which include the lines:

   > . . . I wish men to be free
   > As much from mobs as kings—from you as me.
   >
   > The consequence is, being of no party,
   > I shall offend all parties:—never mind!

5. The commentaries on the Turkish Tales in McGann, op. cit., Vol. III,
   imply at least a gesture towards political allegory in the plots of the
   poems. See also above p. 169.
6. F. L. Jones (ed.), *The Letters of Percy Bysshe Shelley* (1964), Vol. II, p. 154.
7. The motto from Moore reads:

   > One fatal remembrance—one sorrow that throws
   > It's bleak shade alike o'er our joys and our woes—
   > To which Life nothing darker nor brighter can bring,
   > For which joy hath no balm—and affliction no sting.

8. A random selection: *The Bride of Abydos*, I, [x], 253–56; *The Corsair*, III,
   xxiv; *Lara*, II, xxiii; *The Siege of Corinth*, xxx; *Parisina*, xviii.
9. Though there are signs of a self-conscious weaving of cross reference at
   least, the running Promethean imagery having often been noted; as the
   merest hint of others one might note the words 'gazing' and 'glow' in vi
   and lxxv; or the 'eddy' and 'vortex' images of vii, xi and elsewhere.

10. W. P. Elledge, *Byron and the Dynamics of Metaphor* (1968), *passim*; K. P. A. Drew, *The Meaning of Freedom* (1982), p. 187. Drew's discussion of *Manfred*, pp. 183–90, sees the hero firmly as a Childe Harold figure. As I shall argue, this does not seem to me wholly true. His reading of *Don Juan*, pp. 190–203, makes an interesting comparison with that of *Beppo* above, pp. 181–84.

11. Kierkegaard, thinking of Byron, believed that the Continent 'no longer need be initiated into the secrets of boredom by some English lord, the travelling member of a spleen club' (*The Concept of Irony*, trans. Lee M. Capel, 1966, p. 302), yet his *The Concept of Anxiety* links freedom and *angst* in a remarkably Byronic way. See the new translation by Reidar Thomte *et al.*, 1980.

12. I am assuming that the old red-herring of the female figure in Act I *not* being Astarte is well and truly buried—Manfred collapses before his sister other-self, and in the Incantation is condemned to eternal selfhood.

13. Elledge, op. cit., p. 94.

14. Jessica and Lorenzo are also indulging in self-dramatization in the passage following 'The moon shines bright. In such a night as this . . .' (*Merchant of Venice*, V, i).

15. Nabokov, *Pale Fire*, Shade's poem, 803–15: '. . . It sufficed that I in life could find . . . some kind of correlated pattern in the game. . . .'

16. Faulkner, *The Sound and the Fury*: Quentin attempts to escape time by the self-dramatization of imagined incest. His father characterizes the impulse as a desire to be 'symmetrical above the flesh'.

17. Stanzas xii–xv on Giorgione's *Tempestà* (which Byron thinks of as the *Famiglia di Giorgione*, see Ian Scott-Kilvert, *The Byron Journal*, Vol. 9 (1981), pp. 85–8) are another case in point. The painting is admired, yet treated as a tourist object:

> . . . when you to Manfrini palace go,
> That picture (howsoever fine the rest)
> Is loveliest to my mind of all the show;
> It may perhaps be also to *your* zest,
> And that's the cause I rhyme upon it so.

It does not portray 'love ideal', and yet it is 'Like the lost Pleiad seen no more below'. Perhaps most to be remarked is the way in which even the approach to the transcendent is now not realized in static terms, or at most this is only very tentatively touched in (in the 'One' and the 'fix'), but as a 'momentary gliding' of someone truly beyond our knowledge, free of speaker and text:

> One of these forms which flit by us, when we
> Are young, and fix our eyes on every face;
> And oh! the Loveliness at times we see
> In momentary gliding, the soft grace,
> The Youth, the Bloom, the Beauty which agree,
> In many a nameless being we retrace,
> Whose course and home we know not, nor shall know. . . .

9

Byron and the Cult of Personality

by J. F. HENDRY

The late Sir Herbert Read distinguishes in one of his essays[1] between personality and character, as did Goethe. Personality to Read was labile, or flexible, and character—inflexible. 'Character is the product of a disciplined education . . . and the result is a firm dependable set of ideas and reactions upon which a definite type of society can be based.' Perhaps to-day we are less impressed by this than we should be, in view of our knowledge of brain-washing techniques, but Read goes on to point out that character 'cultivates a taste, but this taste is rational rather than aesthetic, retrospective and historical rather than experimental and contemporary'.

As for personality, it is 'distinguished by immediacy, and what I would call lability, or the capacity to change without loss of integrity. . . . The values of the personality are neither moral nor social: they are religious or aesthetic.'

But it is Read's conclusion that is his most valuable contribution to the subject. 'The tautness of the social fabric depends on their dialectical counterplay.' In other words, they must be allowed to interact, because dominance of one or the other may upset the social structure.

Goethe's view was not dissimilar. To him, personality, or talent, was the private factor in creation, whereas character was formed by experience in the world:

Byron and the Cult of Personality

Es bildet ein Talent sich in der Stille
Sich ein Charakter aber in dem Strom der Welt.[2]

(Talent takes shape in quiet,/ But character in the stream of the world.)

Goethe managed to reconcile both of these reasonably well in his lifetime. Not so Byron, whom he admired, born in a less propitious era. Goethe's world consisted of a formal society which, he failed to see, did *shape* character, instead of being shaped by it also, and shaped it not always in a positive way. Good and bad characters, even at odds, become too often, not themselves but 'real characters', in the popular sense, i.e. unreal, because they identify totally with their various precepts and concepts, imposed by the society in which they live. It was easier for Goethe, after *The Sorrows of Werther* had helped unleash a cult of feeling in Europe, to settle down to the role of Counsellor at the Court of Weimar, than it was for Byron to try for a Parliamentary career in a growing industrial society still dominated by concepts, or myths, of character. The social currents in Byron's world were overwhelming and threatened to drown anyone rash enough to try to swim *against* the stream.

One might almost say that these currents were becoming too strong to allow much in the way of character formation at all. After the French Revolution had come Napoleon—an example, if you like, of a cult of personality, but at what cost, and through what resistance? Byron's admiration for the man is understandable. Goethe, Schiller and Rousseau had already launched the movement in Europe of *'Sturm and Drang'*, which was more an expression of personality than of rationalism and was as much an expression of individualism as the *'Je pense, donc je suis'* of Descartes. Did not Byron repeat: 'I feel, therefore I am?' The value attached to feeling and sentiment was therefore to some degree already a cult of personality, as well as a demonstration against economic and social inhibitions. Character, as a concept, had begun to flake badly. Yet though private life in England, among the aristocracy, was as cruel, repressive and profligate as in France, it was given no publicity, and scandal rarely became public. Yet the division which some critics perceive in Byron's *nature* between his character and his

187

personality actually existed therefore, before he was born, in society as a whole.

In saying that Character, as a concept, had begun to 'flake', we mean that the governing classes had lost *insight* into events. Cromwellian action and the French Revolution are proof of that. What began to take its place was cant. 'Cant is the currency of false opinion, a profession of belief in something which no one really believes, but which everyone finds convenient.' Cant, or myth, is equally widespread to-day. To Byron it was the *primum mobile* of England, *perfidious* Albion, and made it loathed abroad. He soon adopted his opposition to 'cant political, cant poetical, cant religious, cant moral, but always cant . . .'. And one is justified in saying that cant was responsible for the first piece of criticism against him, which has lasted until to-day: that he was a 'poseur', a cultivator of personality, an actor, and therefore *did not mean what he said.*

There were other criticisms, that he was egocentric, 'mad, bad and dangerous to know'—according to Caroline Lamb—a radical in politics; a satyr and impractical revolutionary; as well as a poor versifier; his own humbug, and morbid son of a mad father; who nevertheless managed to achieve a passing fame, or notoriety, by exploiting his name and reputation.

To deal with these accusations of self-dramatization and cultivation of personality it is necessary to examine both the meaning of the phrase 'cult of personality' and its various ramifications, and later to trace whether these have any application to the poet's life and work. For what it is worth, what should be borne in mind is Vuillamy's phrase that 'It was Byron's defiance of cant rather than any alleged enormities of conduct which eventually brought upon him the enmity of his respectable countrymen.'[4]

It was Byron's misfortune to live in a period when social concepts were breaking down in the face of social images, and with them 'character' and institutions, before individual destiny, interpreted as 'cult of personality'. It was a period of transition, with a rising merchant class, and industrial disruption producing misery among the working class that seemed to threaten Jacobin revolution, as in France. A hero was demanded, like Napoleon: or a scapegoat, like Byron.

In recent times, the phrase 'cult of personality' has been

applied by Mr. Krushchev to the adulation given Stalin and later Mao-tse-Tung, in China. This of course was an artificial 'social' cult accorded leaders who had little personality in themselves, if plenty of 'character', good or bad. Yet the phrase masks the problem facing Russian thinkers, especially Marxists, for a number of years: does society produce great men? Or is it shaped by great men? Lenin, one might say, is at the heart of the problem too, since he unmistakably shaped the revolution. Is it personality or character that makes great men, one might also ask? There is no doubt that opportunity is a factor, but it takes a supreme leader to seize that opportunity, as Napoleon did, and Lenin. So, is the hero an aspect of the cult, individual or social, of personality? In the case of Byron, it is fairly certain that society's contribution to his career was the privilege it accorded him of becoming a titled member of the aristocracy, since otherwise he would scarcely have been heard of. On the other hand, his personality might have broken through in other and more revolutionary directions. Just as Empire prevented Revolution at home (as absence of Empire produced fascism in Europe), so foreign travel distanced the poet's mind from social issues at home, to a great extent.

Nevertheless, it is impossible not to admit that his hostility to society contained a personal note. His own personality was in constant conflict—some might say adjustment—between sensitivity and insensitivity, rebellion and conformity, sin and remorse—a conflict which society merely fostered and embittered. To attain wholeness in himself he had to try to achieve a vision of wholeness for society. It was a gigantic task, and one not to be achieved by any simple cultivation of society and personality. His crippled foot, like Achilles's heel, became a symbol of his *mortal* weakness; and his own estimate of himself was that he did not possess any character at all. It was to Lady Blessington that he confided his thoughts: 'I am so changeable, being everything by turns and nothing long, that it would be difficult to describe me. . . .' This is Read's 'flexibility' all right, but it was not understood as such, even by the poet himself, and certainly not cultivated, but, if anything, a reaction to the growing speed of social change. Yet there *were* fixed points. 'I have two constant sentiments, a love of liberty and a detestation of cant, and neither is calculated to gain me friends', he told her.

That was true. What he faced in society is typified by the blimpishness of the Duke of Wellington: 'I hate the whole race of them. There never existed a more worthless set than Byron and his friends', he said in conversation with Lady Salisbury. Others felt differently about the importance of feeling, and linked it to individual destiny, as did Novalis: *'Oft fühle ich jetzt . . . (und) je tiefer ich es einsehe, dass Schicksal und Gemüt eines Begriffes sind.'*[5] This is translated as: 'I often feel, and ever more deeply realize, that fate and character are the same in conception'; but the translation is hardly accurate, for *'Gemüt'* does not mean character, nor does *'eines Begriffes'* mean 'the same in conception', implying an extraneous agent. What is meant is no doubt a comparison between *destiny* ('Schicksal') and what might be called *disposition*; but T. S. Eliot repeats the other version, in line with his own inclinations. Whichever is preferred, it cannot be said to prove in Byron any cult of personality, like Coleridge's alleged cult of sincerity. *'Gemüt'* in fact is 'mind', 'spirit', or 'soul'.

It does indicate, however, a *conjunction* between the individual, in this case, and the social history. Read puts it this way, that as a symbolic figure, or myth, a poet has to fit into the spirit of the age, or *Zeitgeist*. 'In the Elizabethan Period, Sir Philip Sidney was that man; he too had an heroic death.' Sidney was a 'natural centre', in a free society, and Byron a free spirit in a conventional society; and Byron's *Weltschmerz*, Read goes on to say, 'was genuine enough,—*unless we are prepared to accept the view that his whole life was an affected pose.'*[6] But people are always inclined, whether or not they believe in an Absolute Divinity, to condemn their own friends and enemies in absolute terms, as being a —— or a ——, and Byron has continued to be castigated in such terms by critics who ought to know better.

The clearest exposition of Byron as an egotistic poseur is given by Vuillamy, discussing what he terms the Byronic 'fugue'. It is 'a transformation and enlargement of personal emotion, an escape into the realms of autonomous fantasy. What is desired is . . . an escape from the intolerable pressure of environment . . . of conflict.' He continues: 'Byron was

190

disturbingly *egocentric.*' This second accusation contradicts the first and is less serious, since any creator must concentrate on his work, and scientists are not as prone to such criticism as artists, for some reason. 'What interested him was his own emotional experience. . . .' It does not occur to Vuillamy that this should be a natural process in any type of self-analysis or analysis of the only reality an individual may know—himself or herself.

Read recognizes the poet's need to withdraw, as he says in his own words, 'himself from himself', which seems to express a distancing, we might say, of his personality from his character.

Then what, it will be asked, about his abominable behaviour towards women? Is it not here that an accusation of ego-centrism and posing, as cold and distant, is justified? Edwin Muir seems to think so when he retorts, to statements that it was Byron who was pursued, that 'the rabbit does not pursue the trap.' But in the main, especially after the publication of *Childe Harold*, Byron was pursued by women as much as many a modern pop-singer, so that Muir's remark about his 'film-star' attitudinizing is neither fair nor accurate.

Though he cannot be accused of merely posing, however, and was undoubtedly sincere in many of his affairs and ventures, even if in others he was the victim of his passions, one can legitimately talk of a growing cult of the personality *during* the period in question, the era of Gentleman Jackson, the boxer; of Beau Brummell; and Dandyism in general; and above all, of the spread in Europe of the Romantic Movement, in which personality was to play such a great part. In Russia, Pushkin's *Yevgeny Onyegin* owed much to Byronism, with the proviso that in the novel in verse (as skilful, or even more so, than Byron's similar works), as in much Russian literature, it was the woman who was superior. And in *A Hero of Our Time*, by Lermontov, the coldness in love and war or duelling exhibited by Pechorin is such that there does seem to exist the blood-relationship between the author and Byron that is sometimes claimed. Lermontov was said to have descended from another Scot, or half-Scot, named Captain Learmont.

Finally, Byron's *Weltschmerz*, accepted by Read as genuine, was far more than the romantic stress on feeling and more of a Faustian attempt to change the world. It was no less than

Goethe who introduced Byron into his Faust II as Euphorion, on account of the heroism of his death and of the fact that Byron was neither Classical nor Romantic, but *a man of the present*. 'To understand and realise what this moment in 1827 *is*, and what to-morrow will be, is to understand and realise what Byron is.'[8] There could hardly be a greater compliment to the man's prophetic insight and sincerity, in work and in life; and if we must go beyond the poetry to the life, it is more convenient perhaps to examine the work first, as a proof of Byron's commitment to literature, which he sometimes professed, through modesty perhaps, to despise.

But this commitment to the *present*, or the *actual*, by no means ignored history. To Byron, it could be said history was omnipresent. It is here that the question of the cult of personality again enters, in a strange way.

He had been proud of his ancestors, among whom were crusaders, and medieval knights, living in the times of Romance and Courtly Love. Love and Heroism were always to be inextricably connected and even confused in his mind, together with the gallant, Platonic and less Platonic amours of the poet-troubadours of those far-off times. These heroes were essentially, in his view at least, *liberators*, freeing genuine love from the trammels of arranged marriage and tyranny, and even the Holy Land from the infidel. The Grail was a quest for the absolute, and Byron's own quest for identity had something of the same obsession. Yet a line must be drawn, for the cult of personality stopped short of tyranny, as far as the poet was concerned. Caesar and Napoleon both lost their glamour as liberators when they assumed a crown and became victims of history, when they lost it.

This martial or heroic phase comes out most strongly in 'On leaving Newstead Abbey', as far as his early work is concerned, with its glance at the Crusades and French and Civil Wars:

> Shades of heroes, farewell! Your descendant, departing
> From the seat of his ancestors, bids you, adieu!
> Abroad, or at home, your remembrance imparting
> New courage, he'll think upon glory and you.

Together with his innumerable love-poems, his early martial and Highland poems clearly constitute a kind of rehearsal for his later career, especially in their dramatic tone, which must be regarded therefore as an attitude, rather than an empty pose, and as search for and identification with the Absolute.

It is, of course, in *Childe Harold*, and *The Bride of Abydos*, *The Giaour*, and *The Corsair*, that Byron finds and expresses the heroic role, while denying that the heroes were self-portraits. The first two cantos of *Childe Harold* were published on 29 February 1812, when, as he wrote, 'I awoke one morning and found myself famous.' 'Projected on to the world-stage' would have been a more accurate description. These cantos ended enticingly and aroused curiosity as to what might follow, especially after the lines in I, ix:

> Yea! none did love him—not his lemans dear—
> But pomp and power alone are women's care. . . .

These lines are significant, because pomp and power, as aspects of tyranny, were his enemies, and to identify women with them was to reduce women to enemies also, contemptible enemies who had prostituted themselves to the power of a '*soldateska*'.

Childe Harold, like the other poems and especially *The Corsair*, is full of the description of foreign countries that probably led to the institution of the Grand Tour beloved of Victorians, but contains a real insight into character and national traits which later produced Byron's intense interest in history.

There is much emphasis on freedom and on sailing, a symbol of sex. Vuillamy maintains that the work represents a 'type of romantic individualism where the individual claims the rights of a freedom which is to be as wide and wild as he pleases',[9] but this is contradicted by the bounds set in the poems to the exercise of complete freedom and the apparent punishment that attends it. Vuillamy's terms are all concepts, but the poet is concerned with images and with particulars, not with constricting rules and generalities.

His fondness for thunderstorms, earthquakes, battles and shipwrecks is also commented on, as indicative of the poet's need for relief from his inner conflict; but they are surely Eliot's familiar 'correlatives'. Vuillamy goes further: 'The sound of cannon or the roaring of a gale fills him with joy.'

Anyone reading this would think that nuclear weaponry was the creation of romantics instead of realists, and that down through history writers, even like Wilfrid Owen, had promoted and delighted in war. Byron's list of 'heroes' at the beginning of *Don Juan* should dispel that idea. His descriptions of violence, storm and passion correspond to his own feelings but do have an objective basis, and appear to offer an external solution to personal as well as social problems. His battles were with himself, on the whole, but did not exclude social questions. Most people's lives in modern society are governed by events over which they have little or no control: events that disrupt their existence or imprison them in a situation they cannot alter and which they call 'reality'. Byron's world was like our own in many ways, full of change, war and violence, *reflected in his work*, though to-day few writers follow his example in coming to grips with the present. Byron would not accept or evade:

> The fire and motion of the soul which will not dwell
> In its own narrow being, but aspire
> Beyond the fitting medium of desire. . . .

as he said in *Childe Harold*, expressing his attitude to history:

> This makes the madmen who have made men mad
> By their contagion; Conquerors and Kings,
> Founders of sects and systems, to whom add
> Sophists, Bards, Statesmen, all unquiet things
> Which stir too strongly the soul's secret springs. . . .
>
> (III, xliii)

History, a contemporary Russian poet[10] has said, is the story of human relations. If so, Byron would have retorted, it certainly is a bloody business, for *human* relations are not the same as *social* relations revolving round wealth and welfare. *Public* history—full of concepts—pullulating over and over again about prosperity, or dramatizing its own greed and lust as somehow 'instructive', a quarrel in a brothel almost, was to him not worth study and demanded action.

It is nonsense, therefore, to allege that by 'withdrawing into himself', i.e. dissociating himself from a world bent on its own destruction, the poet was *escaping from reality*, because if that *be* (or *were*) reality, there *can* be no escape. Had Byron really shrunk from it, he would have deserved the epithet of coward, which was in fact launched at him, or of vapid moralizer, which was implied. That he went to meet it earns him the award of 'a violent temperament'; a renegade; a worthless scribbler; a devil incarnate; yet he had written: 'To fly from, need not be to hate, mankind.' And of the loneliness around him:

> Is it not better then to be alone
> And love Earth only for its earthly sake?

In other words, to accept the natural world, free of human concepts and theories, but rich in images that feed the mind? He was developing fast when he penned the lines:

> I live not in myself, but I become
> Portion of that around me. . . .

The same sentiments were acclaimed when repeated by Rupert Brooke, but in Byron's case they and others lead to the charge of solipsism.

The constant struggle within him was expressed in terms of Eros and Agape: 'I cease to love thee when I love mankind', and despite the ambiguity, the conflict is the same.

To Edwin Muir, Byron dates. To Auden he has no imagination; he is a comedian. Notice again the *absolute* categorization. We all date, as part of our time, but these lines do not date, and the wit and insight is far beyond any Auden ever displayed:

> I speak not of men's creeds—they rest between
> Man and his Maker. . . .

So much for concepts. No wonder Bertrand Russell places him in the pillory for indulging in the Romanticism that, in Russell's view, brought about Hitlerism, though in fact it was *conceptual rationalism*—so predictable in its terms—which did so. Byron's history is almost apocalyptic:

> There is the moral of all human tales;
> 'Tis but the same rehearsal of the past,
> First Freedom, and then Glory, and when that fails
> Wealth, vice, corruption—barbarism at last.

We ought to know about that, but this is not all. The cure lies in the mind. There is more of the apocalyptic to come: 'Of its own beauty is the mind diseased . . .', or 'Our life is a false nature—'tis not in/ The harmony of things. . . .' Compare: 'The graph of history's a chart of the disease embodied in humanity'.[11]

To complain of the violence of Byron's verse in the period that saw Waterloo, Peterloo and the stand of the Guards in the Russian Decembrist Movement, is indeed to be blind: blind to the depths of the Byronic contribution. English dislike of rhetoric and histrionics obscured from its understanding much reasoning, history and even prophecy. The Romantic movement was decadent and discredited, in the end, as barbaric and baroque; but one poem, 'Darkness', strangely neglected, is definitely apocalyptic in its portrayal of a world dying after some cosmic catastrophe, in a kind of Wellsian or Orwellian 'pre-historic', or rather 'post-historic', savagery. It is pointless to regard this as merely another aspect of the famous Byronic gloom, or as the expression of some remnant of Calvinist predestination, because it really sums up his view of human history, judged *in its own terms*, from Cain to Waterloo. The Holocaust, in fact, carried one stage further.

This is the answer to those who, like W. H. Auden, accuse Byron of lack of vision and imagination, or to the others who allege lack of sincerity, meaning the cultivation of a pose. He himself was aware of his apparent inconsistencies, which, as if anticipating Read, he ascribes to *mobilité*[12] or 'excessive susceptibility of immediate impressions': in other words, the labile nature Read associates with personality. As for the Imagination:

> This is Byron's social version of the Romantic term 'Imagination', for mobility also reveals itself in the balance or reconciliation of opposite, or discordant qualities. . . . The great Romantic contraries—emotion and order, judgement and enthusiasm, steady self-possession and profound or vehement feeling—all find their social balance in the quality of mobility.[13]

Constant adjustment to circumstances, in other words, to ever-changing images, instead of unvarying opposition to change, *on principle*, and a clinging to abstract concepts, seem to demand just that vision, imagination and sincerity which Byron is said to lack, though the lack may be ascribed to his detractors on the grounds that often we accuse others of our own faults. It is the expansive nature of his *imaging* and vision, indeed, which makes any metaphysical doctrine anathema to him, and renders ridiculous the charge that he was no philosopher.

It was this quality that earned for him the appellation of 'chameleon', and made it difficult for Lady Blessington to understand what she felt was his dual personality, and his 'scoffing at himself' and others, soon 'after he has aroused great interest', though this is clearly a relief from tension and a healthy distrust of his own as well as others' reactions. The latter, too, is probably the explanation of his often repeated assertion in his work that he could not be loved, or did not in fact deserve to be loved. He had insight, in other words, into his own failings, a quality that does not seem to merit the belief in a dual personality, unless we accept the implication that to have *no* insight into one's failings is healthy and normal.

There are, on the other hand, certainly times in his work when theatrical attitudes can be observed clearly, though after all he was also a dramatist, and so had to be aware of his own poses, on occasion. In *The Corsair*, for example, can be read his description of:

> . . . the closed hand, the pause of agony
> That listens, starting, lest the step too near
> Approach intrusive on that mood of fear. . . .

Anyone as creative as he could not avoid a feeling of being besieged by impressions, objective as well as subjective, producing the chameleon aspect which Yeats attempts to describe as 'The Multiple Man', Phase 26, in his interpretation of history, expressed in *A Vision*.

Any dualism in his personality derived from this confrontation with *himself*, as compared with his confrontation of the *world*. The pirate portrayed in *The Corsair*—a man of action— compares with *The Giaour*, to whom 'Love is light from heaven', and is expressed even in *The Bride of Abydos*, in which the theme of incest is dealt with rather ambiguously, since Selim does inform Zuleika that he is *not* her brother. Augusta, with whom Byron had an equally ambiguous relationship, to say the least, was his half-sister. Dualism is thus involved *here*, but again as confrontation between 'himself' (in the person of a half-sister, another Byron) as an *aspect* of the external world and his own *person*, individual and alone, *facing* that external world. It had always been his problem to unite the two—personality and character; image and concept—in Life. Passion for Augusta must have been inspired by that feeling of other-worldly *unity* with *her*. Others have seen the task of Byron as being to reconcile the contradictory elements in Romanticism, and, one might add, in himself: namely, aspirations and ambitions, social and individual, with what is ever termed the *realities* of the social situation and the human condition; this to be done perhaps by some form of action, but at least using form, symbol and imagery to reach by means of myth the unconscious mind, striving to free itself from the rigid prison of rule. Thus in form, he is classical but in content romantic, a factor common to other poets, such as Pushkin and Lermontov, but also found in reverse, as in Eliot, where the form is romantic but the content classical. Byron, of course, denied that he was either. One reason for his revival, again, is the fact that apart from his social commentary, and the comic aspect of *Don Juan*, his verses are made to be recited in public, as essentially spoken poetry. The popularity of poetry in Soviet Russia is due to the same fact, that the existing culture is essentially an oral culture. In Byron's case it may be assumed that, in its early stages at least, his work appealed especially to the rising merchant class, which had less time and inclination for perusing print.

Yet the Romantic/Classical dualism is also an aspect of others probably more extreme in Byron than in any of his contemporaries outside of Russia. It was in fact his Fate, the destiny which overcame him at times with gloom, and yet inevitably introduced also the other side of tragedy, comedy, in *Don Juan*, where even Fate is treated with some scepticism: '(Fate is a good excuse for our own will).'[14] In other words he was aware of how much of his destiny depended upon himself. T. S. Eliot, citing Novalis, citing perhaps Heraclitus, that 'Character is Destiny' or Fate, overlooked the dichotomy between personality and character, so that in Byron's case, as can be seen from his life, it was the character that ultimately began to emerge and to involve him in the final scene at

Missolonghi. And this dichotomy is the same as the other examples of his 'dualism', or the dialectic interplay even between the elements, in his life, of Venus and Mars.

So interwoven indeed are his life and his poems that at times it is difficult to disentangle the two, as in the alleged portrait of Lady Byron, his wife, at the beginning of *Don Juan*; but an examination of his personality and his cult of it, or society's cult of it, is best made finally from the details of his life.

The balance he was seeking all his life to achieve between these various aspects of dualism—or conflict, depending on one's attitude—was a vital necessity to him when one considers the events of his childhood. The early beatings and precocious sexual initiation in Aberdeen were enough in themselves to have upset the balance of his nature, quite apart from the mixed blood he had inherited from his Calvinist mother in the Highlands and his debauched English father. Transfer from the reality of life in Scotland, knowing poverty but a real sense of personality, to the (to him) unnatural wealth and self-indulgence of England only deepened that division. Where the old life had been real, in the sense that one was committed to events—this being a form of identity, or the balance he sought—the new one was artificial, a masque of masks, where any commitment, erotic or political, was a source of amusement, or sometimes fear. Commitment must have become to the poet a form of the identity he sought, and the reconciliation of the opposites he discovered in himself and in society. In other words, it became commitment to oneself, and to one's personality, first of all, and not unthinking dependence on institutions or creeds of one sort or another.

To win through to that, however, he had to rediscover the old realities, of relations between men and women, as another part of the same search for identity. Numerous love-affairs were the inevitable result, at school and Cambridge, and, in the end, travel abroad; but it was not until the publication of *Childe Harold* that he found himself literally besieged by the fair sex, and confronted by the erotic challenge of Lady Caroline Lamb. The melancholy he suffered from was dissipated in her presence. Not only was she attractive, but light-hearted and witty in the way he needed, and with a sense of the theatrical as well.

It has often been said that all his life he wanted to be loved. The phrase is as cynical, or as tragic, as one wishes to make it. What seems reasonable to assume is that, in a partner, he hoped to find that reflection of himself which most couples find, one which would help him in his search for that unity of being which is what is meant by identity. Absence of such an experience necessarily threw him back on himself.

Caroline Lamb thus tested both his personality and his character. Notorious before she met the famous poet for her lack of either insight or inhibition, she prided herself on her ability to manipulate *homo sapiens*. Curiously, however, on the day after he met Caroline, Byron was introduced to Miss Anne Isabella (Annabella) Milbanke, the country cousin of Caroline's husband, William Lamb, and was strangely intrigued. She was the counterpart of Caroline in every way, withdrawn and rather scholarly in outlook.

Between them these two ladies were to turn his life upside down and finally drive him abroad. Throughout his affair with Caroline and his marriage to Annabella, however, his behaviour reveals much more character already than one would have expected. The proof is contained in his published letters to them and to friends.

The alleged affair with his half-sister, Augusta, on the other hand, is less easy to discuss. Specific proof of incest is not available, and the charge may or may not be part of the legend of his wickedness. There can be no doubt, in any case, that Byron's attachment to Augusta was sincere and permanent, as compared to his feelings for the other two women, which were often ambiguous and subject to considerable self-control. To regard the poet solely as an unprincipled seducer of all and sundry is perhaps simply to accept him as he wished the public to regard him. His relations with his half-sister would then assume the pattern exhibited in that classic of sexual intrigue, *Les Liaisons Dangereuses* by Choderlos de Laclos, the theme of which is the fascination of deliberate, conscious evil. Valmont, the central character, aided by his mistress, sexually corrupts an innocent girl and delights in watching her degradation. Not even Byron's most hostile critics accuse him of that. Yet some incestuous passion almost certainly existed in him, whether realized in practice or not.

Reference is made from time to time, nevertheless, by serious critics to some 'dark secret' in Byron's life, which they apparently rarely associate with Augusta, but make use of to explain his terrible coldness and 'hauteur' in public, which can hardly be accounted for as an attempt to avoid adoring women—since in fact it attracted them even more—or as a repressed homosexuality, or incestuous feelings. Most probably it was the fact that he himself could not love wholeheartedly, like other people, that made him subject to gaiety and melancholy by turns. His essential coldness of *intellect*, as he began to discover, was the alarming trait, since it questioned everything and has few parallels in literature other than in Lermontov's *A Hero of Our Time*, where Pechorin is, if possible, still more devilish, in the sense of cold and even calculating, than Childe Harold, or Don Juan, whose humour he lacks. In both cases there is the definite feeling that the coldness is in fact the author's own. So Caroline too, is accused of coldness. 'I fold a statue in my arms', he writes, which must have been quite maddening for a man whose ability to love depended on the woman's stimulation and faith:

> You may be prudent, fair and chaste
> But ah, my girl, you do not love!

His loves were thus a compound of peculiar feelings. He felt that he was awakening *souls*—or personalities—in women; *they* could have been more or less the same to him as they were to the early introspective philosophers. What he awakened in Caroline Lamb was, in the end, raging jealousy akin to madness. She denied that she was cold. He had drawn her, she said, like a magnet, though she had thought him 'mad, bad and dangerous to know': in other words, a reflection of herself.

The affair that ensued became the scandal of London, particularly because it was carried on in public. Caroline's play with a fruit-knife at Lady Heathcote's was the last straw. Whatever her motives, murder, suicide or dramatics, she had disrupted a reception by a display in public of deep feelings, that might have been overlooked had they been kept private, like countless other love-affairs known to all but not displayed in that way.

Byron's coldness had been made evident, and he had

renounced her in a letter, asking her to 'correct' her vanity, and 'exercise her caprices upon others'. But the affair had become a dangerous erotic *gamble*. And his real affection was engaged, no doubt about that. This is shown by his irascible reply to the message she scrawled on a book he was reading, after she had broken into his flat when he was out—'*Remember me*':

> Remember thee! [he wrote] Ay, doubt it not.
>   Thy husband too shall think of thee!
> By neither shalt thou be forgot,
>   Thou *false* to him, thou *fiend* to me!

Involved, as he always was, in emotional scenes, it is reasonable to assume that Byron was, finally, personally horrified and even terrified by Caroline's unpredictable and reckless behaviour. Coming on top of his own bitterness on his return from Greece, and his elevation to fame, this sudden transition to the centre of the stage in a petty melodrama, which threatened to destroy his name, reputation and even life, must have produced in him a madness almost equal to hers. He has been accused here, and in other cases, of behaving 'like a "cad" '. The romantic cad was a well-known figure, of course, exemplified in Lovelace (Lucifer), lover and destroyer of Clarissa Harlowe in Richardson's novel. The poet was no cad in that evil sense.[15]

That Byron had a personality, and a charming one, there can be no doubt; that he cultivated it, was only to be expected; that at times he did so consciously, and with an air, like a poseur, is not surprising, considering his dramatic character; but that throughout he was merely an actor is not tenable, despite the strictures of Edwin Muir. More probably his apparent aloofness and depression were ways of safeguarding his privacy and reflective nature. That women should feel it to be due to unhappiness, because he lacked the solace only a woman could give, and that his wickedness cried out for conversion, was also 'in character', since women have often felt they know the answer. At least Byron could deal with them, and could hardly be averse to taking advantage, even unfair advantage, of their protestations of affection—in which he could not believe—but Caroline Lamb was something quite different and constantly invaded his privacy, entering into his most secret thoughts and confidences, so that he had actually to defend himself as if it were really a struggle to the death.

It may indeed have been Caroline's contribution to his wealth of experience that in the end made him the master of satire he became. Just as his childhood had been a rehearsal of the parts he had to play in later life in love and war, so the Caroline episode probably produced the mastery of *Don Juan*, once he had recovered confidence in himself.

He was in correspondence, meanwhile, with Miss Milbanke, who was opposite in every way to Caroline. Outwardly she was all he admired: intelligent, serious, and a woman of principle who did not indulge in affairs. Marriage, he may have thought, would lend him respectability, and no doubt the lady's virtue was also a challenge. She might even change him. She clearly thought he could be changed, and noted his various qualities in her Diary, including nobility of character. Miss Milbanke was no fool and may have noticed what others overlooked. Life after all is not static, nor are people, and Byron was more changeable than most. There are grounds for believing that he hoped she would be able to change him. But a letter he had written to her should have put her on her guard: 'The great object of life is sensation—to feel that we exist— . . . It is this craving void which drives us to gaming—to battle—to travel. . . .'

The 'craving void' has been felt by countless other artists and philosophers, not to mention ordinary mortals. It is often referred to as 'the abyss', 'nothingness', and all that is negative. Herbert Read dismisses this feeling as '*Angst*', perhaps with justification, for the era was not so different from our own, with Napoleon occupying Europe and invading Russia, as did Hitler, and the Congress of Vienna muzzling development, much as East-West relations to-day still do. And has this not already been called The Age of Anxiety? One feels, however, that Byron's 'craving void' was personal, which was why he hoped that marriage would fill it. Loss of a sense of identity is part of the '*Angst*' feeling, and Byron had not found the role he expected in Parliament, or even in society, where he regarded his poetic reputation with some disdain, real or otherwise. Read concludes that Byron was a nihilist, a word which is very ambiguous when applied, as it is, to such disparate characters as Tolstoy and the Russian revolutionary, Nechayev, whom everybody feared, including revolutionaries. Those who reject their society are not necessarily nihilists. Byron comes, indeed, perilously close to nihilism in his philosophy of history, but he nevertheless constantly questions himself about his own identity, and the meaning of life, and never denies freedom. In a period that saw the failure of the Reform Bill, the action of the Luddites and Peterloo, there was ample reason for his periodic dejection. He had never been a systematic thinker, being opposed to most systems; but the fact that Miss Milbanke *was* a thinker, disciplined as well as attractive, must have fascinated him. She seemed an ideal foil: a student of geology, and mnemonics, as well as of poetry; a woman with iron principles, and none too happy about the desires of the flesh. It has been alleged that Byron may have wanted to arouse the passion in her, or to subdue her reluctance; but from his point of view, he may just as well have thought he was in fact freeing her from her ridiculous concepts, by showing her the value of emotions and of real living. As it was, what should have been mutual adjustment became mortal combat.

They were married on 2 January 1815, and separated a year later. For once, Byron was caught in a part he could not act. He seems to have played the fool, as one might call it, by exercising his sense of humour on his wife, in an attempt to arouse her from her rigid attitude, but without much success, and in the end she brought out all that was worst in him, in baffled rage. Yet he appears to have behaved better than she did, and to have been genuinely in love. It is odd that Caroline should have called him 'mad, bad and dangerous to know', and that for a time Annabella Milbanke, too, thought him insane. It is the reward of those who step outside of social norms and exhibit some frustration because others do not follow. A daughter Augusta Ada, born in December, gave him much delight, and brings up the question as to why she was named after Byron's half-sister Augusta. The riddle as to how Annabella could show so much affection for Augusta, whom she suspected of having an affair with her husband, has not been solved, and can help little in enlightening us as to

Byron's feelings in the matter. Augusta too had borne a daughter, who was brought up to believe that Byron was her father. Once this became public knowledge, Byron was ostracized. The only solution was to escape abroad.

Evidence of his sincerity appears, all the same, in a Journal entry for 29 September 1816 when he writes that bitterness has followed him throughout his travels. Nothing, not music, or mountains, 'the Glacier, the Forest nor the Cloud, have for one moment lightened the weight upon my heart, *nor enabled me to lose my own wretched identity* in the majesty and the power and the glory around me above and beneath me.' Only the fluency of the language hints at a certain dramatic pose.

There is reason for suspecting that the 'loss of identity' he sought in drink and sex was not really a loss, but the feeling that he had never achieved stability of *character*. It was in action that he felt he could achieve it, in line with the statement of Goethe that it was formed in the currents of life; and it might almost be said that his personality was the real, and any *cult* of it a public rather than a private phenomenon, like so many cults in the entertainment 'business', especially in America. Byron was in fact, in that case, cultivating *character* when he went abroad, and there are witnesses to testify to this. Shelley in Venice in 1821 thought he was becoming a 'virtuous' man. 'There was a sharper awareness of the symbolic role that circumstances had thrust upon him, and for the rest of his life he never lost sight of it.'[16] Here is an admirable example of the fact that life is *dynamic*, and that it is useless to talk of human beings in terms of absolute qualities. It was, indeed, character he was developing, but a character imposed on him by society as well as by circumstances, a kind of *negative* personality, or negation of the cult of personality thrust on him in London and meant to destroy him, as it did. It is a complex situation. Only strength of character and revolutionary sentiment could in the end defeat the efforts of society to destroy him by portraying him as an immoral monster.

Yet there are his amours in Venice, amounting to frenzied sexual activity in every class of the population, which if true— and the statistics available, his own, are not exactly worthy of credence—appear to confirm, and glory in confirming, his evil nature and grossness of appetite. Was that his real self? Was he a raving seducer of the young and innocent?

> Less harm would have come to him from the creatures who composed the vagrant harem of the Palazzo Mocenigo, had he possessed the cynical hardness and spiritual grossness to think of them as animals. . . . However dissolute she might be, the woman he regarded with passion became for a moment the object of an affection that was no less tender than transient.[17]

Compared to Byron's own version of his Venetian amours, this is mild.

> Some of them are Countesses, and some of them are cobblers' wives; some noble, some middling, some low, and all whores. . . . I have had them all, and thrice as many to boot, since 1817.[18]

Tenderness? Rampant rape? There is a conflict here, but there was, of course, a growing conflict within himself, perhaps at the gradual awareness of the new role engulfing him. Whatever the reason, he now plunged into debauchery, since, as he concluded in his letter: 'The night cometh.'

One of the affairs—that with a 'tiger', La Fornarina, wife of a baker—became a curious admixture of sexual and physical combat, repeating on a higher, or lower, level, that of his marriage to Annabella. The result left him weak, but not so emasculated as to be able to resist a married lady, Teresa Guiccioli. To her, and it is an interesting follow-up, he was the most wonderful of men, one whose character was more fascinating than his personality even. If the finest of characters was that which gave much and exacted nothing, then Byron was the finest of characters. In this, contempt for others and for what was called life was also a factor. But she thought him also modest, granting superiority to others in cases where it seemed merited. In addition, he remained astonishingly faithful to her, and seemed to try hard to fit into the picture she saw of him.

If she did not understand that he was a free spirit, a free personality, exemplifying freedom for all mankind, she must have begun to realize it when he left Venice for Greece and the fight for Greek independence, to which he had sacrificed a great deal of time and money. It was hard for him to leave her, as his letters prove. The disconcerting fact is that he was capable of really loving, as opposed to seducing, so many women. He was impressed by the East and his poetry is full of harems, but it is the genuine love, so often discovered, that confounds, because it seems to strike at the virtues of monogamy.

His motives in going are clearly the result of his lifelong love of Europe and of freedom, as well as of the opportunity offered. That might have been his epitaph. 'He was a lover of Europe', of whom there are few, even in the European Community. But even in his final gesture detractors cannot resist their own temptation to make the poet less real, by playing on the word 'mask'.

> Byron wore perhaps the last of his many masks, not now that of an aloof aristocrat or unprincipled lecher, not that of a hectic lover, dandy or melancholy poet, but that of the man of action, the warrior or hero, *thus attempting once more to command reality*.[19]

The italics are mine.

What this implies is that some divine or demonic force enabled the man to assume these masks at will, and that he was, presumably, evil, since all along he intended to *command reality*, whatever that means. The repetition of such cant is sickening. Lady Longford, in her introduction to the work cited, puts matters straighter: 'He hoped to force the world to take off its own masks, look him straight in the face, and acknowledge his existence and worth.' The fact is that any heroics at Missolonghi had no audience to speak of, so that the mask was in fact himself. Dying, he showed the greatest of courage in the most wretched of conditions and in a cause more or less betrayed by the people who were supposed to help. He displayed the character behind the personality, if by character we mean living by a set of principles, or reactions, which may be good or bad.

It was when the personality was displayed, in his attacks on cant and corrupt politicians, and in multiple love-affairs—including the alleged relations with Augusta—that he had to assume the role of the enemy and be ostracized, for society, then as now, battens on personality of any sort, owing to its insatiable appetite for sensation, and hastens its own downfall.

A personality-cult is thus produced by *society*, and unless moderated, becomes destructive and extended to wider areas.

Byron is an example. We can fancy the origin of the cult. 'Fellow had it in him to be a real sporting gentleman despite his gammy leg. Friend of pugilists, no mean boxer himself, an all rounder; why should he shut himself away, insist on being a loner unless he had something to hide? All came out of course. Something to do with his sister. And by gad if you believed the rumours! Deserved horse-whipping. Best thing he ever did to go away and get himself killed. All the same, these dreamers!' English calumny does not have to be specific.

What comes under attack then, ascribing the cult to the individual involved, and not to society, is 'romanticism' as such and concern with freedom and spiritual values, as against quiescence and universal materialism.

The romantic has been under attack for a long time, especially in England, where it yields to 'realism', or 'things as they are', the stability of quietism: in other words, to an acceptance of whatever attitude at the moment appears to furnish the greatest short-term stability, irrespective of right, wrong or certain long-term disaster. The romantic attitude represents, instead, constant mutual adjustment of personality and society—constant movement, therefore, and change, not of course *per se*—ensuring stability over the long term, in place of the imposition of a classical concept, as expressed for instance in totalitarianism.

It is a pity that Read gives up the attempt to understand and regards Byron as 'beyond good and evil', a pernicious doctrine which still assumes these as absolutes and fails to bring out their roots in the human mind. To Byron, it was living and loving that were important, not moral absolutes. He could never have held that evil was pardonable, like some character in a Dostoyevsky novel.

And Read could not be more wrong than when he alleges that the poet contracted the current '*Weltschmerz*', which tempted him to philosophize, in sceptical terms. 'During the greatest horrors of the greatest plagues', he writes, '... men were more profligate than ever.' Should this surprise a generation which has learnt of the loutish profligacy in the Berlin bunker? Nihilism leads naturally enough to nothingness and bankrupt oblivion, but Byron was no nihilist, as Read implies. Despite despair and doubt of any worthwhile historical goal, and of the impossibility of a creature like himself ever being loved—because he knew that his own dissatisfaction with life was not a basis for emotional ties—his life and death are those of one who never ceased struggling and fighting for true freedom in the world.

It may give a wrong picture, but his portrait of a bullfight in Spain comes to mind:

> Foiled, bleeding, breathless, furious to the last
> Full in the centre stands the bull at bay
> Mid wounds and clinging darts . . .

and then the finale: 'Once more through all he burst his thundering way.'

It is a pity that those who brought him down still show no sign of understanding what *cant* means, and thus confirm the horrifying vision he had of the human future.

NOTES

1. *Annals of Innocence and Experience* (Faber, London, 1940), pp. 90–1.
2. Goethe, *Torquato Tasso* (1790), i, 2.
3. C. E. Vuillamy, *Byron* (Michael Joseph, London, 1948), p. 3.
4. Op. cit., p. 26.
5. *Heinrich von Ofterdingen* (1802), Bk. II.
6. Herbert Read, *The True Voice of Feeling* (Faber, London, 0000).
7. C. E. Vuillamy, *Byron* (Michael Joseph, London, 1948), p. 286.
8. Francis Berry, 'The Poet of Childe Harold', in *Byron: A Symposium*, edited by John D. Jump (Macmillan, London, 1975), p. 35.
9. C. E. Vuillamy, *Byron* (Michael Joseph, London, 1948), p. 285.
10. Yevgeny Yevtushenko, *A Dove in Santiago* (Secker and Warburg, London, 1982).
11. J. F. Hendry, *The Orchestral Mountain* 2nd Edition, (1st edn., Routledge, London, 1943).
12. Note to *Don Juan*, Canto XVI, xcvii.
13. Harold Bloom, *The Visionary Company* (Doubleday and Co., New York, 1961).
14. *Don Juan*, Canto XIII, xii.
15. For a brilliant analysis of the Romantic Cad see the essay 'Robert Lovelace: The Romantic Cad', by H. T. Hopkinson, in *Horizon: A Review of Literature*, Vol. X, No. 56, August 1944, 80–104. Though Annabella Milbanke and even Caroline may have been affected by the figure of Clarissa Harlowe, in Richardson's novel of the same name,

Lovelace can only have contributed to the Byronic Legend, as a preparatory myth, whether or not Don Juan may be said to approach the cad syndrome.

16. Gilbert Phelps, 'The Byronic Byron', in *Byron: A Symposium*, edited by John D. Jump (Macmillan, London, 1975), p. 73.
17. John Cordy Jeaffreson, *The Real Lord Byron* (London, 1884), p. 264.
18. Peter Quennell (ed.), *Byron, A Self-Portrait*, Letters and Diaries, 1798 to 1824 (John Murray, London, 1950), 2 vols., II, p. 440.
19. Peter Brent, *Great Lives: Byron* (Weidenfeld and Nicolson, London, 1974), p. 213.

Notes on Contributors

ALAN BOLD was born in 1943 in Edinburgh. He has published many books of poetry, including *To Find the New*, *The State of the Nation* and *This Fine Day* as well as a selection in *Penguin Modern Poets 15*. His *In This Corner: Selected Poems 1963–83* represents his best work over the past two decades. He has edited *The Penguin Book of Socialist Verse*, *The Martial Muse: Seven Centuries of War Poetry*, the *Cambridge Book of English Verse 1939–75*, *Making Love: The Picador Book of Erotic Verse*, *The Bawdy Beautiful: The Sphere Book of Improper Verse*, *Mounts of Venus: The Picador Book of Erotic Prose* and *Drink To Me Only: The Prose (and Cons) of Drinking*. He has also written critical books on *Thom Gunn and Ted Hughes*, *George Mackay Brown*, *The Ballad*, *Modern Scottish Literature* and *MacDiarmid: The Terrible Crystal*. He has exhibited his Illuminated Poems (pictures combining an original poetic manuscript with an illustrative composition) in venues as varied as Boston University and the National Library of Scotland.

J. DRUMMOND BONE was a Snell Exhibitioner at Balliol College, Oxford, from 1968–72. From then until 1980 he was a Lecturer in the Department of English and Comparative Literary Studies at the University of Warwick, and since 1980 he has been with the Department of English Literature at the University of Glasgow. He has lectured widely on Byron, in conferences at such institutions as the Universities of Bordeaux, Salzburg, and Mannheim. In 1975 he became an editor of the *Byron Journal*, and since 1980 has edited its academic content. He has published articles and reviews on Byron and Shelley in *Notes and Queries*, *Modern Language Review*, *The Keats-Shelley Memorial Bulletin*, and the *Byron Journal*. He is the editor of a forthcoming history of the Romantic period, to which he has contributed the chapters on Byron and on Coleridge's poetry.

JENNI CALDER was born in Chicago in 1941 and came to England with her parents when she was 9. She read for her B.A. at New Hall, Cambridge, and for her M.Phil. at Birkbeck College, London. She is married to the writer, Angus Calder, lives in West Lothian and works in the Education Department of the Royal Scottish Museum.

211

Her publications include *Chronicles of Conscience*, a study of George Orwell and Arthur Koestler, *There Must be a Lone Ranger*, on the myth and reality of the American Wild West, *Women and Marriage in Victorian Fiction, Heroes: From Byron to Guevara, The Victorian Home*, and *R.L.S.: A Life Study*.

GEOFFREY CARNALL has worked in India and Ireland, and now teaches English at the University of Edinburgh. He has written *Robert Southey and his Age*, which appeared in 1960, and he completed the late John Butt's volume of the Oxford History of English Literature, *The Mid-Eighteenth Century* (1979).

J. F. HENDRY was born in Glasgow in 1912. He co-edited the wartime anthologies *The New Apocalypse, The White Horseman* and *The Crown and Sickle*, and edited *The Penguin Book of Scottish Short Stories*. He is the author of a volume of short stories *The Blackbird of Ospo*, a novel *Fernie Bras*, and a forthcoming biography of Rilke entitled *The Sacred Threshold*.

PHILIP HOBSBAUM was born in London in 1932, grew up in various parts of Yorkshire, studied at the Universities of Cambridge and Sheffield, has published eleven books including four collections of poems, and is Reader in English Literature at the University of Glasgow where he has taught for the last sixteen years.

EDWIN MORGAN was born in 1920 in Glasgow. He was educated at Rutherglen Academy, Glasgow High School, and Glasgow University. He took his degree, in English, after war service with the Royal Army Medical Corps mainly in the Middle East, 1940–46. He lectured in English at Glasgow University from 1947 until 1980, when he retired, as Assistant Lecturer 1947–50, Lecturer 1950–65, Senior Lecturer 1965–71, Reader 1971–75, and from 1975 as Titular Professor. He has written many books, including *Essays* (1974) and *Poems of Thirty Years* (1982).

WALTER PERRIE was born in 1949 in the Lanarkshire mining village of Quarter. Educated locally and at Hamilton Academy, he took an M.A. in philosophy at the University of Edinburgh. Full-time poet and essayist, his last two volume-length poems have attracted considerable attention. The recipient of various literary prizes and awards, he lives in Edinburgh. His first collection of essays on the philosophy of literature—*Out of Conflict*—was published in 1982.

Notes on Contributors

TOM SCOTT was born in 1918 in Glasgow. His first poems were published in 1941, since when he has published five further volumes of verse (with as many yet to publish), a critical study of Dunbar and some children's books. He has also edited several anthologies, including *The Penguin Book of Scottish Verse*, and contributed to many journals. In 1957 he went belatedly to Edinburgh University taking first an Honours M.A., then a Ph.D. in literature.

RONALD STEVENSON is a Scottish composer/pianist and writer on music. His 80-minute *Passacaglia on D.S.C.H.* for piano is published by Oxford University Press and recorded by John Ogdon on the E.M.I. label. Commissions include a MacDiarmid song-cycle *Border Boyhood* (Aldeburgh Festival 1971: Peter Pears and the composer) and two B.B.C. commissions, *Peter Grimes Fantasy* for piano (B.B.C.2, 1971, the composer) and *Piano Concerto No. 2* (B.B.C. Radio 3, London Proms 1972, N.P.O./Del Mar/the composer). His most recent commission is from Yehudi Menuhin for a *Violin Concerto*. Stevenson has composed some 200 songs. As concert pianist he has performed in Australia, Austria, Britain, Bulgaria, Canada, Germany, Italy, South Africa, the U.S.A. and the U.S.S.R. He has contributed many articles to *The Listener, Books & Bookmen* and the leading music magazines, and is the author of *Western Music: An Introduction* (1971) and *Busoni: Aspects of a Genius* (1983).

213

Index

Index

Index

Mickiewicz, Adam, 86
Milbanke, Annabella *see* Byron, Lady
Millais, John Everett, 68
Milton, John, 28, 60, 71, 134, 135
Moira, Countess of, 79
Molière, J. B. P. de, 82
Moore, Thomas, 21, 26, 38, 58, 80, 86, 113, 115, 116, 132, 149
Mozart, Wolfgang Amadeus, 113, 122
Muir, Edwin, 21, 26, 191, 195, 202
Murray, John, 37, 41, 69, 118
Musset, Alfred de, 142

Nabokov, Vladimir, 181
Napoleon, 64, 86, 104, 137, 160, 176, 187, 188, 203
Nathan, Isaac, 87–8
Nechayev, 204
Neild, James, 130
Nelson, Lord, 64
Nero, 76
Nerval, Gerald de, 142
Nietzsche, F. W., 142, 152
Novalis, 190, 198

Olson, Charles, 62
Ossian *see* Macpherson, James
Owen, Robert, 132
Owen, Wilfred, 83, 194
Oxford, Lady, 20, 131

Paganini, Niccolo, 89
Parker, Margaret, 153
Pasley, Charles, 126
Percy, Thomas, 127
Phelps, Gilbert, 152
Phillips, Thomas, 84
Pindar, 80
Poe, Edgar Allan, 86–7
Pope, Alexander, 17, 21, 38–44, 47, 163
Pound, Ezra, 62, 87
Pulci, Luigi, 22, 29–30, 45, 47–8, 51, 85
Pushkin, Alexander, 28, 86, 143, 191, 197

Racine, Jean, 82
Raff, Joachim, 88
Raphael, 182
Read, Herbert, 186, 189, 190, 191, 196, 203, 208
Redesdale, Lord, 130
Richardson, Samuel, 202
Rickman, John, 126
Rogers, Samuel, 38
Romilly, Sir Samuel, 130, 132, 133
Rose, William Stewart, 47–8, 50
Rousseau, Jean Jacques, 125, 157, 177, 187
Russell, Bertrand, 142, 143, 195
Rutherford, Andrew, 78, 143

Salisbury, Lady, 190

Sand, George, 86
Sappho, 76
Schiller, J. C. F., 187
Schoeck, Othmar, 86
Schoenberg, Arnold, 90
Schumann, Clara, 89
Schumann, Robert, 89
Scott, Sir Walter, 18, 21, 26, 28, 34, 38, 128
Sgricci, Tommaso, 63
Shakespeare, William, 17, 89
Shelley, Mary, 144
Shelley, Percy Bysshe, 17, 37, 128–29, 132, 143, 155, 159, 168
Sheraw, Darrell, 52
Sidney, Sir Philip, 190
Skinner, John, 22
Smith, Adam, 126
Smollett, Tobias, 26
Southey, Robert, 24, 25, 27, 30–2, 35, 37, 46, 126, 127, 139
Spenser, Edmund, 17
Stael, Madame de, 107
Stalin, Josef, 189
Stanhope, Colonel Leicester, 63, 166
Sterne, Laurence, 131
Stevenson, Robert Louis, 116
Suetonius, 76
Swift, Jonathan, 18

Tasso, Torquato, 26, 45, 85, 91, 159
Tchaikovsky, P. I., 90
Thomson, James, 18
Tolstoy, Count Leo, 204
Trudgill, Eric, 154
Turner, W. J. M., 86

Underhill, John, 46

Verdi, Giuseppe, 87
Villon, François, 33
Virgil, 71
Voltaire, 125
Vuillamy, C. E., 188, 190–91, 193

Waller, R. D., 45
Webster, Frances, 114
Wellington, Duke of, 104, 190
White, Maude Valérie, 80
Whiting, Nathaniel, 46
Williams, William Carlos, 62
Wilmot, Mrs., 108
Wilson, John, 128
Windham, William, 125
Wolfe, James, 64
Woolf, Virginia, 21
Wordsworth, William, 32, 37, 38, 75, 128, 143, 163, 164, 168

Yeats, W. B., 197
Young, Edward, 70

216